SOFTWARE FOR THE MIND
Opening the Inner "I"

Emmett E. Miller, M.D.

SOFTWARE FOR THE MIND
Opening the Inner "I"

Discover healing imagery
through selective awareness

CELESTIAL ARTS
Berkeley, California

ACKNOWLEDGMENTS

This book, *Software for the Mind*, would not have survived were it not for the faith of those who kept encouraging me, insisting that the ideas contained herein were not only valuable but also very much desired—especially by the community of health care professionals.

Among my earliest supporters were Russel Wills and Arthur Hastings, who was one of the book's very first editors. Many thanks to Ed West, who resurrected the material and developed the title. I would also like to acknowledge Sandra Smith whose enthusiasm for the material helped keep my spirits up. And finally I would like to thank David Hinds and Paul Reed of Celestial Arts for seeing the value of the manuscript and helping me get it between covers, Kathy Kaiser for her splendid eye and high degree of craftsmanship in the final editing stages, and Nancy Austin for the clarity and simplicity of her work in designing the interior.

CELESTIAL ARTS
P.O. Box 7327
Berkeley, California 94707

Cover and text design by Nancy Austin
Composition by HMS Typography, Inc.

First Printing, 1987 (under the title *Software for the Mind*)
Second Printing, 1991

Library of Congress Cataloging-in-Publication Data

Miller, Emmett E.
    Opening your inner "I": discover healing imagery through selective awareness / Emmett E. Miller.
        p.   cm.
    Rev. ed. of: Software for the mind.
    Includes bibliographical references and index.
    1. Medicine, Psychosomatic. 2. Mind and body. 3. Mind and body therapies.   I. Miller, Emmett E.   Software for the mind.
II. Title.
RC49.M498   1991
616.08—dc20
ISBN 0-89087-642-8
                                                                90-19811
                                                                CIP

Manufactured in the United States of America

2   3   4   5 – 93   92   91

Dedicated to my wife, Sandra,
and my children, Emmett Jr., Yuval, and Lauren.

CONTENTS

PREFACE

The fable of the five blind men and the elephant is a well-known story. Each man, asked to describe the animal, did so in terms of that part of the elephant he had touched. The one who had felt the tail said, "An elephant is like a rope"; the one who had felt the leg argued, "An elephant is like a tree"; and so forth. Today many of us who once thought we understood what good health care was have become uneasily aware that we may have been enjoying the same false kind of understanding—that we may have had the beast only by the tail, so to speak. Yet it does not seem easy to find a new perspective, one offering a more integrated view.

Certainly the past two decades have witnessed a major change in health care practices and in attitudes toward disease in our culture. Chiropractors, faith healers, and health spas are enjoying a new surge of popularity. Practitioners of acupuncture have suddenly appeared on the American scene. Those who practice homeopathy and diet therapy have found their ranks greatly swelled. Treatments as different as exercise therapy, Rolfing, and primal scream therapy are being cited by patients as instrumental in the resolution of diseases such as hypertension, migraine headaches, and hay fever. To add further to the confusion, literature on healing diets in any local bookstore will include five or ten distinctly different, often contradictory, methods purporting to treat the same physical condition. Some proscribe all meat, some proscribe all dairy products, some suggest a high-protein, lean meat diet, and some recommend prolonged fasting.

Even more frustrating to the scientifically trained investigator, the proponents and originators of these different approaches claim theirs to be the only true way. Small wonder that university-trained physicians tend to dismiss such approaches as rubbish, and smugly return to their more predictable world of scalpels and syringes. In regard to current therapies for emotional and mental problems, the situation appears even more chaotic. When one considers the welter of behavioral therapies, self-hypnosis classes, Eastern gurus, and est-like trainings, one is indeed reminded of the blind men and the elephant.

It would be tempting to join the conservatives who classify alternative approaches as nonsense, if it were not for certain undeniable facts. There is clinical evidence that virtually all of these approaches, at least in certain cases, have been associated with dramatic mental, physical, and emotional cures—the resolution of problems that physicians in the best institutions had been unable to alter significantly.

I probably would have been able, like most physicians, to avoid this controversy, if my original medical practice had not been in Carmel, California—midway between the avant-garde San Francisco Bay Area and Big Sur's Esalen Institute, the spawning ground of Gestalt and the body therapies. The theories and concepts that formed part of the intellectual environment of the area kept me sensitive to the clinical evidence—daily available to me in my family practice—of the importance of psychological factors in illness and in healing. At the same time I could not accept any one of the various alternative approaches to which I was exposed as being a satisfying framework within which to fit all the facts, ideas, and questions I had gathered from my reading of medical research and from the world of clinical evidence.

Faced with contradictions and my own confusion, I began the search for a model. I recalled the story of the discovery of digitalis, a story recounted to me in medical school. Although the efficacy of the plant foxglove for cases of cardiac weakness had long been known to herbalists and others practicing outside conventional medicine, it was Dr. Withering who isolated the relevant active ingredient, thus making its use available to a broader range of healers. In doing so he accepted a useful technique of a folk healing tradition, without embracing every aspect of that tradition. Clearly, in the past it proved beneficial to conventional science to look carefully at practices of other traditions. To accept the possibility that good might indeed be effected by approaches that lay outside my own background, training, and present understanding; to learn more about these approaches, constantly looking for the active ingredient that might underlie that effectiveness—these guidelines shaped my investigations. The results of these explorations furnish the ideas shared in this book.

The Changing Face of Disease

In understanding the present emergence of so many different techniques of healing, I have found it useful to consider things in a historical perspective. The patients in a physician's office today are quite different from those of a century ago. Infectious diseases were then plentiful and deadly. A child with meningitis would almost certainly die. Hundreds of thousands died of tuberculosis each year, and millions more were crippled by it. Smallpox took a deadly toll, and polio mutilated those it did not kill. Diphtheria, plague, and other infections of numerous types decimated humanity. Gastrointestinal problems that today are cured swiftly and easily by surgery were at that time deadly. The mortality rate from wound infection after surgery and from the anesthesia itself was sometimes 50 percent or more. At that time there were often no specific cures available for a disease, and the mainstay of treatment, as it had been for untold centuries before, was to build up the patient's body, get the patient to rest, reinforce the self-image and will to live, and strengthen the spiritual reserves. Bedside manner was crucial to a physician's success.

In rapid succession, then, came Lister's techniques for sterilization, the discovery of safe anesthetic agents, and antibiotics. Microorganisms were cultured, and specific cures and immunizations were developed. Today plague, smallpox, and diphtheria are rarely seen. Immunizations prevent polio and measles, and surgical diseases are swiftly treated by ultramodern tools and techniques. Modern medicine has been eminently successful in eliminating those problems caused by invaders from without.

The killers today are of a different class. Hypertension, heart disease, lung cancer, and many important chronic diseases, such as arthritis, diabetes, asthma, and migraine, are all problems that develop not through outside agents but because of the interaction of genetic factors, personal habits, way of life and emotional state— none of which is much affected by drugs or surgery. The most we can hope to do with these tools of modern, or technological, medicine is to suppress the symptoms.

The age of technological medicine and specialization has thus led us into a paradox. In our efforts to atomize and fully analyze every part of the human body, we have developed superspecialists. Some, such as the dermatologist and the cardiologist, limit their practice to a single organ or organ system; others, such as the surgeon, focus on a single approach; yet others, such as the parasitologist, concentrate on a single class of disease—there are even certain ophthalmologists who limit themselves to diseases of the lens of the eye. Alas, most medical schools no longer teach the time-honored tools of the physician that might enable us to cope better with the complex *roots* of today's killers. Most medical schools select the highly competitive and technically oriented student and drive him or her to the limit learning facts; they tend to reject the more easygoing and humanistic student who might better be able to relate in the symbolic manner necessary for the treatment of today's diseases. But nature abhors a vacuum, and there are many indeed who are striving to fill it. In surveying the differing approaches, I find myself led to a conclusion that will be accepted by many, misunderstood by some, and perhaps resented by a few.

My belief is that *although each discipline probably has at least a few substances or techniques that directly affect the body or disease process, for the majority of diseases the common pathway to improvement is probably a psychophysiological change resulting from the belief, motivation, and commitment of the patient, and catalyzed by the personality of the practitioner, who uses an approach that gives the patient a feeling of having something active to do with the healing process.*

This conclusion is not one that leads me to dismiss the significance of these alternative approaches to health. Rather, it inspires me to explore more deeply this core common to the many disparate disciplines. It has become my goal to develop ways in which, divested of irrelevant trappings, the power inherent in this core can be made more widely available—to the healers in the medical mainstream, as well as those in the varying alternative disciplines, and to the individual desiring to enhance his or her own wellness. This book, I hope, will help to meet that goal.

CHAPTER 1

The Psychophysiological Approach

"The Physician should not treat the disease,
but the person suffering from it."

A brief survey of healing practices throughout history and throughout the present world is both illuminating and thought-provoking. From the "miraculous" cures of the faith healers and the witch doctors to the curious successes of homeopathy and acupuncture; from the chemically oriented treatments of the allopath to the strict dietary proscriptions of the naturopath; from the operations of the surgeon to the manipulations of the chiropractor or osteopath: we seem to find almost every kind of contradiction in theory. To make matters even worse, there appear to be chronicles of undeniable success using all these methods.

Even within a single healing discipline, huge variations in response are found. Two persons, in apparently the same health, will respond differently to the same medication, one experiencing side effects or an allergy, the other getting well. The same incision in two similar individuals can produce results as different as rapid, complete healing; the development of internal adhesions; or an infection, which may require repeated surgery.

Moreover, a single disease process such as diabetes, migraine headaches, or asthma can range from a mild annoyance to a severe affliction. And because there are few indicators at the outset of a disease as to what its course will be, watching and waiting are often our only means of determination. Many physicians have learned to avoid predicting. Who has not heard stories of people who were told by doctors they had a fatal disease, only to recover fully, or those who were told their problem was minor, only to find a lifelong handicap develop.

Among the most interesting of all the healing disciplines are those that produce a physical change by focusing on mental processes. Most of us are attuned to the concepts of Western medicine: we recognize the rationale behind the use of scalpel, antibiotics, plaster cast, and anticancer poison, and can see the results of the use of artificial kidneys, cardiac valve replacements, and laser beam treatment of eye disease.

Yet the family practitioner has long known the ploy of offering a child a quarter for his or her wart. The psychological motivation to gain the quarter would, in many cases, be sufficient to enable the body to eliminate the virus that was responsible for the wart. The smiling child would then collect the reward from the doctor a week later. Where do we look to find the physiological explanation for this?

Consider also the case of the man with gangrene in his toes who, when scheduled for surgical removal of the foot, became "miraculously" well within a week after visiting a faith healer. How do we account for the many reports of cancer and tumor inhibition or regression when patients are taught meditation and deep relaxation? What is the basis for the many drugless cures reported by members of the Christian Science Church?

These represent examples of the psychophysiological approach to disease. Most people recognize that such diseases as asthma, ulcers, and migraine have psychological connections, but on close examination it is difficult indeed to find a disease for which there has not been some report of healing or improvement through approaches such as those described. But why does this kind of approach fail in some cases and yet succeed in apparently identical ones? And, even more interesting, what is the mechanism by which it works in those cases in which it is successful?

One thing is clear: all these approaches draw upon the psychological resources of the patient. The cooperation of the "patient" is paramount. In other words, rather than simply manipulating the person's physical structure, inner, neural processes are enlisted to aid in the fight against the disease. Somehow changes in the mind are ultimately translated into molecular change.

After studying those aspects common to all these seemingly different disciplines, I attempted to wed this knowledge to the physical and psychological facts about the human mind–body complex I had learned in medical school and verified in my own practice. Slowly there began to emerge a consistent picture relating physical stressors, mental and emotional states, and disease. I recognized that in many ways the human mind (particularly the unconscious) may be viewed as functioning as a device for reducing the equivocality or ambiguity that the higher conscious centers must endure. To accomplish this it learns new material and reproduces things previously learned so as to protect us from experiences that are painful and to enhance our ability to experience rewarding ones. This aspect of mental functioning works in the way that a computer does, and so we may call the brain a biocomputer. Although the analogy is neither complete nor strictly accurate, it will enable us to investigate certain of its operations more efficiently, especially those that transform thought and imagination into emotion and physical change.

We will experientially investigate the conscious and the unconscious. Then we will explore ways of transferring material between these two, developing efficient states and modes of awareness to facilitate this transfer.

We will then explore the laws of positive and negative conditioning (programming), look at our personal memories, and develop approaches that will allow us to strengthen those aspects of our behavior, experience, and attitude that we desire and to deprogram those we find maladaptive. These approaches comprise what I call "software for the mind."

We will see the importance of emotion as both the prime mover and the ultimate outcome of each mental process and learn how it can, when associated with patterns that escape conscious regulation, produce maladaptive states such as depression, low self-esteem, or uncontrollable anger; habit patterns such as overeating, alcoholism, or procrastination; or even physical disease.

Emotions and Physical Change

It was the study of these physical disease patterns that originally led me to develop the concept of coherency—that the biocomputer evolved to provide effective, nonambiguous relations with self and environment, and that incoherent or faulty programs produce disease states by maladaptively interrelating both mind and body and conscious and unconscious.

Throughout this book we will look at diseases as verbs rather than nouns. By doing this it will become obvious that most diseases are in fact *processes*, and as such are potentially reversible. When we look at diseases as nouns it tends to produce a crystallization of thoughts and we thus become identified with a disease.

How this works is most easily seen in the stress-related diseases whose final expression involves muscle tension. Conceptually, it is much more difficult to "get rid of a headache" than to relax the muscles in the back of the neck or let go of the tensing there. Many of the positive responses to imagery in diseases of muscle tension (such as asthma, high blood pressure, and gastrointestinal disturbances) are accounted for by the ease of conceptualization. It is usually easy to visualize something tensed becoming relaxed.

Yet in other diseases, such as disorders of glandular functions, infectious diseases, allergic responses, abnormal growth of bodily cells (tumors and cancers), and the degenerative diseases, a mental picture of them as processes is possible, and healing can, in many cases, be facilitated.

Getting rid of a cold may seem difficult to imagine; it is perhaps easier to imagine allowing the body to increase its healing rate to eliminate bacteria that are trying to multiply. Arthritis can be viewed not as a thing, but as a situation in which the joints are inflaming—

blood vessels are enlarging and carrying certain elements to these areas. Viewed in this way, it is now possible to create imagery of this process reversing.

Critical, then, to the utilization of the imagination for healing is the imaging of the disease as a process. Healers in native cultures know this quite well—possession by a demon is reversible through exorcism. What the chiropractor calls pinched nerves can be visualized as being relieved through an "adjustment." Similarly, dietary therapy reverses the disease process by fasting to "eliminate the toxins from the body."

Unfortunately, the Latin-based nomenclature in use by the medical profession tends to make diseases sound like permanent attributes—we call a person a diabetic or arthritic. We say that a person *has* migraine, and a person given a diagnosis of cancer often does not experience this as a challenge to increase the body's defenses against cells gone awry, but hears the pronouncement as a death sentence, which produces a depression that actually decreases the body's ability to fight the disease.

One fundamental hypothesis of this book, is that when viewed from the proper perspective it is possible for a person to direct his or her thoughts to influence physical processes that are ordinarily considered to be beyond conscious control.

The Evidence for Conscious Control of Diseases and Normally Unconscious Processes

The past few years have allowed me ample opportunity to observe the many physical effects of deep relaxation, hypnosis, guided and positive programming.

I have seen chronic problems of stomach and intestinal pain, spasm, and hypersecretion become resolved. People with long histories of allergies, hay fever, and repeated colds have put an end to these patterns. Those with continuous anxiety, pounding heart, sweaty palms, and high blood pressure have experienced a resolution of these problems. Even Parkinson's disease and visual problems have dramatically improved.

Other investigators have found that acne and even tumors may respond to relaxation and suggestion. James Esdaile, M.D., found, as have many other surgeons, that a simple hypnotic induction with suggestions of health will speed healing, retard infection, eliminate postoperative swelling, and provide excellent anesthesia during and after surgery.

Biofeedback researchers assure us that gastric secretion, EEG characteristics, blood flow to selected organs, skin temperature, and metabolic rate are among the many parameters that previously untrained subjects can learn to regulate.

An oral surgeon I know says that during a complicated extraction of a tooth, suggestions will serve to inhibit bleeding so that the area being worked on stays clear and dry. He also tells me that following the extraction, when blood is needed in the area to form a clot, suggestions to this effect can be given to the deeply relaxed patient. At this point the blood will flow until the tooth socket is filled exactly to the brim, then stop! (Other oral surgeons have shared my friend's experience.)

Still others have found that even a process as complicated as blood sugar control can be affected through thought. Hypnotized subjects will have a rise in blood sugar after imagining they are eating a candy bar. Advanced students of yoga add even more to the list of normally unconscious activities that can be brought under conscious control.

Nearly twenty years ago I attended a professional seminar at which a man named Jack Schwarz demonstrated a remarkable feat. While I held his arm in my hands, he inserted a thin, saber-sharp needle about the length of a knitting needle through the belly of his right biceps muscle. Prior to doing this, he had visualized himself sitting across the room, watching his own demonstration. As a result, I could detect no tensing of the muscle as the needle passed through it and out through the skin on the opposite side of his arm. He showed no sign of pain, and continued to lecture to the group that was present. After about three or four minutes he removed the needle, and in spite of intense squeezing of his arm by one of the people present in the seminar, no blood was shed through the wounds of entry and exit. This feat was even more remarkable in view of the fact that prior to putting the needle into his arm, Schwarz had thrown it to the ground and stepped on it to ensure that it was dirty. His claim was that through mental imagery he was able to prevent infection.

So remarkable were Schwarz's feats in autonomic self-control that Elmer Green, Ph.D., from the Menninger Institute studied him intensely and wrote several papers concerning his abilities. From all scientific tests available to us, it seems that Jack Schwarz is constructed exactly like every other human being—he bleeds and hurts normally, unless he enters a certain state of concentration and produces mental imagery to change these normally unconscious reactions.

While visiting Green at Menninger, I was able to view his experiments wherein Swami Rama demonstrated his ability to throw his heart into and out of atrial fibrillation at will. I also watched a movie that Green had made in India of an Indian yogi being buried alive for eight hours. He was able to slow his breathing to less than once every few minutes, and to decrease his metabolic rate to such a low level that the meager amount of air in the coffin was able to sustain him.

Numerous books have been published in the past decade presenting an ever-increasing amount of evidence in favor of the hypothesis that the development and course of most commonly encountered physical diseases are dependent, at least in part, on

1. The amount of stress the individual has been experiencing. In general, the greater the amount of stress, the greater the likelihood of disease. There are also indications that the negative effects of stress are cumulative—the number of changes a person has had to deal with, mentally and emotionally, over the past two years is directly related to that person's likelihood of developing a disease within the next six months.

2. The individual's ability to effectively deal with stress, and return the body to a healthy equilibrium.

3. How the person view himself or herself and the disease—his or her self-image and the image he or she forms to represent the disease to the conscious mind.

4. Way of life. The person whose way of life includes smoking or drinking as an outlet for tension is paving the way for diseases he or she would be protected from to a greater degree if he or

she found other ways to eliminate accumulated tension in the body. Similarly, people who eat for emotional reasons may find that excessive weight vastly increases their likelihood of becoming ill and dying from diseases such as hypertension, coronary thrombosis, or musculoskeletal problems.

The evidence at present, in my opinion, does not imply that *all* human diseases are the result of stress, the inability to cope with stress, attitude, or way of life. Those that are, however, should obviously be approached through the mind and emotion in addition to physically. This, of course, creates a dilemma—in any given case, it is impossible for anyone, including the patient, to tell to what degree, if any, psychophysiological factors are playing a part. One can either assume they are not, and resign oneself to a life of repeated attacks and symptomatic drug treatment, or explore the unconscious connections and attempt to facilitate the healing process. This latter decision seems to be an especially reasonable one in view of the experiences of those who have shown that the healing rate of even such obviously externally induced problems as animal bites and surgical incisions can be markedly altered through a simple relaxation or hypnotic induction combined with the proper imagery or suggestions.

If unconscious activity, then, is fundamental to all healing, and if it can change the functioning of different organs, what is the mechanism by which this is accomplished? Is there some way, other than the nineteenth-century hypnotists' "universal Animal Magnetic Fluid," to conceptualize this process? Finding this would lead to a better understanding of human disease as well as provide a mechanism through which we could eliminate or ameliorate many diseases and prevent others from ever occurring.

The Conscious Control of Chemical and Physical Changes

Have you ever stopped to consider that you can, by the use of your conscious mind, initiate, halt, or alter the rate of the complicated cemical reactions that take place in your body cells?

The chemist never "sees" the chemical molecules interact with each other, but merely adds substances together under certain conditions and exerts a limited control over only such minor factors as whether a chemical reaction starts, stops, or changes its rate. The physicist requires the most complicated equipment to detect small quantities of substance, and when it comes to speaking about a single molecule or atom, the physicist's knowledge and reasoning become highly speculative.

Our bodies, however, don't suffer from these limitations. Our cells are familiar with atoms and electrons, and deal with them constantly throughout our entire lives. During every minute your body is combining oxygen molecules and sugar molecules in a specific manner so as to produce energy. If each of us (assuming we were all healthy) were to take a small amount of phenobarbital, it would go to the same place in each person's body and be detoxified through exactly the same kind of chemical reaction. If you catch a cold this winter, it may be a form of virus that has never before been present on the Earth; yet your body will likely be able to analyze its chemical structure and produce an antibody molecule that fits it so exactly that the foreign entity is completely inactivated and the disease soon eradicated.

One thing we all take for granted is the means by which we contract and relax muscles. When you contract a muscle, you are actually producing many specific chemical changes according to a certain specific pattern.

The contraction occurs because of a specific chemical reaction that is repeated over and over again at certain points along the fibrils. When the muscle maintains a certain degree of contraction, the chemical reaction must continue. When you relax the muscle, chemical reaction ceases. If you now consider the speed and delicacy with which your eyelids may be fluttered, the power of the legs of a sprinter, and the extraordinary control of a watchmaker's fingers, you can get an idea of how intricate is our molecular control of these chemical reactions.

If, while you are sitting alone in your bedroom at night, you hear what sounds like stealthy footsteps somewhere in your house, you might begin to perspire. You might also have noticed that you perspire when speaking in front of a group of people or when being introduced to an important person. In both of these cases, the chemical changes represented by the production of perspiration are produced because of what you are thinking rather than because of a change in temperature. Once again, your body is initiating certain chemical reactions: each sweat cell must move molecules of sodium and chlorine out of your bloodstream, mix them with water, and discharge them onto the surface of your skin.

Perhaps you can recall a time when you almost fell off a roof or when you narrowly avoided an automobile accident. A few seconds later you felt a shocklike tingling throughout your body, followed by rapid heartbeat and respiration. The cells of your body had manipulated chemicals, releasing adrenalin into your bloodstream. Your experience resulted from the changes in your nerve endings, changes produced by this chemical.

During World War II a study showed that people who read the newspaper during breakfast developed ulcers much more frequently than a similar group of people who did not read the newspaper while eating. The emotions produced when the reports of the war were read caused chemical changes, such as changes in gastric secretion and spasm and tension in involuntary muscles.

You can probably think of hundreds of other ways in which a person's thoughts or imaginings can produce or inhibit chemical reactions in the cells of the body. You will find that you are quite familiar with the ability of your body to outperform even the most well-equipped chemical or physical laboratory in this respect. You may, however, have given little thought to the fact that you can actually learn to control these chemical reactions consciously. Although the bodily responses discussed in the examples just mentioned seem to be related to the external environment, it is actually the imagination that is ultimately responsible for initiating these responses. For instance, you will not perspire if you recognize immediately that the nighttime noises are made by your dog. It is your imagination of danger that gives rise to the perspiration, not the danger itself!

Perhaps the role of the imagination will be understood clearly through a little experience. Sweat! That's right—start sweating!

You are probably finding this impossible to do. Yet if suddenly your door flew open and an angry grizzly bear walked in, you would probably find it easy to sweat. Yet nothing would have been physically done to you! Your imagination, or mental image of what might happen, would be producing the response. And if your ability to produce fantasy is strong enough, you can picture that bear in your mind's eye so clearly that your sweat glands will respond to the image.

The Evolution of Imagination

The sciences of archaeology, biology, and physics indicate that the earliest forms of life on our planet seem to have been organisms of only one cell. This cell was responsible for obtaining food, digesting it, and eliminating waste. It was responsible for reproduction and respiration and defense. All of its processes were centralized and controlled by its nucleus.

As time passed, groups of cells began to join together, forming clumps and even hollow balls. Each cluster-forming organism, or colonial organism, was equal to its neighbor. Each was also responsible for its own life processes, and journeying together was mainly a convenience.

Still more time passed, and the animals and plants living on the Earth became more complicated. Specialization began to take place: certain cells were responsible for obtaining food, others for locomotion, and still others for defense. Around this time a problem arose. For those animals that had developed the ability to move, to feel, and to react to sensations, it became necessary to coordinate the activities of these different groups of cells. To put it simply, the eye had to communcate to the foot the location of the food so that the mouth could be taken to it!

Thus was born the need for a communications system or, as we call it in biology, a nervous system. The nervous system consists of specialized cells whose job it is to carry messages back and forth to other groups of cells (organs).

As organisms became more and more complicated, a central area for coordinating activities became necessary. If you imagine a town in which all the phones are connected to each other without going through a central switchboard, you have an idea of the confusion that might have occurred in animals or plants if some kind of brain had not been developed.

Nature found this new organ most valuable for coping with the changing conditions in the world. Areas were developed to store information gleaned from the surroundings, so that it could be used if similar conditions arose later. In other words, animals gained the capacity to learn.

The development of a fixed body temperature led to the appearance of the mammals. Delicate, finely controlled brains could now be developed, and the lives of these animals became dependent more upon their ability to learn and adapt in their individual surroundings than upon limited sets of reflexes passed on genetically, such as those that govern the life of paramecium or a mosquito.

These abilities seem to have reached a zenith with the human, whose versatile body and complex brain are crowned by the specialized function of the nervous system that we experience as the conscious mind. As mammals evolved more adaptable, flexible bodies, nature found it necessary to develop this special part to control the brain itself. Just as the lower centers of the brain, or unconscious mind, is responsible for maintaining the coordination of your body during such activities as swimming or playing tennis, the higher centers, or conscious mind, is responsible for maintaining the overall coordination of the unconscious mind. It is the conscious mind that decides whether to have the unconscious mind play tennis or simply sit and watch because you are only a spectator at a championship match. And, tracing it all the way back, this elaborate cortical structure still serves the primitive function of allowing all the cells of the body to communicate with each other.

Nature has given us a special freedom. We are not bound to simply respond to immediate life situations, as are the lower animals. Freed of these patterns, we can transcend time and respond to events as they occur, to events that have already occurred, or to those that have not. For example, a soldier may reproduce feelings experienced in last week's battle or may experience feelings related to what he imagines will happen when he is shipped home next week. In the first case he will likely feel fear and anguish and, in the second, he will likely feel happiness. Either reaction could take place as he lies in his sleeping bag at three in the morning. Similarly, we may take the knowledge we possess at this moment and project onto a future situation, thereby planning our response, a procedure well known to any good quarterback. Furthermore, we can project into the past, recall how we handled a given situation, and make a decision to handle similar situations in the future in the same or in a different way. In other words, we can use conscious feedback to help us make decisions.

In the following chapters we will focus on the aspect of conscious imagination that I call Selective Awareness—the process of focusing on certain thoughts and taking the focus away from others, temporarily, in order to use the brain and nervous system more effectively. The techniques for accomplishing this grew out of the synthesis of many objective scientific disciplines, including mathematics and computer theory, cybernetics, psychiatry, behavioral psychology, and many subfields of Western medicine. The findings and conclusions of these objective sciences are used to bring the mind–body complex into internal harmony through the use of subjective self-observation and self-regulation methods derived from medical hypnosis, autogenic training, biofeedback, and meditation techniques.

The ultimate goal of this work is to place you in control of yourself to the degree that you choose and are motivated to achieve. I hope that in learning to eliminate maladaptive symptoms, emotions, and habits, my readers, students, clients, patients, and friends will further develop access to that internal guidance system that, through guiding the evolution of life, has transformed a harsh terrestrial wasteland into a planet of luxuriant greenery, supporting an almost limitless variety of flying, walking, and swimming creatures. But for the belief that such an internal guidance system still remains beneath the confusion in each of us, this book would never have been written. Perhaps it will, in some small way, help to create an inner awareness commensurate with the achievements of twentieth-century technological science; an awareness that might stem humanity's blind, headlong, inhuman rush toward an unthinkable nothingness.

CHAPTER 2

Flux, Flux, All Is Flux . . . .

C hange is in the air; the world is taking a new look at itself. The age of the throwaway society is being ushered out as the age of ecology and recycling is being ushered in. It had seemed self-evident that natural resources were almost limitless, that technology would compensate for any limits that did exist, and that economic growth would continue forever. The evidence is now being reexamined.

Many in the healing profession seemed to think that gradually technology would extend our lifetime further and further, that more health expenditures would automatically give rise to better and better health, and that ultimately a person could go to a fully automated "doctor"—machine that would totally analyze a patient's body, give a readout of diagnosis and treatment, and send the patient on his or her way. Hans Selye's book *The Stress of Life* began to awaken us to the idea that our interactions with the social world and our reactions to it are primary in the development and course of most of our busy years. Now it's commonplace to see men and women jogging, riding bicycles, or running par courses in an effort to improve their cardiovascular functioning. A new professional has appeared on the scene, the health educator, whose duty it is to teach people to relax, enjoy our foods, and develop a healthy way of life. Corporations are finally discovering that it's cheaper to keep personnel healthy than to replace them when they wear out prematurely, and stress reduction workshops and clinics are burgeoning in virtually all industries.

Even American medicine, slow-moving and cautious behemoth that it is, has begun to change its attitudes and procedures. The number one killers, high blood pressure and heart disease, have been inextricably linked to psychological precipitants. For years there has been a *Physician's Desk Reference*—now at last there is a *Patient's Desk Reference*. Patient education is becoming more and more a part of the medical job. Psychosomatic and holistic approaches to healing are rapidly gaining in popularity. Acupuncture, biofeedback, autogenic training, meditation, yoga, and psychic healing are being explored by an ever-increasing number of people.

The standardization of assembly lines made the industrial revolution a success, and we thought the gods of technology and specialization would continue to guide us. But human beings have revolted against being folded, spindled, and mutilated and are pressing on toward a new world of individual responsibility, consciousness, and self-determination. The East and West are coming together, economically and philosophically, and increasing numbers of Westerners are exploring the Eastern view of the self and its relationship to the universe.

The Reemergence of Relaxation and Imagery Therapy

Some form of relaxation therapy was in common practice in almost every period of history. Greek, Egyptian, and Persian healers used it routinely to help the well-born achieve higher states of consciousness and freedom from disease. The yogi lying comfortably on a bed of nails is using a similar mental process.

Hypnosis: The Imagery Therapy of the West

Tens of thousands of patients were treated with hypnosis, a form of relaxation and imagery, during the nineteenth century in both Europe and America. In *Hypnosis in Medicine and Surgery* (Julian Press, 1957), James Esdaile, a Scottish surgeon working in India, reports on hundreds of operations performed with patients in deep hypnosis. Though many of these involved major surgical procedures, no pain was experienced by the patient even in the absence of any other form of anesthesia. Even more startling, these operations were preformed in the filth of the Indian jungles, with no possibility of using sterile procedures, yet the infection rate following surgery was equal to that of the best hospitals in London! His report describing the fall in surgical mortality from 50 percent to 5 percent after he began using hypnosis is most interesting.

How, then, did it happen that hypnosis has come to most of us shrouded in mysticism and is routinely thought of as a tool for the manipulation of the minds of innocent people by Transylvanian vampires, Svengalis, brainwashing experts, and sideshow charlatans?

There seem to be several reasons for this. First, the term *hypnosis* was coined from the Greek word *hypnos,* meaning "sleep," by a well-meaning physician who thought it was a form of sleep. Of course one of the times we are most vulnerable to harm is during our sleeping hours. Small wonder then that people were suspicious of a treatment that promised to "do something" to them while they were asleep! The facts are that hypnosis is, as far as awareness is concerned, the opposite of sleep. Though the body is relaxed and the eyes are closed, the person in hypnosis is actually in an alert state of *hyper*-consciousness. The subject merely appears to be asleep because he or she is not reacting to unimportant stimuli, as we do in normal wakefulness. The subject is motionless because there is no reason to move, not because he or she is unable to do so; the eyes are closed because he or she is looking within.

Moreover, the theories advanced to explain the remarkable feats possible for the subjects in hypnosis were childish and unscientific. Franz Mesmer believed the hypnotic state was due to magnetism produced in the body by placing it in a magnetic field. Historical accounts of Mesmer's experience indicate that originally he produced his "magical" cures by passing boxes over patients' bodies. Within these small boxes were iron magnets. His patients went into convulsivelike states, following which they fainted and awoke cured. One day he forgot to put the magnets in the boxes, but found that the patients went through exactly the same process. It was then that he began to develop his theories of "animal magnetism."

As Mesmer became more and more popular, he was persuaded by the Marquis de Puysegur to "magnetize" a tree on the Marquis's estate so that people could come to it and be cured. This was done and people who came to the tree for treatment continued to have convulsions and to faint just as though Mesmer were there himself.

Once a retarded peasant boy was brought to the tree by his family to see if his dullness could be improved. Many new patients were awaiting their turns at the tree behind him. The pressure of the situation and standing in front of all those people apparently proved too much for the boy and, in order to escape the situation, he collapsed in a faint and went to sleep. The others, observing the "power" of the tree, immediately began to swoon themselves.

It was noticed that any verbal instructions given to the people in this strange "sleep" would be carried out in an automatic, robot-like way. Thus was born what we now call the hypnotic trance.

New theories began to spring up that focused on this aspect of the state, and such constructs as "universal fluid," which sup-posedly flowed from one person to another, began to arise. This, of course, did more harm than good to the idea, because the march of science soon showed these theories to be untenable. As the theories were disproved or rejected, skeptics tended to throw the baby out with the bathwater, and disbelief in the hypnotic state fol-lowed disbelief in the theories.

The final blow was delivered by Sigmund Freud, who began his study of psychoanalysis by using hypnosis. It is said that Freud was not a good hypnotist, and mistakenly believed that the patient had to go into a deep state for therapy to work. His authoritarian approach to hypnosis was rejected by most patients, but Freud seemed unable to use more permissive, patient-centered techniques. He finally dis-missed hypnosis as not generally useful in psychotherapy, and developed a format of therapy, using a couch and free association, a process that is, in effect, an indirect hypnotic induction.

Hypnosis almost completely disappeared from the medical scene, with only a few physicians using it, and then it reappeared as a tool of charlatans and mountebanks. The techniques that could have been useful in the healing of the sick were now misrepresented to be the hypnotic "power" of the stage performer. And good use he made of those "powers."

At his performances, which were well attended by a gullible public, "Mr. Mysto" would suggest to a volunteer that the volunteer's body was as rigid as steel. Then, placing the volunteer's heels on the seat of one chair and his head on another, he would demonstrate that three people could sit on the volunteer's stomach without causing him to bend or feel any discomfort. He would then have a subject read a newspaper while in a trance and later repeat it, verbatim, with no mistakes. Having no other place to learn about these amazing feats, the onlookers had little choice but to believe that Mr. Mysto and his mysterious ability to hypnotize did indeed have some access to some fantastic secret power.

The movie business and the writers of popular novels, always alert for any popular fears they might capitalize on, began to present hypnosis as a black art. This was quite effective for their money-making purposes. There was plenty of evidence that there was something real about this "hypnotic power," and it was a simple matter to extend the fact that people could accept suggestions that were in keeping with their moral and ethical standards to the *superstition* that people could be forced to accept diabolical ones as well. The Svengali-Trilby story in which a helpless girl was brought under the hypnotic power of an evil wizard set the stage for decades of misunderstanding and fear.

Of course, we know that the "power" is in the subject, and the stage performer merely used the subject's own belief to channel it. In many states the stage or entertainment use of hypnotism is actually banned by law at the present time to prevent it from becoming even more associated with trickery. *All hypnosis is self-hypnosis.* The hypnotist is merely a skilled guide and teacher. The strength unlocked on the stage, like that accessed in the hypnotherapist's office, lies dormant within each of us and is available to us, as you will discover in later chapters.

Today people of science and medicine are taking a new, unbiased look at this ancient art. Such universities as Harvard and Stanford are investigating the effects of hypnosis. The American Medical Association has recognized it as an accepted medical technique and method of treatment. There are now numerous professional journals devoted exclusively to hypnosis, and professional associations such as the American Society of Clinical Hypnosis and the Society of Clinical and Experimental Hypnosis have members throughout the nation.

An increasing number of physicians, dentists, psychologists, and psychiatrists are now using hypnosis, autogenic training, meditation, biofeedback, and other approaches that rely primarily on the techniques of deep relaxation and guided imagery in their practice. Once again thousands of patients and clients are experiencing the benefits that can be achieved only through the use of this state of consciousness. Many former drug users have found their own internally accessed states preferable to their experience with drugs and infinitely more under their control. Alcoholics have found a better way to relax. Surgeons using preoperative preparation with guided imagery cassettes note a remarkably increased speed of recovery and freedom from infection. No one can guess how many persons now feel free to fly in airplanes, climb the Eiffel Tower, speak out in groups, or swim in the ocean as a result of individual hypnotherapy, a group seminar, or the information gleaned from a book on hypnosis.

My introduction to the potential of deep relaxation and imagery came through my experiences with medical hypnosis. It was several years after my graduation from medical school. In a social gathering of physicians, a colleague was describing how he had treated the back pain of a patient we both knew with a relaxation technique based on hypnosis (essentially the same process that we will discuss in the muscle spasm section later on). My eyebrows flew up in surprise. Medical hypnosis? Why, I had just finished my studies at one of the world's finest medical schools, and not once had those words been mentioned. Even during my studies in medicine, psychiatry, and psychology I could recall it being mentioned only in an historical sense, and in a derogatory context at that.

But I had been warned that sometimes general practitioners located far from university centers practiced certain "dubious" forms of medicine. Still, I had witnessed the remarkable recovery of our patient with my own eyes! I lowered my eyebrows soberly and gave my colleague my most scientific look. "Where can I learn about this hypnosis business?"

Within a few hours I had seated myself in front of my tape recorder and was listening (in the most critical manner I could muster) to the tape recording my friend had loaned me. On the tape Dave Elman, a lay hypnotist, was teaching a group of physicians and dentists how to incorporate hypnosis into their work. It was their first lesson and from the questions they asked, they were as skeptical as I. Pretty soon he asked for a volunteer, and, after briefly inducing relaxation, one of the doctors was given the suggestion that his lower jaw would become numb as if he had just received an injection of novocaine. Elman then invited one of the dentists who were present to test the "anesthesia" with a dental probe. After a few moments he blurted out. "Why, I'm scraping the periostium (the covering of the bone)." The astonishment in his voice was understandable, because this usually painful procedure (which feels like a bad toothache) brought forth no response from the subject. "What are you feeling?" asked the hypnotist. "Just a little pressure" replied the subject, who, in his relaxed state didn't sound at all surprised.

As I listened to hour after hour of instructions and demonstrations on the tape, I found I was undergoing one of the most profound changes in my thinking I had ever experienced. Memories of pain echoed through my mind: women screaming for hours in the labor and delivery rooms, postoperative patients and cancer victims who required round-the-clock narcotics for freedom from agony, young and old alike who would rather allow their teeth to rot than spend a few hours in the dentist's chair. And here, contrary to the self-promoting claims of the vaudeville charlatans, was a remarkably simple technique that could be used by *anyone* who wished to eliminate his or her own physical pain! I had to try it to verify these almost unbelievable claims for myself.

Fortunately, at this time I was working in an emergency room, an excellent proving ground. But here a problem arose. It was easy enough to tell someone with a lacerated hand that I was going to inject some medicine to numb the area before suturing it, but could I risk the embarrassment of failing after proclaiming that I could deaden the area with hypnosis? After all the bizarre propaganda about hypnosis in the past, the patient would probably think I was a nut for even suggesting such a thing. (This took place in 1970, before the public was as informed and accepting as it is now concerning the benefits of medical hypnosis.) I thought about how I had felt a few weeks earlier when *I* had first heard about it.

So I studied alone for weeks and practiced with friends, trying to summon the courage to use it in actual medical practice. At last the moment of truth arrived.

Late one night a seven-year-old girl was brought to the emergency room with a laceration of the left upper eyelid. Sutures would be needed to close the wound, but she was so scared I knew that she would never let me come near her eye with the anesthetic needle. Even by tying her down (a primitive procedure often used in such cases), we would never be able to keep her eyes still enough for the delicate procedure necessary to prevent permanent scarring. I had to make a choice: I could pick either the frightening process of admitting her to the hospital for twenty-four hours and using general anesthesia, with all its physical and psychological side effects and possible complications, or I could pick hypnosis, trusting Dave Elman's statement on the tape that."Children make the best subjects."

Now I figured that I was really risking very little with this girl. If hypnoanesthesia failed, I could always call the anesthesiologist. I wouldn't be too embarrassed if I failed in front of a child, and by not using the word *hypnosis*, she could not explain my failure to her parents, who were in the waiting room. So, in my most authoritative tone of voice, I turned to the nurse and said, "Please draw the curtains, Miss Bennett, I'm going to use hypnoanesthesia," and set to work.

"OK, Barbara, would you like to do this the easy way or the hard way?"

Children seldom have trouble with such questions.

"The easy way!"

"Great. Now you must do exactly as I tell you. Close your eyes and pretend you can't open them . . . . Good . . . . What's your favorite TV program?"

Any parent whose child has begged for a toy seen on television will attest to the remarkable ease with which television programs the child. Studies indicate that the television watcher is in a very suggestible state—similar to, or identical with, hypnosis. This holds true even if the show is an imaginary one. I proceeded to repeat the children's induction that I had heard on the tape and practiced so often in the privacy of my home. The smile on her face as she watched "The Beverly Hillbillies" and the tiny fluttering movements of her eyelids told me the time had come.

Gingerly, I passed the needle through one flap of skin. The lack of any movement encouraged me, and I passed it through the other side and pulled the suture thread through. She was still smiling and felt nothing.

Suddenly, the silence around me was broken by what sounded like ten people exhaling simultaneously. I turned, and to my surprise the entire staff of the emergency room, alerted by the nurse to the strange goings-on, had silently slipped inside the curtain. They had all been holding their breaths in anticipation of the inevitable scream of pain and were staring at me and my young patient in wide-eyed amazement. The suspense was over; I had passed my test, and so had hypnosis!

I finished the job and carried her smiling to her parents. A new day had begun.

For the next six months I used my new skill with confidence. I employed the technique in many of the cases in which I would ordinarily have used a chemical anesthetic. In addition, I found that a patient could often slow or stop even fairly severe bleeding if he or she was told to do so in this state. Healing time was speeded up, scars seemed reduced in size, and the wounds almost never became infected.

But for me this was only a beginning. A more far-reaching idea was developing in my mind. If the decreased tension and increased awareness of hypnosis could be used to eliminate pain, perhaps it could be applied with equal success in other areas. Pain is one of the most dominating sensations we can experience. A person with a painful postoperative wound will be unable to get up to get a cigarette, a glass of alcohol, or extra candy, no matter how bad his or her habit is. Regardless of how angry, depressed, or frightened a person is, he or she will quickly forget the emotion, at least for a while, if he or she steps on a nail. If pain could distract people from these habits and problems, and hypnosis could block out pain, I reasoned that hypnosis might at least temporarily relieve these emotionally based problems. Perhaps with temporary freedom from these compulsive habits and emotions and the physical symptoms they cause, a person could focus on the process at the source of these problems and eliminate them forever.

A form of age regression analysis that I developed, called the Selective Awareness Exploration, was the tool I was to use in investigating this hypothesis. It has long been known that deep relaxation produces a remarkably enhanced ability to relive events, remembering subtle details and even feeling the original emotion. We are not born with problems such as recurring depressions, a cigarette addiction, or tension headaches, so we must have *learned* them somewhere along the way. Logic suggested, therefore that these patterned reactions were like computer programs that we have learned without realizing it. As my undergraduate degree was in mathematics I had studied computer programming in the early sixties and was able to see the parallels clearly. I hoped that perhaps I could trace these unwanted programs to their source (much as I had learned to trace a signal in a radio receiver to find the source of an unwanted hum) and eliminate the causative emotions just as I was now able to help patients relieve pain. Deprived of the driving motivation, I reasoned, the program and its resultant habit pattern would vanish. What's more, because the actual source had been removed, there would be no tendency for recurrence or for substitution of other symptoms (such as substituting overeating for cigarettes).

As you read on you may discover concepts you have encountered before in books on transactional analysis, meditation, or drug experiences. Principles you may be familiar with from your studies of yoga, biofeedback, autogenic training, faith healing, and psychosomatic medicine will appear. On the other hand, you may encounter concepts different from anything you have read about before. But please try not to simply pigeonhole the information in order to finish this book so you can rush on to your next task. It has been said that some books are to be tasted, others to be swallowed whole, and others to be carefully chewed and digested. This book is of the latter type. If you simply skim it or spend your time merely comparing philosophies, you will miss its main point—*your experience.*

Unlike most you have ever read, I have attempted to construct this book in a way that will enable the reader to experience relaxation and deeper levels of consciousness and learn to tap those inner resources and abilities that are neglected in formal education but that lead to greater health, wellness, satisfaction and personal fulfillment. The process will be easy and enjoyable to the reader who follows along, step by step, *taking time to understand* each point and each experience as it is presented. It is constructed like a carefully designed house. Each brick is essential and set down in the proper place. If, to save time, you do not permit yourself to follow the instructions in the Experience sections, but just content yourself with "knowing" that you *could* experience this, you will finish the book with a possibility and not an actuality. And if curiosity should lead you to rush ahead to more advanced imagery experiences before it is suggested that you do so, you will be building the second floor before the first has been completed; the integrity of the structure may be lost, and the results may be merely a pile of interesting bricks.

You can be assured of a most enjoyable and profitable trip through these pages if you remember that one word, *experience.*

CHAPTER 3

Exploring the Conscious Mind

The concept of *consciousness* is a useful one. Unfortunately, the word *conscious* has been used in so many contexts and has been defined and redefined by so many thinkers in psychology, psychiatry, and philosophy that the meaning of the word has become unclear.

Those who study the operation of the mind realize that the distinction between the conscious and the subconscious is actually arbitrary and artificial. It is useful to learn these concepts, but the distinction between them will disappear as we gain more facility in experiencing and using them.

Thus, at this point, we are faced with the difficult decision of whether to develop an entirely different set of words to introduce the experiences or to merely use related ideas that are already partially familiar to most people. I choose the latter approach, but each concept is to be understood as your *here and now* experience rather than as a mere recollection and a sorting into preexisting categories.

Let us start by becoming aware of the conscious mind. Of what sorts of things are we aware? What do we find in our conscious experience? How do we perceive everyday happenings?

Information (Data)

One thing that is immediately evident is that our minds have stored a great deal of information—facts, events, memories, names and ideas. We do not keep them all in our awareness at all times, but if we want some piece of information, we may simply bring it to mind and become aware of it.

EXPERIENCE ONE

Allow yourself to become conscious of the period at the end of this sentence. Now become aware of your middle name. Without moving become aware of your right ear, your navel, and your left big toe. Become conscious of the town in which you were born, your telephone number, a food that you enjoy eating, your eyelids, and the sounds you are hearing at this instant.

It is obvious that most of these items may be brought to mind with great speed and ease. When they are brought to mind, we say that we become *conscious* of them.

Now attempt to bring to consciousness all those items simultaneously! You will find that even this small number of items overloads the conscious mind unless some mechanism, such as a jingle or mnemonic, is used.

This little experiment shows that although the conscious mind has limited storage facilities, its selectivity and retrieval ability is extraordinary. You are able to focus upon individual memories such as the ones suggested by merely willing yourself to do so.

Consider now a common situation, such as entering your living room. As you walk in the door and scan the familiar scene, a magazine on the floor, a vase out of place on an end table, or a pen in an unusual position on a desk will attract your attention immediately. Your eyes and mind have taken in thousands of stimuli when you entered the room, yet the single element out of place has been noted automatically and presented to your conscious mind for consideration. You can tell immediately that someone else has been in the room since you left it.

You can imagine the extremely complicated list that would be necessary to enable you to make such detailed observations if you were unfamiliar with the room. Instead of a relocated magazine, there might have been an armchair, a wastebasket, or any number of items out of place. If you were to check a written list as accurate as your memory, it might take hours for you to realize what the mind, familiar with the setting, sees instantaneously. In a split second your mind can perform all these activities, inspecting each of the individual items and comparing them with previously stored information concerning the room. All this was performed with as little effort as it takes to recall your phone number. The information about the living room, like the information in the first Experience exercise, was stored in the *unconscious mind*.

Bring to mind your mother's maiden name, the location of the post office nearest your home, and the size shoe you wear.

Again, with no difficulty, these pieces of information can rapidly be brought to consciousness. Obviously, they have not come from any mysterious place, but have been stored in your mind throughout the reading of the preceding paragraphs, even though you were not consciously aware of them at that time. During that time they were stored in the unconscious mind, available for your conscious retrieval at a moment's notice.

Activities (Programs)

Let's explore the wider scope of the unconscious mind. You leave your house, drive downtown, park your car, walk across the street, and enter the door of a bank. You have carried out a series of complicated activities. Yet these activities were carried out automatically, with a minimum of effort from your consciousness. Your eyes, for example, may have changed focus thousands of times, and it would take many volumes to describe the multitude of muscular contractions and relaxations necessary to maintain your balance as you proceeded on foot. You were aware only of the overall activity (such as crossing the street). Nevertheless, each of these activities represents an extraordinarily complex network of simpler activities and movements performed by the body, all of which, at one time, had to be painstakingly learned through conscious experience by trial and error, and recorded and coordinated by the unconscious mind. This happened so long ago that you do not even consider it learned information, but somehow accept it as automatic action. But watching a baby take its first halting steps or miss in an attempt to pick up a rattle immediately reminds us that we were not born with these skills.

EXPERIENCE TWO

Many examples of this type of activity of the unconscious mind can probably occur to you. Choose an activity that you usually perform almost automatically, such as writing your name, throwing a ball, or brushing your teeth. Begin to dissect it into its component parts, first noting the different organs of the body being used, then dividing the action of each of these parts of the body into smaller and smaller units. You might pretend that you are instructing a robot in how to carry out this activity. Spend about a minute or two doing this.

Before escaping from the complexity of that task, you probably experienced an awareness of how accurately timed, coordinated, and intricate even the smallest of these movements was. One of the major characteristics of the unconscious mind, then, is the ability to carry out relatively complex but automatic activities generally considered to be routine. The conscious mind, on the other hand, is used primarily for planning out major activities and for detailed appraisal of any situation differing significantly from the usual, expected experience. Through this monitoring activity of the conscious mind, we may, through the use of our will, make a decision overriding previous mental patterns or programs and cause a new, more adaptive solution to be initiated. For example, upon finding our favorite armchair missing from the living room, we might decide to trace the cause of this alteration or, if we choose, simply sit in another chair.

The important fact here is that the unconscious memories, parts, and functionings of the mind are exactly that—unconscious. The moment we become aware of them, they become conscious also, though they are still present in the unconscious. That an item or activity is at one moment unconscious says nothing about whether we may be capable of bringing it to our consciousness. (Freud referred to such items and activities in the unconscious that could be brought to consciousness as being preconscious.)

For instance, both our rate of speech and the size of the pupils of our eyes are usually controlled by the unconscious. It is easy to become conscious of and alter the rate of speech we are using at any given moment, whereas it is difficult to control the size of the pupils of the eyes. The yogin who lies on a bed of nails without pain or walks on hot coals without harm and the person who has learned to lower his or her blood pressure through the use of a biofeedback machine have both learned to bring activities that are normally *only* unconscious under conscious control. The factors that determine whether we can do this with any particular piece of unconscious material and ways of improving our ability to do so will be discussed later.

Emotions (Internal Behaviors)

So far we have focused on the information and the control of activity that can exist in our minds. We will now investigate a third area, the emotions.

Our emotional lives are extremely important to us. Consider how your emotions would reflect the news that your pet dog had just been struck by a car. How differently you would feel if, instead, the news was that you had won the Lottery or that a beloved friend had suddenly appeared after years of absence! Similarly, two o'clock in the afternoon of a working day feels completely unlike two o'clock on a vacation day. The major difference is the emotion you feel at that instant. The emotion is automatic. You don't have to figure anything out or decide what to feel. Like many other items that are usually unconscious, you have an emotion at every moment of the day, and at any moment you may become more or less aware of your emotions and their changes.

The general trend and changes in your emotional life often give a much more accurate picture of the quality of your life and your development as a person than an achievement or performance test can, and the emotional area of thinking is much more difficult to understand or measure. We seem to have much less control over it than over other areas of our mental functioning. Who has not behaved in an uncharacteristic way while under the influence of a strong emotion?

Chemical agents demonstrate this dramatically. The psychoactive drugs, such as stimulants and tranquilizers can leave the items and activities of our thinking untouched but have marked changes on our feeling states. Regardless of what we are doing, uppers tend to make us happy and downers may make us sad and lethargic.

Usually your emotions are selected by your environment and thoughts. You have the ability to feel happy, sad, lonely, relaxed, fearful, bored, guilty, calm, angry, or any other emotion on a long list of feeling states. Your emotions ordinarily bear some predictable relationship to your surroundings. Laughing, for example, may be associated with being in a carnival fun house and panic with being in a situation of danger.

Our emotions, however, may depend on more than just the situation at hand. A person who is feeling depressed will not laugh at a joke that ordinarily would have struck him or her as funny. Your emotions, then, can affect your response to a present situation as well as be affected by it. Further, a person's memories, be they from earlier in the day or several weeks ago, are important in determining his or her emotional response and, in most cases, his or her physical response to any situation.

EXPERIENCE THREE

Close your eyes and for a few moments become aware of the quality of your emotion at this time. Begin by trying to describe to yourself exactly how you are feeling. Such words as happy, sad, lonely, empty, fulfilled, disturbed, angry, worried, *or* satisfied *may be appropriate to this description. You may become aware that these words are inadequate to describe the more subtle qualities of your emotion. Go beyond them and experience the nature of those feelings that cannot be put into words. You will then become aware of the personal qualities of your emotions, which cannot be described to another person, and yet in this wordless way you can experience them. Indeed, the English language is often unsuited to expressing the quality of emotions—begin to learn to let your experience transcend your vocabulary. Try not to give reasons or search for causes of your feelings in this exercise. Be as objective as you can. Merely experience your feelings in the here and now.*

It soon becomes apparent that in order to talk about feelings we must judge our emotions relative to a nonfixed scale. It is simple to describe yourself in terms such as feeling "happier than yesterday." On an absolute scale, however, it is difficult to say what the quality of happiness is in general or to tell if one person is happier than another.

We often seem to be in between two or more different emotional states. The words used to describe emotions are not exact in their meanings as are, for example, nouns that describe more tangible things. Calling something an orange or an apple leaves no question as to what we are referring to. The qualities of emotions are more complex however, and the words used to describe them can be thought of only as reference points to which an individual may turn in attempting to locate himself or herself in emotional space.

To further complicate the picture, there are differences in the way individuals perceive outwardly similar feelings. My idea of what a happy or an angry person looks like may differ considerably from yours. You have probably had the experience of commenting that a friend appears to be sad, only to have him or her reply, "Oh, I'm not sad, I'm simply thoughtful." Either the friend isn't being completely honest or your definitions of sad and thoughtful differ. Actually, this descrepancy of definitions is usually in the *degree* of the emotion experienced. Probably both you and your friend have generally the same ideas of the directions in which the feelings of sadness and thoughtfulness lie.

Also, different people have different levels of response. Some people seem to need only a little pleasurable stimulation before they will state that they feel happy. Others may need to be in a state of near ecstasy before they will call themselves happy.

A devastating failure in some important undertaking or the sudden illness of a loved one might cause you to be depressed for days, but the same event might cause only a few moments of unpleasantness for a person similar to you in many other respects. Your depression might prevent you from performing with your usual efficiency, and the other person might actually be stimulated by the circumstance, working harder to get his or her mind off the problem.

The variability of emotions depends upon even more factors. Some people love milk chocolate, others find it loathsome. "One person's meat is another person's poison." "To each his or her own." This stands in marked contrast to the lack of disagreement as to whether an object is a tree or a rose. Emotions, then, are distinctly personal reactions to perceptions, and the same stimulus (such as chocolate) can cause different reactions in different people.

EXPERIENCE FOUR

Your emotional reaction to a situation depends on more than the character of the situation and the time at which it occurs; it is also determined by your own personal history, memories, and experiences. Let's take the experience of being in a large group of people, such as at a crowded motorcycle championship race. Imagine the emotions you would feel as you were jostled and shoved as you tried to push your way closer to the track to see the racers.

Now imagine that you are a prince or princess of a European country and have always been surrounded by guards and transported in regal comfort. What might your emotional reaction be to the sweaty people, the dirt, and the noise of the motorcycles?

Now imagine that you are in the same situation, but your life has been spent as a Midwestern farm boy or girl who has always longed for the excitement of crowds and the thrill of riding a motorcycle.

Now imagine how completely different your emotions would be if you were a member of Columbus's crew, suddenly transported from the deck of your ship in 1492 to the edge of this same track. How might you react to the different styles of dress and the profusion of engines and equipment that you had never before imagined?

Although in each of these cases you would be confronted with the same objects and activities, your emotional reactions would be different. Your emotions, then, are fundamentally rooted in your personal memories and their relationship to present events.

Often we find that a memory is unchanged, but the emotional reaction to it may be altered. The woman who buys a shiny new car may feel proud and happy when she remembers this for the first few weeks while the car is working fine. When she discovers, somewhat later, that she has purchased a lemon, and that many costly repairs are needed, her feelings on remembering this purchase will be markedly different. If you are sitting in her living room when she tells you about her car, you will be aware that she is feeling an emotion at that moment. Because her car is not there, however, her emotion is obviously a reaction to her memory. Thus memories may have emotions attached to them.

EXPERIENCE FIVE

Choose two events in your memory, from the recent or distant past, that you can recall vividly. Let one be a pleasant memory and the other an unhappy, frustrating, or painful one, Recall them, one at a time, with your eyes closed—going through the experience just as though you were describing it to a friend in an emotional manner. Do it with the energy of a young boy describing an exciting movie to one of his friends. When we try to convince someone of something we feel strongly about, we generally allow ourselves to experience much of the emotion of the issue. Allow yourself this experience now, and see how vividly you can bring in the emotion of these two past experiences. Try, as much as possible, to exclude any thoughts other than those directly associated with the experience in order to further strengthen this effect. If you wish, you might describe these two memories to a friend, noting your ability to feel the attached emotion.

You have now used the process of remembering to retrieve both the objective (the physical facts of the memory) and the subjective (emotional recollections) from the unconscious mind. At the same time you demonstrated how it was possible to use the mind to alter one's emotional state to a perceptible degree, by reevoking emotions associated with a memory. Though the incident is no longer occurring, you can respond to its memory as though it were.

The process of remembering is an interaction between the conscious and the unconscious mind, which may occur when the conscious mind requests a certain response from the unconscious mind. You may ask it to recall names, ideas, or other factual information from its storage. You may also ask it to perform some activity, such as directing your hands to brush your hair, type, or open a door. Again, this performance depends upon its ability to remember learned behavior. We make these requests of the unconscious because we desire certain things, and a desire usually includes an emotion of one kind or another. Thus an emotion is usually present as a precursor to willing activities from the unconscious. You can probably remember the names of several of your schoolmates from years ago, yet, unless there is some emotion that impels you to do so, you will probably not bother to make the effort.

If you have the choice of reading a science fiction book, eating a carrot, or playing a trumpet, your selection will depend upon your guess as to which will produce the most favorable emotion. If you have never learned to play a trumpet, you may look forward to the excitement of experimentation or, conversely, choose not to try because you dislike the frustration of not being able to produce a clear note. In a similar manner, your likes and dislikes in food and literature will be fundamental in determining whether you will desire the carrot or the book. Your present emotional state and the emotions you imagine in the future are the keys to your selection.

On the other hand, actions, memories, and emotions may be triggered, so it seems, not by the conscious appraisal of a situation, but by the activity of the unconscious mind itself. You have perhaps experienced the sensation of walking down the street and suddenly finding the name of a friend come to mind, a friend you may not have thought about for years. Though you were not looking for his or her name, and though it seems to bear little relationship to the other thoughts you have been considering, it nevertheless pops into your consciousness. In like fashion, we often find ourselves automatically doing such things as scratching an itchy spot, wandering into the kitchen for a snack, or tapping a foot, never having consciously directed the unconscious mind to carry out this activity. In a similar manner we frequently experience the injection into our consciousness of an *emotion* by the unconcious mind, though we are usually unaware of its source. Sometimes this emotion seems reasonable when we stop to examine the circumstances of our current lives and environment, but often it comes up for some unknown reason, and doesn't seem to fit. A day of depression may be described as one in which "I got up on the wrong side of the bed." Likewise, sometimes we find ourselves extremely happy and full of energy for no apparent good reason.

Our emotions, then, are determined primarily by our previous experiences interwoven with the experiences of the present. Any new perceptions or actions thus create a new set of emotions that impels us to make new decisions and initiate new actions.

Though at any moment we may become aware of our emotion and decide to alter things so as to produce a more satisfactory and productive emotion, few people take the time to do so. As a result, maladaptive emotional states, such as depression, anger, frustration, and anxiety can produce an ever-tightening spiral in which we can become more and more trapped.

A friend of mine provides an excellent example of this. His unhappiness with a difficult assignment given him one morning caused him to be touchy, and before long an argument with a co-worker had erupted. He developed a tension headache later that morning, and because he fell behind he had to rush through lunch. His mood became even more sour when he developed indigestion a little while later, and he began to make more mistakes in his work. By the time he reached home, he was so irritable that the discovery of his three-year-old child's lollipop stuck on the corner of a chair was sufficient to throw him into a rage directed at his wife, who "must have been gossiping with her friends all day long" and at his child who "ran amok through the house" while he was at work breaking his back to make a good life for them.

It is obvious that his reaction to each successive event was dictated more by his emotional state of consciousness than by the situation itself. A few days later he was embarrassed and ashamed of his irrational anger of that day. You can probably supply multiple examples of similar occurrences in your own life. When we are in these mental states we feel as though the situation is controlling us. Yet, looking at them from our present, rational viewpoint, we can see clearly that a simple alteration in emotion could change the entire outcome. Few people, however, even consider that this can be done, fewer still attempt it, and an even smaller number are successful.

If something so simple can so profoundly alter the path of our life, why do we not make use of it? Not only would the immediate situation be changed, but the future would also probably be much different. Because my friend will undoubtedly have difficult assignments in the future, he will probably in the future experience the same emotions that he experienced in the example given, only stronger, and less under his control.

I once was driving my car in a heavy New York rain when I had to stop for a stoplight. Next to me was a man in a small foreign convertible. He was red in the face and swearing loudly. I asked him what was wrong and he said that he was angry because he was getting wet. I asked him why he didn't put up the roof on his car, and he said that the car was borrowed and he didn't know how to work it.

I was familiar with the procedure, and it took me only a moment to point out to him the lever that had to be released in order to accomplish this simple task, a task that he performed rapidly.

My observations over the past few years indicate a similar fact about people and their feelings—we have simply never been taught how to alter our emotional state. There is also a simple mental latch that can help us out of our emotional storms. Next we will learn to find and operate it.

CHAPTER 4

Developing Selective Awareness

U p to this point the experiences suggested have been short and used the Selective Awareness capabilities of the conscious mind to focus on specific mental items and processes. You experienced minor alterations in your state and focus of awareness, and these changes were generally related to the images being reviewed at that moment. The techniques in this section, are also simple to apply, and will enable you to reach states profoundly different from your ordinary waking consciousness.

Each of the experiences suggested contained a set of instructions. After you read them you requested your unconscious mind to perform them, and probably obtained the expected results. If we view the unconscious mind as analogous to a computer, then we can call the instructions a program that you gave to this computer. This program instructed your bio-computer to focus on physical sensations, memories, and emotions, and gave guidelines to follow in this activity. To guide you to the states of awareness commonly associated with deep relaxation, hypnosis, and meditation, we will use a similar approach.

We must somehow define the state for which we are aiming, a more complex task than defining the simple memory goals of the previous chapter. Also, the unconscious mind must carry out the program on its own so that our awareness may be free to focus on the results, rather than on the program itself. And keep in mind that the development of an emotion takes, in general, much longer than the development of a thought, idea, or memory. This is partly because a biologically older part of the brain is brought into play, and many more structures must be utilized, so the length of time spent in the experience of an emotion will, of necessity, be somewhat longer, at least at first. We can begin by tapping our experience to determine just what is meant by a state of awareness.

States of Awareness

A multitude of different states of awareness is possible for any person. When you are happy your state of awareness is quite different from when you are sad. Anyone who has experienced the effect of tranquilizers, diet pills, cigarettes, alcohol, marijuana, or psychedelic agents such as LSD or mescaline is aware of the different states of awareness that can be reached through these means. Other ways of changing one's state of awareness include meditation, prayer, dreaming (day or night), and hypnosis. As mentioned in the preceding chapter, happiness, fear, loneliness, sadness, and anger each produce a characteristic alteration in awareness (resulting in a change in our response to ongoing reality). The well-known "runner's high" is yet another way of shifting states of awareness.

A particular state of mind occurs when a person's thought processes continue to follow along a specific pathway. Listening to a sad story or seeing a depressing motion picture often alters our thought processes and produces sorrow or depression in us. An inspiring discussion or happy movie can likewise create a pleasant state of consciousness. More dramatic changes can be attained through meditation, hypnosis, or prayer. These require a certain degree of training, after which, by following certain prescribed thought patterns (programs), a person is able to reach specific *desirable* states of awareness. These are most interesting because they are *chosen by the person himself or herself;* the person controls his or her own experience *voluntarily.*

The method we will use is similar in many respects to these techniques. It is called guided imagery, and its goal is to produce a calm, relaxed state. This state of mind is produced by thinking certain calming thought patterns and eliminating other, unwanted thought patterns. Even as we can be selectively aware, at any given moment, of names, parts of our bodies, places, and memories, this same capability of the conscious mind may be used to bring up memories and ideas that have a calming and relaxing efffect.

Sometimes called a relaxation induction, this process is a means of *leading into* a particular state of awareness. The state of mind experienced following any given guided imagery experience will vary from one individual to another and even vary within the same individual from one induction to the next. The goal is not to achieve a rigidly defined or unchanging state of consciousness. All of us have an idea of what a nice home is like, but in designing our most desirable home we would not all design the same house in the same location. You might enjoy being near the seaside; I might find the fog there undesirable. Likewise, you might find my beloved pine trees not to your taste. Ideas of what constitutes a handsome man or beautiful woman, good music, or a pleasant vacation also vary markedly from person to person.

Similarly, the state of mind for which you are aiming will be as uniquely yours as is the sum of your likes and dislikes and will vary depending upon the time, surroundings, and purpose. Obviously, then, the state of mind reached through the induction will differ among different people.

It is not a state that we work to achieve, but one that we allow to temporarily superimpose itself on our minds; we are open and receptive to it. In the same way that heat induces water to boil and a lower temperature induces it to form ice, following the pattern of images and having an open mind permits the appropriate state to develop. Any attempts to *evaluate* the state of mind reached through the induction may unlock a long series of memories and comparisons that may rapidly destroy it. Striving is not necessary in order for the water to change its form, nor is it necessary to *aim* for a particular state of mind during the induction.

In fact, we should not specify the exact state of mind or aim for a specific quality, because we might then be limited by the very concepts we choose. We realize that a talented or intelligent child has a potentiality for developing. We do not know what field he or she will enter later in life or what his or her experiences will be. The training (programming) we give the child, then, should be as general and as flexible as possible. Nor should we try to push the child along preconceived lines; we should try to allow him or her to experience and learn in as free a manner as possible, thereby permitting him or her to develop in the most natural fashion.

Let yourself, then, be free from any preconceived notions regarding your experience. As you repeat the imagery each day, merely observe and learn from the many states you will experience. Relaxation feels different on different days!

There are some qualities of awareness that have been experienced by nearly everyone and that have certain features in common. They may give you an idea of what to expect. You may remember the feeling of awakening in the morning on a weekend or holiday when there was no work ahead. If you remained in bed, perhaps with the sun shining in on you, and allowed yourself to awaken slowly, you may have noticed that before your eyes opened you were aware that you were awake but as yet you hadn't placed yourself in any particular location. You could have been on the bed, you could have been floating in the air, you could have been in any of five or six different places that came to your mind at that moment. You could feel your body, but it seemed to be some distance away, almost as though it were enveloped in a cloud. Though you knew that you could end the mystery rapidly, you may have tried momentarily to maintain it and avoid the inevitable awakening. Only gradually, as you became more awake, did you become aware of where you were. Slowly, the real world began to tumble in and limit your mental freedom and imagination.

This far-off feeling is similar to the feeling you have when you are lost in thought and staring off into the distance. On such an occasion someone may notice the curious look in your eye and ask what you are looking at. At this point you suddenly realize that although you have been staring in the same direction for several minutes, you have not been "seeing" what has been in front of you. Though your eyes have been open, you mind had decided to focus instead on other, more internal thoughts. If a jack-o-lantern or a peacock had suddenly appeared right at the point where your eyes were focused, you would have seen it immediately, but because nothing so interesting was happening, your mind preferred to slip into what is often called daydreaming.

Perhaps you can remember being so engrossed in a book that you simply did not hear your name being called, although the sound was quite audible. Again, so interesting was the material in that book that your mind had turned off most of its attention to the rest of the world. You might compare this to the markedly less relaxed state your mind is in when you are trying to learn every detail in a book for an examination. At an unpleasant time such as this, even the distant sound of a passing car will be a most annoying distraction. This tends to happen more often when the mind is not really interested in the task before it.

The early morning state, daydreaming, and being engrossed in a book are all similar; they represent a *passive* concentration of the mind on thought patterns passing *through* the mind. At such times one abandons the task of remaining directly aware of one's external environment. In each of these cases, no effort was needed to achieve this state of mind. The thought processes were merely allowed to flow on unhindered.

If we were to ask several people to describe the feelings they have at these times, they might use the word *relaxed*. The precise feeling associated with this relaxation, however, may be described differently by each person. It may be perceived by some as a heavy feeling in the arms and legs, by others as a light feeling. Still others may feel as though parts of the body have completely disappeared. Some may sense a gentle rocking motion; others may feel firm and steady. Obviously, no particular set of feelings is superior to any other set. The "correct" set of feelings is simply that which you are feeling at the time. After performing the induction you will feel relaxed, perhaps more relaxed than you can remember ever being before.

Another feature that all these states of mind share is that they may be interrupted by certain kinds of thinking: *analytical thinking* or *critical thinking*. If you become interested in examining the quality of the printing or the typeface in the book you are reading, become interested in the weight of the pages, or are forced to continually turn back to check and see if you have remembered the story correctly, the receptive, relaxed pattern of thought flow will be interrupted. During a daydream, if you are suddenly concerned with what is in front of you and bring it into focus, your reverie will be halted. If you awaken early in the morning and begin immediately to think about your chores for that day, you may find that the pleasant feeling you have been experiencing disappears rapidly.

Similarly, while inducing relaxation, if you become overly concerned with the exact words being used, the accent or speech traits of the voice, or the noise that is present in the background, the proper thought flow will be impossible. If you continually criticize and evaluate your progress during the induction, this will hinder the progress.

There seems to be a part of the mind that tends to question everything and bring in memories of other experiences during an induction. It is the part of the mind that has been trained to analyze, to worry, to mistrust, to doubt, and to divide experience into parts. It is a linear process, closely associated with the function of speech. It has become fashionable to refer to this as left brain thinking, because the left cerebral hemisphere is usually primary in this kind of functioning (at least in most right-handed people).

This little voice should be recognized as being an unwanted one and the question ignored for the time being. No attempts to figure out anything are necessary during an induction. Such attempts will, in fact, detract from your ability to get the maximum benefit from the experience. Of course, having grown up in a culture where analytical and critical thinking is highly valued, and relaxed self-acceptance practically forbidden, you may need to practice before you get the knack.

Imagination

Imagination is one of the most important factors we use during an induction. And, for anyone who might be tempted, don't say you "have no imagination." When it comes right down to it, everyone has a pretty good imagination, although many of us have learned to suppress many of the activities of the right brain.

Take, for example, a man sitting in the movies. He is in an enclosed room, with perhaps the sound of air conditioners humming in his ears. There are several hundred people sitting around him, some eating popcorn, some chatting among themselves. Others are walking up and down the aisles, searching for seats. But his eyes are fixed on a plastic screen hung in the front of the room, and he is watching shadows being produced from a film being run through a projector. Yet during his stay in the movies, he will probably spend only a few minutes thinking about the realistic aspects of his environment.

Instead, as the cowboy star rides across the desert, he feels that he too is riding across the desert. When there is a dive beneath the sea and multicolored fish swim by, he believes that he is underwater seeing the fish. He doesn't consider the reality of the situation: that he is seeing only a pattern of light and dark images on a screen, and his imagination is creating their reality. They are not moving; they are still images being projected sequentially—his imagination supplies the movement. He is under the illusion that the fish are real and may act as though they were real, even to the point of feeling fear as the giant squid attacks the diver. The curious thing about this illusion is that he is not really being tricked. He has merely made the conscious decision to suspend his usual critical factors, to suspend disbelief. Rather than continually analyzing the situation, he decides to permit his imagination to follow the course suggested by the movie.

The imagination used during a guided imagery experience is similar to the imagination we use to bring to life characters in movies or in books. In books the only stimuli we have are little black marks on white pieces of paper. These black marks are not perceived as letters or words but as ideas, people, and places, and at times you may become very emotionally involved with these ideas, people, and places.

In a like manner you may learn to experience the emotions and situations that you imagine during the induction as "real," just as they are when you are deeply involved in a book or movie. The major difference is that rather than following the exact colors, shapes, images, and sounds a story or movie dictates, during guided imagery the imagination is given a range of situations and feelings from which to choose. In addition, because the subject of the experience is you yourself, not a character, the experience can be all the more valid. Of course much less concentration and creativeness are needed to make movie or TV images "real," because visual stimuli are so compelling to the imagination. But therein lies the difference—the smaller the amount of imagination used, the less personal are the images and the less useful they are for catalyzing personal change. It does, however, help, especially when first learning these techniques, to have the experience induction recorded on tape. Most people find that when appropriate music is included the effect is stronger. You may make your own tapes by reading the Experience onto a cassette, or by using prerecorded experiential cassetes. Excellent tapes to start with are "Rainbow Butterfly" or "Letting Go of Stress." (See the list of tapes on pages 284 and 285.)

Allowing Spontaneous Imagery

EXPERIENCE SIX

A most vital process in developing selective states of awareness is the experiencing of spontaneous thinking. Be sure to spend at least one full minute on this exercise, and take care to follow the instructions explicitly. Do not give yourself any additional instructions. If you find it difficult at first, start again, giving yourself more time.

Close your eyes and imagine a tree, allowing the images and details of the tree to arise spontaneously in your mind.

Notice that in imagining a tree you may have been able to actually "see" a tree in your mind's eye. Perhaps you imagined the sound of the leaves waving in the wind. You may have imagined it as it appears in a particular season—such as winter, spring, or fall. You may have imagined a tree during a storm, or one dropping its seeds to the earth. It may have been large or small, growing in the woods, or it may have been growing on a busy city street corner. Different people will, of course, imagine different things. We can be pretty certain, however, that you didn't imagine sharp fangs, hooves, ears, wheels, or an underwater plant. With the instruction to imagine a tree, you found your mind effortlessy filled with one set of images, and as a result, many other possible images were automatically excluded.

Regardless of whether you saw, heard, tasted (some people may have thought of a fruit tree), or sensed with the intellect what you imagined, the act of imagining has been sufficient to bring about the desired results: *the selection of certain items and the exclusion of others—Selective Awareness.*

In using the imagination people tend to fall into one or more of several categories, including visualizers, feelers, and hearers. Some "see" the images, others "feel" them, and still others "hear" them. Each way of sensing with the mind has its advantages, and we will explore how you can experience all ways. For now, however, simply accept the imagination the way it is.

EXPERIENCE SEVEN

Close your eyes and once again spend a minute imagining a tree. Let your mind fill in more details of the tree, its activities, environments, sounds, and so on.

Notice that this time your mind provided many more images for your consideration, even though no more effort was expended than the first time. Notice how much more freedom your mind has to paint a picture now that you better understand what is meant by spontaneous imagery.

EXPERIENCE EIGHT

Now spend a minute or more imagining a tree, but this time, rather than simply allowing your mind to do it, try to be very conscious and exact. Start out either at the roots or the highest branch, or some other point of departure, and imagine it as fully as possible, trying not to miss any details. Then continue to imagine very precisely in your mind its environment.

Most people find this Experience less pleasant than the previous one. It requires a certain amount of effort and a certain amount of analyzing and cataloging to get the information into a preconceived order.

This kind of concentration and imagination tends to create tension in the mind and body, a vaguely unpleasant sense of "having to do something." For this reason forced concentration such as this must be avoided during a relaxation process as it would interfere with the relaxation. Allow yourself instead to experience a more relaxed, passive concentration, as you did the first two times.

Just about the only conscious program necessary during an imagery Experience is the desire to allow the mind to fix on an idea and eliminate all others. Your spontaneous imagination will supply the details. As details are noted by your conscious mind, it isn't necessary to analyze, criticize, or evaluate them; just passively observe them and continue to follow along with the suggested images. If you find yourself getting hung up on a particular thought or part of an image, just let it go and follow the next suggested pattern in the induction.

Preparing for a Guided Imagery Experience

1. Find a comfortable place where you can feel relaxed. For most people this will be a reclining position, but if you tend to fall asleep very easily, a sitting position with the head unsupported by a head rest, as in meditating, may be preferable. Although

it is possible to experience an induction standing up or in any other posture, lying down will probably be the most comfortable position for you at this point.

2. Before sitting or lying down, make sure you have no obligations for the next fifteen minutes. Any concerns about parking meters that may run overtime, phone calls you may be expecting, or even timers due to go off soon would serve as significant distractions. The state of mind you will be experiencing is a delicate one, and even minor worldly concerns such as these could serve as interruptions.

3. As you assume a comfortable position, make sure that your surroundings are as quiet as you can make them. Dim the lights if possible. Make sure that you are not restricting the blood flow in your arms or legs. It might also help to loosen your clothing. Use the toilet if you feel this sensation might interfere later.

4. Remember, above all, do not evaluate your progress, the process itself, or anything else that comes to mind during the process. The induction will be critically evaluated according to a specific method *after* you listen to it.

5. Carry out the Experiences as suggested. If you do not have one of the tapes suggested on pages 284–288, the most effective methods are having a friend read the instructions to you or listening to your voice reading them on a tape recorder. Alternatively, you may memorize the procedure in a loose fashion, then close your eyes and let yourself drift through it; it is the overall flow that is important, not the little details. The voice (including your own internal voice) should be relaxed, interested, and pleasing. Adequate time should be allowed for completion of each suggestion.

   The times indicated are rough guides that you may change to improve your Experience.

6. The first Experience is the one I have found most useful. Practice it several times a day. As you become more familiar with

using the concepts, less and less time will be required to produce the same state.

Pause in your reading following the Experience, and be sure to practice the process a few times a day, until you feel you have mastered it, even though days or weeks may elapse before you continue your reading. This is an excellent form of meditation and will aid in decreasing your internal stress, as well as teach the technique—and future Experiences will be based upon this Experience.

Each imagery Experience consists of four main parts: physical relaxation, mental relaxation, imagery, and returning from deep relaxation to your usual waking awareness. At different points in the book I will present various methods for accomplishing each of these actions. Try them all, then choose the ones most effective for you. Of course the physical relaxation from one Experience may be used with the mental relaxation from another, and more than one type of physical relaxation may be used in a single Experience. As you read on, feel free to experiment with different Experiences and groups of suggestions as you wish. Remember, you are talking to yourself; your own ideas, words, and expressions will ultimately prove even more effective than those of another person. If you are listening to a tape, feel free to mentally change words or images into those that are more effective for you. The important idea is to produce deep relaxation and clarity of mind before the suggestions are given.

I have given suggestions as to how much time to spend with each phase of the Experience. These are general, and some people may wish to take two or three times as long to perform certain of the phases and only a fraction of the time for others. Generally speaking, as you become more Experienced with the induction of relaxation, you will be able to perform it more rapidly. Thus the entire experience, which took fifteen minutes the first few times, may be completed in three or four minutes. The thing you must be certain of is that you reach a deep level of relaxation each time, even as you progressively shorten the induction procedure. It is essential that your body can be as relaxed as it can and your mind be as quiet as it can.

EXPERIENCE NINE
SOFTWARE ONE

Remember—make sure you memorize the procedures or, better still, read the instructions onto a tape (or have them read to you). It's a good idea to carry out the induction and suggestions without having to return to wakefulness and open your eyes to read the next step. You may use the first experience on tape 10 (see p. 285) in lieu of the following induction, but this is the method of choice.

A. Physical Relaxation

This method of physical relaxation employs the technique of first relaxing the muscles in your eyelids, the smallest muscles in your body, and then letting the other muscles in your body imitate this same feeling. The process is repeated until the desired level of relaxation is reached.

1. *First, loosen all constricting clothing and find a comfortable place in which you can sit or lie. Find a position in which you can remain comfortably motionless for a few minutes. Then, with your eyes open, find an object or an area on the ceiling or wall opposite you upon which to focus your attention. Once you have chosen this, keep your eyes fixed on it. The tendency of your eyes to want to wander around the room are signs of anxiety from your mind; keeping them fixed on one single object is a way of telling your mind there is nothing else in the room of which you need to be aware.*

   You will notice that you can bring the object in very clearly at first, seeing the colors, shape, size, and lighting, and you can even imagine what its texture might be if you were to reach out and touch it.

   Pretty soon you will notice a tendency to drift into that state of mind that we call daydreaming. Although your eyes are still open, the object is "out of focus." This is a sign that your mind has become more interested in looking inside at your thoughts than looking outside. Let it happen.

2. *Soon you will find your eyes beginning to sting, burn, or blink more frequently. Take this as an indication that your eyes would feel more comfortable closed. Because you are allowing the most comfortable things to happen, let them close when they feel ready. As they close, imagine the muscles in your eyelids are letting go after having to carry those heavy eyelids for so long, and focus all the attention that was focused on the object outside on the inside of your eyelids. Become aware of their warmth and relaxation.* (About one minute)

3. *Now let the relaxation in your eyelids increase all the way to the point where they just won't open at all. You might find it comfortable to gently roll your eyes upward a slight bit behind your closed eyelids. Imagine that you are looking at a little screen on the back of your forehead, and on that screen you can see printed the word* Relax. *As you see that word,* Relax, *imagine your eyelids are so relaxed they just won't open at all. Then, very gently test them, proving to yourself that you can leave them relaxed and closed.* (About thirty seconds)
    Of course if you really wish to open your eyelids you can, but in order to do so you would have to unrelax them. Because the object is to allow any relaxation you have to stay, keep your eyes rolled upward and test gently at first.

4. *As you test your eyelids, let the relaxation flow throughout all the rest of your body, one part at a time, starting with your forehead and letting it flow down to the muscles of your face, neck, shoulders, and fingertips.*

5. *Take a deep breath, drawing the relaxation up from your fingertips into your chest. As you let that breath out, imagine you are a balloon letting out all the air, becoming completely flat.*

6. *Stop breathing and let the air breathe for you, as it does when you are asleep or not thinking about it. As it breathes, feel the relaxation flowing into the abdominal muscles and the internal organs.*

7. *Allow it to continue to flow through the pelvic area and all the way down your thighs and legs to the tips of your toes. You have now reached the first stage of physical relaxation.* (One to two minutes)

8. *Next, you will double your relaxation. Do this by opening and closing your eyes. The opening and closing of your eyes will be the signal to let your relaxation double. Wait until you feel as though the relaxation in your eyelids is twice what it was before you opened them. See the word* Relax *behind your forehead again, then very gently test your eyelids to make sure you have doubled your relaxation. And, as you test them, let that doubled relaxation flow throughout the rest of your body. Allow this to happen rapidly, as though you were being covered with a warm blanket of comfort.* (About one minute)

9. *Double your relaxation once again by opening and closing your eyes. As your eyelids open and close, let their relaxation increase to the point where you don't have to test them anymore. When you are certain your eyelids are so relaxed you don't even have to test them, and when you are sure that they just wouldn't budge if you were to test them, let the feeling of not having to test flow throughout your eyelids, down your body, and right out the soles of your feet. You have now reached the third stage of relaxation.* (About one minute)

10. *You may stay in this state for about five or ten minutes. You are now ready to receive suggestions for mental relaxation.*

B. Mental Relaxation: Erasing Distractions

1. *Going on to the even more comfortable stage of mental relaxation, count softly, out loud, backward from 100. As you count, your mental relaxation will double with each number. If you imagine you can see those numbers projected on a screen in your mind as you count, let the numbers grow dimmer. By the time you get to 97 or 96, you will find you will be able to let the numbers disappear completely. Of course the numbers are still in your*

unconscious and you can get them back anytime you wish to, but now you can experience the freedom of not having to think them.

2. *In order to help those numbers disappear, you might recall the relaxation in your eyelids and, as you test them, let a wave of relaxation flow through your mind and erase the numbers like waves might erase words written in the sand.* (About one minute)

3. *Anytime unnecessary thoughts, questions, or memories occur, simply see them projected on that same screen, double your mental relaxation, and let them disappear, as the numbers did. You will always be able to recall those thoughts if you ever feel you need them.*

C. Imagery: Image of Relaxation

Now that you are mentally and physically relaxed, you are ready to project desirable images in your mind.

1. *Form an image of relaxation in your mind. Choose a place you have been on vacation or a place you would like to go. Visualize yourself there, looking and feeling just as you would like. Give yourself exactly the mind and body you would like to have. Let yourself be dressed the way you would like to be dressed and doing something that you find rewarding. Feel yourself far, far away from any place where you might have any worries, cares, or annoyances.* (About one minute)

2. *Take a deep breath and, as you let it out, let yourself drift into that image and feel yourself there, using all five of your senses. Look around you and imagine seeing everything just as you would like it to be, surrounded by all the things that make you feel really comfortable. If your body is in motion, feel the movement; if it is motionless, feel the stillness. Hear any sounds there are to hear; taste the tastes; smell the smells.* (About one minute)

3. *After you have allowed this image to come in as clearly as it will, give yourself the message down inside that you can feel this way anytime you want to. No matter where you are or what you're doing, simply recall that little word,* Relax, *and as you bring this relaxing scene to mind, you will reinduce some of the same relaxation you have at this moment. As you think the word* Relax, *or visualize that scene, you will note that whatever you're doing will seem much more comfortable.* (About one minute)

D. Returning to Your Usual State of Consciousness

Always bring yourself out of a state of deep relaxation very gradually. The more slowly you can bring yourself out, the more relaxed you will be the next time.

1. *The best way to do this is to count from one to five, to yourself. With each number, feel yourself floating up to another level of being more awake. Suggest to yourself that you will come up feeling relaxed, comfortable, wide awake, refreshed, and feeling really good.*

2. *After you have counted to five, take a deep breath. Open your eyes and take a few moments to notice how comfortable you feel.* (One minute)

3. *Take a few moments and go back over the experience of the last few minutes. It's most important that your mind learn that any thought it has set aside during the induction, it will be able to go back to during the two or three minutes afterward. Never jump up and run to do something without giving your mind an opportunity to look back and see what has happened during the induction.*

4. *Always make sure you feel completely clear-headed, wide awake, and alert before driving, using heavy equipment, or doing anything else requiring full wakefulness.*

CHAPTER 5

Tension, Anxiety, and Physical Symptoms

Tension and Anxiety

Tension and anxiety are two closely related concepts that refer to our reaction to stressful stimuli and environments.

We will use the word *anxiety* to refer to an emotional state. It's a feeling of apprehension, worry, fear, or even frank panic. We feel it when we miss a train or plane to take us to an important appointment, when we are in danger, when we are depressed, or when we lose our temper. We may also feel it when there is an important task to be done, when something is hanging over our heads.

Tension refers to the physical sensation of tightness—a clothesline, an elastic band, a shirt collar, or a muscle may be tense. A person may feel generalized tension; all the muscles of the body may be tense. We shall soon see how muscle spasm and tension is believed by many to be implicated in perhaps 95 percent of the physical symptoms endured by humanity.

We often use *anxiety* and *tension* interchangeably, and with good reason. It is seldom that we find one in the absence of the other. If you were suddenly awakened at night by a cramp or spasm of a muscle in your chest or leg, you would feel anxious.

Similarly, when anxiety is present the muscles of the body will reflect it. Sometimes this tension may escape our conscious awareness, but a sensitive instrument such as a polygraph or electromyograph can demonstrate it easily.

If a muscle tension occurs repeatedly or continuously, the muscle or organs served by the muscle may begin to undergo damage and symptoms may appear. If the process is allowed to continue, physical death of important cells may occur and irreversible changes can result.

First we will examine how these tensions arise in a muscle and how the symptoms are produced. Then we will examine why we human beings, superior in most other respects to other forms of life, seem to be afflicted with such a huge number of aches and pains and physical disease found rarely, if at all, in other species.

Finally, we will learn how to apply the Selective Awareness induction so that these physical tensions and their symptoms can be relieved without the use of external agents.

The Pain-Spasm Cycle

Muscles come in many varieties; the giant muscle of the thigh and the minute muscle in the wall of a blood vessel; the soft involuntary muscle of the intestine and the tough, fibrous muscle of the arm; the automatic muscle of the heart, and the sometimes voluntary, sometimes involuntary muscle of the diaphragm. Regardless of which muscle we choose, however, the basic function is always the same—movement—whether it is the tightening of the jaw to eat a nut, the smooth peristalsis of the intestine digesting food, or the bristling of a hair with fear or anger.

A muscle cell accomplishes its goal of movement by shortening. Once a muscle has been instructed to move by a chemical or nervous impulse, it contracts, becoming shorter. Once it has contracted, the muscle cell will be unable to perform any function unless there is a relaxation period in which the cell is allowed to elongate again.

EXPERIENCE TEN

Move your hand in the air as though you were alternately pushing and pulling something. As you do so, notice the smooth alternating contractions and relaxations in the front and back of your arm.

Now place one hand on the biceps muscle of this arm. (This is the muscle in the front of the upper arm that contracts when you lift something very heavy or when you show someone your muscle. Straighten, then bend your arm, clench your fist, and continue to tighten this muscle more and more until you feel it bulge. Relax the muscle, straighten your arm, and repeat this. Notice the similarity to the contraction and relaxation felt during the waving. You can feel this both within the biceps muscle and also with the hand that is feeling the muscle.

The kind of contraction you have been experiencing is normal, healthy muscle contraction, and we may refer to it as dynamic tension. Sometimes muscle contraction is not so smooth and controlled. The other kind of contraction is called static, and is responsible for muscle knots, charley horses, indigestion, and headaches. Sometimes this kind of contraction is called spasm. Spasm differs from normal contraction in that the muscle contracted in spasm tends to remain contracted, and the usual relaxation phase does not occur. It may be painful, as in a headache, or it may announce its presence to us through some other symptom, such as diarrhea or asthma.

You might begin to wonder why nature bothered to equip our bodies with processes such as spasms, which seem to be responsible for so many difficulties. Actually, the spasm is a necessary process of the body, which causes problems and diseases only when it gets out of control. We tend to visualize our bodies as belonging to our twentieth-century environment. The truth seems to be, however, that our bodies evolved in a much more primitive setting. Indeed, our bodies are about the same as bodies were thirty thousand to forty thousand years ago, although living conditions have altered considerably.

Back at that time humans were probably living in caves or in the forest, with little or no spoken or written language. It was important for the muscular system and its nervous connectons to function properly, as there were no doctors around to perform surgery or to put on a cast if an injury occurred. Muscle injuries were most likely common, and the injured muscle had to have a way of protecting itself from further damage and repairing itself.

Because primitive people were incapable of making a diagnosis and carrying out treatment consciously, the repair work had to be accomplished through completely automatic mechanisms. One of these mechanisms was pain. This pain caused a person to stop using the muscle. And because a torn muscle is more prone to further injury, it would have been of utmost importance that the primitive person be prevented from putting the usual amounts of stress upon it.

A second automatic mechanism is muscle spasm. This spasm seems to have at least three main functions. If the torn area of the muscle tissue is not somehow protected, this muscle tear would tend to progress just as if it were a stocking developing a run or a piece of paper tearing. As nearby areas of the muscle go into spasm, the effect is like that of a drop of nail polish, which stops the run, or a piece of tape, which halts the progression of the rip. Another benefit of the contraction is that the torn ends of the muscle are brought closer together, so the muscle can reconnect and later have essentially the same capacity as before the accident. Finally, the spasm of the muscle and of the blood vessels in the torn ends tends to halt blood loss.

The injured muscle leaks fluid from within the torn cells and this fluid, with its particular balance of chemicals, stimulates the nerve endings. This information is carried by the nerve to the spinal cord. Two things happen to this information at this point. It is relayed to the brain by other nerves, where it is subjectively experienced as pain. More important to us at this time, however, are the reflex areas and the local neural activity that occur at the level of the spinal cord. The information brought to the spinal cord by these nerves is relayed to the motor nerves, which return to the vicinity of the tear. There they signal to the muscle to go into a prolonged contraction. The automatic way in which these lower reflexes operate will be clear if you recall how your foot involuntarily jumps forward when the doctor taps just below your kneecap in testing your reflexes. The muscle automatically contracts when the tendon is tapped by the hammer. The basic principle is similar, though in the present case pain, rather than the stretching of a tendon by a tap, is used as the stimulus for the tightening.

As the two torn ends of the muscle begin to heal, the chemicals that accompanied the injury are no longer being manufactured. The pain in the muscle disappears and the motor nerves going back to the spastic area cease to fire, because the nerves are no longer being stimulated to trigger them. The spasm has faded, the muscle has healed and is no longer painful, and the primitive person feels as good as new.

Now let's suppose that for some reason a spasm appeared in your muscle but failed to disappear, and perhaps grew even stronger. The muscle cells within the area of spasm would soon be injured because of the pressure and the lack of blood. They would therefore begin to manufacture the usual chemicals manufactured by a muscle cell that has been injured.

This chemical would be picked up by nerve endings in the area and relayed to the spinal cord. You would feel pain and the spinal cord, believing that this pain was due to a muscle tear, would inform the surrounding muscle to go into spasm. This spasm, of course, would produce further muscle injury and more powerful chemicals would be released by the muscle. As the sensory nerves would be stimulated even further, you would feel more pain, and the motor nerves would be instructed to contract the muscles even more. This is called the pain–spasm cycle. It represents one of the most basic ways that headaches are produced (tension headaches). In our culture we usually take muscle relaxant drugs or pain relievers to diminish the spasm or the pain.

Now we will take a brief look at some of the other diseases and everyday problems that seem to be directly related to this reflex mechanism and its resultant spasm.

Symptoms Originating in Muscle Tension

In studying different cultures and languages, we find certain kinds of expressions that pervade nearly every civilized culture. These are expressions that describe emotional and psychological states in terms of physical sensations or symptoms. This is often called organ language.

If you told anyone that your job was "a real headache" or "a pain in the neck," that person would understand what you meant. This is because psychological stress of a certain type is often associated with tension of neck and scalp muscles and, finally, pain in the head.

Physicians often give esoteric names to these processes, depending upon exactly what structures are involved or what seems to initiate the difficulty. The list of names for headaches is one of the longest. The list includes cluster headaches, tension headaches, migraine headaches, hystamine cephalgia, temporal arteritis, trapezius spasm, and many more. Chiropractors have still another set of names, such as cervical spine subluxation and atlas-axis dislocation.

The basic mechanism responsible for the development of the pain in most cases, however, is muscle tension and spasm. They differ only in that in each case a different set of muscles is painful and spastic. For instance, in tension headaches and when we have the familiar "pain in the neck," the muscles that become painful and spastic are often those of the neck; temporal arteritis and migraine involve spasm and pain in the muscular walls of the blood vessels.

EXPERIENCE ELEVEN

Using your fingers, carefully feel the muscles of your shoulders and neck, especially the muscles in the back of the neck. If you press firmly you may be able to detect tiny areas that are quite tender. These are sometimes called trigger points. You may even be able to feel the tension, spasm, and knots like little ropes and nodules. If you press very hard on these areas, you may actually begin to experience

*the beginning of a headache. Anytime that you are worried or under
a great deal of pressure, you may note that the tenderness becomes
more marked and the spasm easier to feel.*

The muscles that are involved in migraine headache and temporal arteritis are not so easy to detect. The muscles in the walls of an artery form a ring around the open channel of a blood vessel. If these muscles go into spasm, the resulting pain may be recorded by the tiny nerves that carry information back from the blood vessel to the sensory areas of the brain. Because this spasm will interfere with the proper blood flow through the vessel, the organs supplied by the blood vessel will undergo changes because of the limitation in blood flow. These changes may be experienced as dizziness and may ultimately give rise to pain stemming from the nerves in that area.

Even though the muscles in the walls of the artery are smooth (involuntary) muscles, the techniques for eliminating muscle spasm, which you will learn, can usually be applied to them with the same success as is experienced when they are applied to the striated (voluntary) muscles of the neck. For most people, however, more practice is needed to learn to affect these involuntary muscles. (See the cassette, "Headache Relief," Appendix p. 287.)

Tension in the Area of the Mouth and Throat

The muscles of the jaw are some of the first to tense up when a person is under stress. If you ask someone to relax his or her hand or foot, you can flop the extremity around with ease. But try moving someone's jaw muscle, or have another person try to move yours! Even when we try, it's hard to let go. You may even find it hard to move your own jaw with your hand.

Many people experience involuntary clenching of their teeth when awake, and some people find that at night they tend to grind their teeth together. The reflex tension in this case is present in the muscles involved in chewing. Persons who stutter have been shown to possess an abnormally high degree of tension in the tongue and in other structures involved with speaking, especially when they are called upon to express themselves verbally. The growing incidence of temporo-mandibular joint pain attests to the tension most of us hold in our jaw muscles.

Spasm in the esophagus, or "food tube," is a symptom that we all note from time to time. We may experience it as a "lump in the throat." This is also the area involved when we feel we "can't stomach it" or we feel "choked up with emotion" or find that we "can't swallow it." Some of these organ language expressions, such as the latter, refer to situations in which we become involved that appear to be safe when we begin but turn out to be difficult as we learn more about them. The physical act of swallowing is one that we begin voluntarily by pushing something to the back of the throat but that then proceeds automatically. The organ language expressions refer to similar psychological situations.

Spasm in the Chest and Respiratory System

One physiological problem that is frequently associated with emotional stress connections is asthma. Contrary to what you might expect, the main problem of the asthmatic is not that he or she is unable to inhale sufficient quantities of air, but rather that he or she has too much air and is unable to let it go fully. The small muscles encircling the smallest bronchioles begin to tighten, often because of emotional factors, allergenic substances in the bloodstream or in the air, or a variety of other causes. This tightening of the neck of the alveoli, little air sacs, serves to prevent the air from escaping fully. Thus the asthmatic feels as though he or she cannot take in air and begins inhaling more deeply. This air becomes trapped and he or she feels even more suffocated and afraid.

The result of this fear is further tension and further spasm of these little muscles, and even more air becomes trapped in the alveoli. The wheezes in the chest of a person with this bronchospasm are produced through the same mechanism by which you may have produced a squeaking sound by stretching the neck of a balloon while the air escapes. Further gasps for air yield less and less relief because the main difficulty is that *the air that is trapped within the alveoli must be let go.*

It is a curious thing that the admission ledgers of every hospital across the country show row after row of patients being admitted for the treatment of asthma, treatment that consists either of injection of chemicals in the emergency room or hospitalization for periods up to several weeks, during which time intravenous medications are given and various forms of physical and chemical therapy are attempted to alleviate the asthma and its complications. Death due to asthma, complications secondary to asthma, or complications secondary to the treatment of asthma are frequent. Yet even following this extraordinarily expensive treatment in the hospital, asthmatic patients may find themselves tied forever to bronchodilators, pills, restricted diets and exercise, and chemical inhalers, to which many develop an addiction not unlike an addiction to cigarettes.

I have seen and worked with many individuals of all ages with asthma. Many of them have been able, on their first attempt, to reduce or eliminate the symptoms by tension relaxation methods. Further exploration into the psychological aspects (fear) associated with their disease often leads to alleviation of the disease and sometimes to its disappearance.

An interesting demonstration of the capability of individuals to alter the course of asthma occurred recently at one of the hospitals for children in San Francisco. A well-known and excellent hypnotherapist was giving a lecture on the use of hypnotherapy with children, and to demonstrate its effectiveness requested that several children be brought from the ward. The ones he chose were those hospitalized for the treatment of their asthmatic attacks.

In order to demonstrate the presence of the disease he held his microphone to the chests of the children and allowed the assembled body of physicians to hear the wheezes. He then induced a state of relaxation in all of the children simultaneously, and he gave them the suggestion that they could "let go." They did so readily, and the disappearance of the wheezes was broadcast over the loudspeaker, to the amazement of all present.

The potential for bringing this normally involuntary set of muscles under control of the will was amply demonstrated when the children were asked to reproduce the wheezes for the audience just to "prove that you have full control."

A similar kind of bronchospasm is present as an integral part of other diseases of the chest, including recurrent pneumonia, bronchitis, and emphysema. There are many who believe that recurrent bouts of these diseases are, like asthma, caused by an underlying reflex mechanism involving bronchospasm. Bear in mind throughout this book that nowhere do I mean to put forth the claim that the mind is wholly or partially responsible for the development of *all* symptoms and diseases. In many cases, nevertheless, reflex-type mechanisms are responsible and the problem can be completely eliminated through relaxation and imagery. In those cases in which psychophysiological factors are only partially responsible, only a partial elimination of the problem will be experienced. In those cases in which there is an organic basis to the problem (such as the production of bronchospasms by an irritating chemical in the air or by an infecting organism), proper medical care should, of course, be rendered as quickly as possible. *Before beginning any of the symptom relief techniques in this book, satisfy yourself that your physician has had a chance to examine you and to prescribe all indicated medical treatment. The methods given herein are an aid to, not a replacement for, prompt and proper medical care.*

The Digestive Tract

If you were to shrink down to the size of an aspirin tablet, it would require courage to take a trip through the digestive tract of a tense person.

Even before you left the esophagus, you might be hit with waves of acid being regurgitated from abnormal contractions in the stomach muscle (reflex esophagitis or hiatus hernia). Your arrival in the stomach and the first part of the intestine could be an uncomfortable one indeed (I can't stomach that). Tensions in these structures produce the well-known nervous stomach, along with its symptoms of nausea and pain (indigestion). If you look carefully you might notice, as does the radiologist who examines x-ray studies of this area, that the first sign of a forming ulcer is a local spasm of muscles.

If you take a glance to your right as you pass through the first section of the small intestine, you will see the sphincter of Oddi, the muscle around the duct through which pancreatic juices and bile flow into the small intestine. Spasm in this muscle can precipitate biliary colic, gallbladder inflammation, and other effects in this system ("it galls me"). The effectiveness of this spasm in causing these difficulties is seen when a person given morphine for pain in some other part of the body develops exactly these symptoms, because morphine causes spasm of the sphincter of Oddi in some people. On occasion, full-blown gallbladder disease has been triggered by this means alone.

As you continue your journey through the intestine, you may see areas of inflammation and the frequent muscle spasms associated with them, especially if you have chosen a person with regional ileitis or ulcerative colitis, diseases in which spasm and inflammation cause severe problems in the small and large intestine. Even the little appendix has a muscular wall, and there is some evidence that an attack of appendicitis may be triggered by spasm here. The spasm may prevent decaying fecal matter from leaving, much as air is trapped in the asthmatic's alveoli. As it decays further, infection and inflammation (*-itis*) develop. If things go this far, surgery may be the only answer.

Other problems of the large bowel, such as diarrhea, colitis, diverticulitis, colic, and some forms of constipation, involve muscle spasm.

At the far end of the digesitve tract you will see the anus, an opening surrounded by a circular ring of muscle called the anal sphincter. Blood from outside the anus drains into the venous circulation.

If this muscle goes into spasm the blood flow is blocked, leading to a swelling of the veins known as hemorrhoids. The tender mucous membrane overlying these abnormal vessels may then become irritated, and hard bowel movements can cause their characteristic bleeding.

The usual medical treatment for nearly all these diseases is to relax the muscles and the patient by proper diet, drugs, and rest.

Spasm of the Heart and Blood Vessels

The most common causes of death in this country are diseases directly related to, and resulting from, spasm of the cardiovascular system. Angina pectoris, pain in the chest because of spasm of the blood vessels in the wall of the heart and in the heart muscle itself, is so often seen to be the direct result of psychological tension that these people are routinely treated with tranquilizers. It has become common knowledge that this problem, as well as the heart attack itself, is found much more often in tense individuals. Friedman and Rosenman, *Type A Behavior and Your Heart* explores the evidence relating a tense way of life and cardiovascular disease. As study after study is performed, the evidence mounts up that these problems are many times more common among persons who live lives in which the psychological stress of time pressure and hostility remains at a high level. Doctors, lawyers, and business executives are prime candidates for the early development of these problems.

High blood pressure, another of the most common diseases in the older age groups, is given the technical name of hypertension. This is an aptly chosen name, because it has been shown repeatedly that the degree of psychological tension that a person is experiencing will affect his or her blood pressure markedly. Because of this, the first treatment given for high blood pressure has traditionally been medication that causes the person to be more psychologically relaxed (phenobarbital or Valium). In the early stages of this disease, the blood pressure will rapidly fall to normal with just this tranquilization. Self-induced relaxation also produces this return to normal.

Anyone who is subjected to a high degree of fear, worry, or self-consciousness will have an elevated blood pressure at those times. For most people the blood pressure rapidly falls to normal as soon as they leave these situations, so flexible are the blood vessel walls. If the stressful situations grow more frequent as the person grows older, however, the tension becomes more generalized, the muscles in the walls of the blood vessels all over the body begin to constrict, and a permanent blood pressure elevation may occur. The narrowed blood vessels produce more resistance to the flow of blood. If you were to try to blow out a candle through a soft rubber tube, and then begin to constrict the tube by pinching it, you would find that more and more pressure was required to deliver an equivalent amount of air out the other end. Because the body's need for blood normally undergoes little change, when the blood vessels become more constricted, more work must be done by the heart. This increased work must be done by a heart that is growing weaker with age, and whose supply of food and oxygen is also being reduced because of a narrowing of the blood vessels that supply its muscles.

The diseases associated with this continual high blood pressure form an almost endless list, because the deposition of cholesterol and calcium in the walls of these spastic blood vessels results in hardening of the arteries. Strokes, kidney disease, and circulatory diseases of the extremities rank high on the list of effects of hardening of the arteries.

In treating these diseases the physician usually prescribes muscle relaxant drugs to open the blood vessels and permit a lowered blood pressure. Usually, however, the life situations responsible for the tension continue and the tension returns, requiring more and more powerful medication to lower blood pressure and avoid its unpleasant complications.

The techniques you are now learning also reduce the blood vessel spasm but because they reduce it through mental relaxation, the techniques strike at one of the actual causes of the disorder. Using them, many people with hypertension have been able to decrease the dosage of medication, avoid progression of the disease, and, in many cases, return the blood pressure to normal.

Muscles Are Everywhere

It is difficult to find an area of the body in which muscles are not present, and anywhere there are muscles, there exists the possibility for tension, spasm, pain, and the subsequent development of inflammation or disease. Spasm in the pelvic area may account for sexual dysfunction, including vaginal spasm and pain on intercourse, uterine spasm, and painful menstrual periods (the uterus is simply another muscle and need cause no more discomfort through its monthly contractions than do the contractions of the biceps muscle). Spasm in the fallopian tubes may be responsible for certain forms of infertility, and spasm has been linked to several types of impotence. The large muscles of the back commonly go into spasm, and many days or weeks may be required for their relief if specific relaxation mechanisms are not available. Whether this spasm is due to psychological tension or to actual muscle injury, any overreaction can be eliminated through the use of our minds. I have even seen people with whiplash injury learn to effectively relax much of their pain and spasm.

Chronic spasm in the back often produces an imbalance of stresses on the vertebral column. This may be responsible for a person's back "going out." This complication may be relieved by traction, osteopathic manipulation, or chiropractic manipulation. If the tension or spasm is being maintained by reflex mechanisms in the central nervous system, however, it will tend to recur and require more treatments. Relaxing the muscles through Selective Awareness may serve the additional important function of eliminating this reflex mechanism and making the relief permanent.

EXPERIENCE TWELVE

Take a few moments and become aware of any muscle tension problems you have had in the past or experience at this moment. Close your eyes and spend a moment searching throughout your body from finger to finger and toe to toe for areas that feel tight. There are almost always areas of muscle tension, and you may be able to feel them better by examining your body, pressing into the muscles with your fingers. Suggestions for relaxation of these tensions will be given later in Chapter 6.

Symptomatic Treatment

The standard medical treatment for all these diseases of muscle tension and spasm, which constitute the majority of problems experienced by patients and physicians, is *symptomatic*. That means we treat the effects of the spasm rather than the spasm itself. We treat psychological tension with chemical tranquilizers, gastrointestinal tract tension with smooth muscle relaxants (drugs), heart disease and cerebrovascular disease with vasodilators (drugs that relax the muscles in the walls of the blood vessels), asthma with chemicals that relieve bronchospasm, pain in the back with drugs that relax these muscles, and so on. Sometimes medications are given that interfere with the nerves conducting these reflexes or with the parts of the central nervous system that perceive the pain. Because we are treating merely the symptoms, the underlying psychological mechanism that produced them is left untouched and free to create symptoms at a future date. The more often the symptoms recur the more persistent becomes the reflex, and the more difficult it is to completely eradicate.

Interestingly enough, physical symptoms can be a solution to a problem. The mind and body of the overworked business executive can gain several weeks of rest if a bleeding ulcer or heart problem can be produced, although he or she might never dream of slowing down otherwise. The actor who develops headaches around bright lights is relieved of the stress of working without agreeing to it consciously. Sudden diarrhea may save a person from a stressful conference he or she would otherwise dutifully attend.

Because the unconscious mind may use these symptoms partly to relieve itself of unnecessary pressure, relieving the symptoms may, therefore, expose the unconscious parts of the mind to further stresses of the kind it has already shown itself incapable of withstanding. Thus we are led to the conclusion that the more often we relieve these tensions without investigating the underlying emotional mechanisms that produced them, the more harm we may be doing to the body as a whole! Indeed, we may actually be doing ourselves more harm than good.

Unfortunately, teaching patients to control the underlying processes of pain and spasm is not a part of the standard medical treatment of their symptoms by most doctors. A few of the methods of achieving relaxation are biofeedback training, self-hypnosis, meditation, and autogenic training.

The Selective Awareness technique that you will learn at the end of this section performs the same function as many of the medicines prescribed by physicians: relief of symptoms. This relief is achieved not by imposing relaxation from the outside through chemical or physical means, but by rearranging the reflexes and unconscious mechanisms that gave rise to the problem in the first place. The freedom from pain and spasm, therefore, may be made permanent and the disease cured rather than being merely temporarily abated.

Civilization and Disease: Strange Bedfellows

The remarkable progress in medical science during the past few decades has all but eliminated diseases due to the microorganisms that have plagued animals since time immemorial. It is seldom that we see a full-blown case of tuberculosis, syphilis, or diptheria, and the young physician is unlikely to ever encounter a case of smallpox or polio in this country. Instead, we suffer from a battery of difficulties that seem to be limited entirely to the human species.

The reason for this is obvious following a little contemplation of the strange predicament in which civilization places us. We did not evolve physically in a civilized world—we evolved in a warm jungle, without tools, with few social pressures.

A prime objective was survival through defense against enemies, competitors, and natural accident. Unlike the vast majority of higher animals, we lack well-developed physical defenses. We cannot fly like birds, cannot swim swiftly like fish, cannot run rapidly like deer. We lack the bear's strength, the elephant's tough hide, the porcupine's quills, the alligator's teeth, the skunk's smell. We even have to wear clothes to avoid scratching ourselves on bushes!

We are almost defenseless. Almost. We have one major weapon: our nervous system. Our nervous system can detect a threat, develop novel and effective defenses against it, and overcome it.

Imagine a tribe of primitive humans living off fruits and roots. Most animals avoid the smell of humans, so they have little danger. They are relaxed. Their muscles are soft, like the soft and relaxed muscles of a calm dog or cat. Let's imagine our hypothetical primitive humans are peacefully munching carrots when a grizzly bear appears. Suddenly they are alerted to the fact that a predator is present, one who ignores humans' protective smell.

Their nervous systems undergo a marked change to prepare them for fight or flight. The blood flow to the intestines is halted by a contraction of blood vessel muscles, and blood flow is shunted to the muscles of the arms and legs. Blood pressure increases to ensure adequate circulation to the brain. The tear glands empty to prevent drying of the eyes, the heart rate goes up, breathing speeds up, and any sexual desire disappears.

Even as a dog or cat assumes characteristic bodily positions when alarmed, the human tenses certain muscles, especially those of the neck and back.

Let's imagine our tribe loses only a few members to the bear, and that it moves on to another hunting ground. As time passes, the primitive humans gradually relax. They can digest food, blood pressure returns to normal, and, after a while, the muscles of the back and neck relax too.

But let's imagine that from time to time the bear decides to come back. We'd see a different tribe of primitive people indeed. They would be tense, wary, and anxious; out of balance with the environment.

Having no inherited physical defense mechanisms, they turn to their brains for help. The motivation to invent is high.

They agree, through sign language and pantomime (for example, the hunting dances of primitive peoples) to lure the bear with bait, then to attack, en masse, with clubs and stones.

As they charge the surprised animal they are again in physical preparation for fight or flight, and display great courage, strength, and stamina. Finally, at whatever the cost, the threat is eliminated and the members of our hypothetical tribe can once again return to their familiar state of mental and physical relaxation.

The Twentieth-Century Human

We no longer live in the primitive environment in which humans evolved, but we still possess the same physical and mental structure. Our muscles tense, our blood pressure goes up, and digestion is interrupted when we are under stress or when we perceive a threat.

The threats, however, are different. We fear nuclear war, economic collapse, mad bombers, sexual frustration, cureless diseases, automobile accidents, oil shortages, and psychopathic skyjackers. We are anxious and motivated, but can find no defense, no solution.

The boss yells at us: we cannot run away, we cannot strike back. Our muscles get tighter, we become more anxious.

A headache develops. Indigestion. High blood pressure. The tension-anxiety cycle is in full swing.

Should we ignore the symptoms? They get worse. Our mind-body complex demands attention.

Take a tranquilizer or muscle relaxant? The problems remain and, artificially "relieved," can become even worse. We need more and more of the medication.

Surgically remove the offending muscle (for example, gastrectomy for ulcer, colectomy for colitis, hysterectomy for uterine spasm)? The anxiety simply finds another target organ.

Develop an escape route, such as alcoholism, overeating, or blind rages? The problems only multiply.

Let organ failure (blinding headaches, bleeding ulcer, heart attack, asthma) make it impossible to go to work, read the newspaper, or otherwise continue to endure the stress? Obviously undesirable.

If the Shoe Fits . . .

The tensions and anxieties we feel tend to amplify each other and may, ultimately, produce disease, compulsive bad habits, and unhappiness. Our reactions are still those of primitive people—yet the problems are those of a civilized society. Our reactions are symbolic, in that extreme degrees of tension and anxiety are no longer helpful; they only produce mental confusion and further difficulties.

In a civilized world the inborn mechanisms fail. You cannot solve a problem at work by punching the boss in the nose! But if the twentieth-century human can step back and take a look at himself or herself, he or she will see that breaking the tension-anxiety cycle is crucial to health, happiness, and problem resolution.

CHAPTER 6

Transforming Tension and Spasm into Relaxation

Fortunately for us, many of the processes of the unconscious mind, as well as their emotional and physical results, are reversible. In particular, muscle tension and spasm such as we have discussed can be eliminated by reversing the mechanism that has caused them. First you will become familiar with the way the deeper mind learns, and then teach it specific muscle relaxation skills.

Everyone's life abounds with opportunites to learn to be tense, but few of us have ever learned its opposite—relaxation. Much of our family, school, work, and social life consists of situations in which others are attempting to force us to behave in certain ways. Whether it is learning to use the toilet, taking a test on long division, or supporting a family, the fear of painful consequences provides the motivation and, with it, tension. Relaxation, therefore, must be taught in a permissive fashion.

EXPERIENCE THIRTEEN

You'll need a friend to help you with this one. Have your friend close his or her eyes and hold out a hand as though he or she were about to have a palm read. Then using the point of a pencil or the edge of a key, trace out on his or her palm a number you have chosen from the digits 1 to 9. Ask your friend then what number you have written. After a little practice you will find that you can write the numbers smaller and he or she will still be able to tell what they are. Now switch around and have your friend write numbers on your palm. You may also try writing on the forehead and other parts of the body for interesting discoveries.

Even if this experience was one that you had never had before, you probably found that after only two or three errors, you were readily able to determine what numbers were being written on your hand. *Though the hand had never had any direct training in reading numbers, the mind was able to "read" the sensory pattern on the hand because there was a pattern of numbers already stored in the mind.* This was done almost instantaneously; there was no particular set of thoughts you had to think in order to get your mind to do it. It was just a matter of letting it happen. In fact, you may have noticed it was harder if you were trying.

EXPERIENCE FOURTEEN

Hold your right hand behind your back and, looking at the pictures that follow, one by one let your hand imitate the pictures. When you feel your hand is in the indicated position, check it visually.

The transformation from the visual images to your hand was probably also easy, even though you weren't looking at your hand. This task was carried out by your unconscious mind, at your direction.

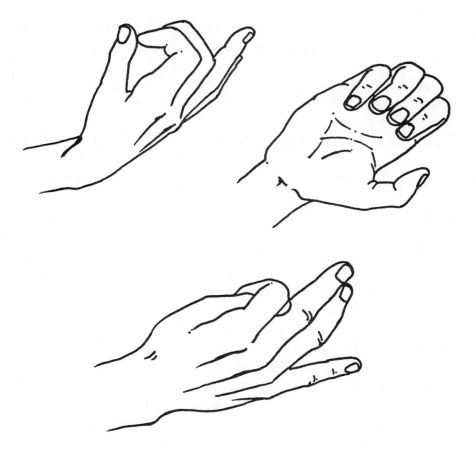

EXPERIENCE FIFTEEN

Now take one of your hands and let the fingers arrange themselves into an unlikely position. You will notice that you can quickly have the other hand imitate this position, although it may have taken you quite a few seconds to figure it out for the first hand. You'll also notice that you can do this equally well whether your eyes are open or closed.

This form of rapid learning and imitation is a basic form of information acquisition and utilization. It is the fundamental way in which children learn. It is through this modeling process that they learn to stand, walk, talk, and behave emotionally like their parents and peer groups. It also forms the basis for symbolic and projective reasoning.

In these exercises, as in the familiar children's game of Simon Says, we see the ability of the mind to become aware of a pattern and to imitate it in such a way that the same pattern may be reproduced in some other part of the body. Using the methods of Selective Awareness, it is possible to transfer intricate paterns from one part of the mind or body to another, even those patterns involving ordinarily unconscious processes. In this section we will learn to transfer the pattern of muscle relaxation by using the hand as a model.

We can imagine that the unconscious mind photographs, or "reads" the desired pattern, stores it in the memory section, and analyzes it. It then converts this information to the proper kind of impulses and sends it to the area you desire. The general relaxation procedure, which you have already learned, uses this same idea to generalize the relaxation of the eyelids so that relaxation is felt throughout the body. Because the pattern used to relax a tense or spasming muscle is slightly different, we must teach the mind a new pattern. We will teach the muscles of the hand and arm how to become tense and go into spasm. Then we will instruct the mind to relax the hand and arm and send the relaxation into any other area of the body that may be tense or in spasm.

Choose a Tension, Any Tension

EXPERIENCE SIXTEEN

Become aware of those areas of your body that are now, or have recently been, in spasm or very tense. Try to be specific. It might help to have someone give you a firm massage or to massage yourself. Those muscles that feel particularly tender, if this is not due to a recent injury or disease, can be assumed to be tight due to some physical or emotional tension. Of course any area of the body whose soreness you suspect might represent something more serious or complicated than muscle tenseness or spasm should first be examined by a physician before you begin symptomatic relief. You may feel the tension in the muscles of an internal organ, such as your stomach or bladder.

You will be able to use the following method to begin relaxing any of these muscle tensions. First choose the most important one, as best you can, whether you are dealing with a muscle that is long and straight or circular. The muscles of the neck, back, arms, legs, and abdominal wall are, for the most part, long and straight. The blood vessels (including those in the head) and the muscles surrounding the stomach and the intestine, the uterus, the vagina, and the fallopian tubes are primarily circular.

When you are going to relieve the tension in a circular muscle, this will be done by modeling relief of tension in your hand. For example, if you want to relieve indigestion, heartburn, or gas, make a fist with one of your hands, imagining that your fingers and palm are the walls of the intestine. As you squeeze your hand tighter and tighter, imagine that it is your stomach or intestine contracting forcibly. Or if you are aiming to relieve the spasm of blood vessels (as in migraine headache or hypertension) or the spasm of muscles around the airways (as in asthma, bronchitis, or emphysema), or tension in any other organ with circular muscles you would imagine that in your hand you are holding a soft hose, and that as you squeeze tighter and tighter it is more difficult for the fluid or air to pass through. As your hand is relaxing, you will instruct your mind to relay this information on how to relax to the other circular muscles you have chosen.

If the muscle you have chosen is of the long, straight variety, then imagine that the muscles of your forearm are the equivalent of this muscle. As you listen to the tape, you can imagine the tension in the muscles of your back, neck, arms, legs, or abdominal walls, and mentally superimpose one upon the other in the same manner that a skillful photographer might superimpose two nearly identical images by double exposing a photograph. Now, just as you were able to associate the number written on your hand with the number in your mind, and as you were able to imitate the position of one hand by positioning the

*other hand in the same way, you will be able to transfer the relaxa-
tion from the arm or hand to the other area of your body that you
have chosen.*

*As you experience the imagery in the next section, tighten the mus-
cles in the hand and forearm to a moderate degree of tension. As you
visualize the area of the body you are working on, mentally superimpose your hand and arm onto this area and imagine that you are
actually causing the tension in this area of your body—that the
squeezing of your hand is actually the squeezing of the targeted organ
of your body, that the tension in your arm is actually the discomfort
in your neck, back, arms, or legs. You may hold your hand or arm
over that part of your body if it is comfortable to do so.*

*As the muscles in your hand and forearm contract, both sets of
muscles will become more and more uncomfortable. All of your attention will be focused on these muscles, and you will feel all of the
changes that are occurring. You will feel the increase in discomfort
and pain. Your mind will then know how it creates the spasm you
wish to relieve.*

*Then you will relax your hand and forearm. As your hand slowly
relaxes, you will feel many changes occur over the course of several
minutes.* Be aware that these are the feelings that are
experienced by a relaxing muscle. *Your mind will be doing the
same thing it did when a number was being written on your hand.
Just as you were able to refer the pattern of the number to your
mind, the pattern of relaxation will be referred and the mind can then
transfer it to relaxation of any other muscle desired. You may notice
that almost immediately some of the muscle spasm will be relieved
and comfort will follow. If a tension has been present for a long period
of time, however, the discomfort may persist even after the muscle is
relaxed. If you have ever been struck in a muscle or have carried an
extremely heavy load, you know that some time passes before the
overworked muscles are completely comfortable, even though the stress
has been removed. A muscle that retains discomfort after the relaxation process should be allowed to recover at its own speed. If you
attempt to pressure the muscle into relaxing faster than is natural for
this particular muscle, you will only succeed in creating further tension around that area, bringing the spasm back again. Remember,
your job is to relax the spasm. Comfort will follow at its proper speed
if you allow that relaxation to come about.*

Spasm and Tension Relief

Let's review what will happen as you experience the next process. The experience I will describe may differ somewhat from *your* experience, but it will give you a general idea of what to expect.

1. First of all, you'll find a place in your body that feels uncomfortable and seems to be related to muscle tension. This must be done before you begin listening to the induction, and there will be no need to think of that muscle again until it is suggested that you do so. We will call this the target muscle.

2. As soon as you are completely relaxed, you will imagine that tense muscle as clearly and as vividly as possible as you roll your hand into a tight fist and tighten the muscles in your hand and forearm. The remaining muscles in your body are allowed to remain as relaxed as possible. As this occurs you will be very aware of the exact feelings in a muscle as it tightens.

3. You will feel a sensation of pressure inside your hand and inside your arm, where muscles, skin, and so on, are being tightly compressed.

4. Gradually, you will begin to experience a kind of discomfort as fatigue and spasm begin to set in. You will be aware of a strong desire to stop squeezing. This is because certain receptors in the muscle are informing you that the muscle is going into spasm. Because it is the spasm and its complications that you wish to experience, these tendencies must be ignored. It is these signals that are being ignored by the other muscle in spasm, and you must do the same with your hand.

5. You may soon become aware of an ache in the hand and forearm as the tension further cuts off blood supply to the muscle cells. The products of overwork that are being given off by the muscle cannot be carried away by the blood, and the nerve endings become stimulated, giving you the sensation of discomfort. You may also become aware of certain unpleasant emotions and a generalized discomfort. This is a good sign. You must

allow yourself to fully experience these feelings; you will later experience how they disappear.

6. After the tension in your hand and arm have reached the same level as the muscle you have chosen, you will slowly allow the hand and arm muscles to relax. When this occurs you may feel a throbbing as blood begins to flow again. This is often followed by a slight *increase* in the pain for a moment as the nerve conduction improves, and further chemicals are released from tissue spaces. A numbness or tingling may also occur around this time. You may feel similar sensations in the target muscle also.

7. As your hand relaxes further, you will become less and less aware of it; it will seem to become weightless and disappear. You will imagine the hand and arm disappearing completely and the other muscle following suit.

The tension and spasm generated in your arm will be produced voluntarily, under your conscious control. The tension in the target muscle is due to an unconscious process. By experiencing the spasm relief in the manner outlined, you will be informing your unconscious mind of which muscle you wish to alter and exactly how you would like it relaxed. This task will be carried out automatically by your unconscious mind. It is unnecessary to try to relax the other muscle. In fact, the less you think of these muscles as being separate and the more you can pretend that your hand and arm muscles and the spastic area are the same, the more effective your experience will be.

Muscle tension relief gained by this method may only be temporary if the original cause is an unbalanced functioning of the muscle in daily life. The relief gained from aspirin, muscle relaxant medication, or massage may also be temporary. Not infrequently, however, the method described here permanently eliminates a tension that has been present for a long time. The breaking of the pain–spasm cycle and the deeper understanding gained in this manner make it much easier to concentrate on the underlying causes through learning to relax. Later in this book methods for understanding and eliminating these causes will be presented.

The following relaxation process is different from the one you have been practicing, but you will note many similarities. Each begins with physical relaxation (A), continues with mental relaxation (B), allows for development of imagery (C), and ends with a return to waking consciousness (D).

At different points in this book I will present various inductions for developing Selective Awareness. Though I have tried to present relaxation inductions that fit esthetically, emotionally, and symbolically with the imagery suggestions given, this is by no means a hard and fast association. Some people find, after practicing a number of times with each induction, that a certain one is especially effective at relaxing them.

Practice and experiment with them all, and then select for regular use those that provide the most satisfactory experience for you. You may use any induction with any set of imagery suggestions. You can also use the physical relaxation from one induction with the mental relaxation from another. Or feel free to use more than one physical relaxation procedure during a single experience. If you wish, you may change the wording to produce a more personal experience.

These changes may be made later. For now, however, adhere to the instructions.

EXPERIENCE SEVENTEEN
SOFTWARE TWO

You may use the second experience on tape 10, "Tools for Taking Charge," (see p. 285) as a guide. Continue use of the tapes as recommended until you have developed sufficient mental concentration and relaxation to carry yourself through the entire procedure.

A. Physical Relaxation Through the Tension-Relaxation Method

Most people think they know what relaxation is, but claim that they can't do it. This is like saying you know how to ride a bicycle or swim or speak Spanish, but that you can't do it! What they're really saying is that they are able to conceptualize relaxation on a mental level, but have not yet taught the unconscious and the body to experience the emotional and physical parallels of relaxation on command. Of course everyone has experienced the process of relaxing, but generally this is initiated by the external environment (for example, alcohol, the beach, or a massage).

The approach here is adapted from the one developed by Dr. Edmund Jacobson, and involves teaching each part of the body to relax by first tensing, allowing the entire body to sum up the effects, then focusing this relaxation on a single muscle or muscle group. Thus before you begin, if possible, locate some area of your body that is presently or characteristically tense. The jaw muscles, muscles of the neck or back, muscles of the stomach or large bowel, muscles of the blood vessels (in hypertension), or muscles of the bronchioles (in asthma) may be chosen.

During the physical relaxation portion of this experience, there are two forms of tension that you may use.

Allow one hand and one arm to rest on a surface with palm facing down. Now tighten the hand into a fist, using about one-half your total strength. Feel the tension and then release, allowing the hand to rest limply again on the table. We will call this active tensing.

Beginning with your hand in the same starting position, slowly lift your hand from the table, allowing your forearm and wrist to remain in contact with the table. As you lift, be particularly aware of the feeling in the back of your arm and the back of your hand. As soon as you detect a feeling of tension, stop lifting, hold your hand in that position for a moment or two, then release. We will call this threshold tensing.

The first few times that you experience the following induction, use active tensing, and then, after you have learned experientially what tension feels like in each part of your body, begin to use threshold tensing.

Begin by tensing your right hand. Feel the tension . . . . Release . . . . Feel the relaxation.

Now repeat this procedure with your left hand. The entire time, from when you first begin to tense until you have experienced the relaxation, should be about seven to twelve seconds. Remember to release the tension as rapidly as possible, at the exact instant you think the word Release.

Now repeat this procedure for each of the other major muscle groups in your body. Following is a partial list. You can expand on this list (for example, by rolling your eyes in different directions to feel the tension before releasing, pressing your tongue against the roof of your mouth and releasing, and so on). Because you may wish to have your eyes closed while you are having this experience, you might find that you forget to tense and release one or more groups of muscles. This is unimportant; do not destroy your relaxation by worrying whether you have remembered every step. You are about to begin relaxing now, so find a comfortable place to sit or lie down, loosen any constricting clothing, and make sure there is nothing that you have to do for the next fifteen minutes or so (you may set a meditation timer or your oven timer for twenty or twenty-five minutes if you have a tendency to fall asleep during deeply relaxing experiences). Take a deep breath in and as you let this breath out, let your eyelids close and let your eyes roll upward behind your closed eyelids. Imagine you can see the word Relax *as though it were written on the inside of your forehead. When you can imagine your eyelid muscles are so relaxed they won't open at all, test them, and let this feeling of relaxation flow throughout the rest of your body. Take a deep breath in, and as you let it out let it be a feeling of letting go, and let the air continue to breathe for you. Let each breath help you become more relaxed.* (Two minutes)

Begin the tension-release relaxation experience with your right hand. Although you are very relaxed, you can remember most of the important muscles in the list on the following page (go down column 1, and then down column 2).

The time for this portion of the experience is variable, depending upon how many muscles you work with and the time you need to really feel both the tension and the relaxation. An average would be five to ten minutes.

After going through your entire body with the tension-relaxation experience, then return to the relaxation in your eyelids, test your eyelids, and send a slow wave of relaxation throughout all the rest of your body, noticing how much more deeply relaxed you are. (Thirty to sixty seconds)

1	**2**
Right hand	*Pelvic muscles, including*
Left hand	* muscles in anal and*
Right entire arm	* genital areas*
Left entire arm	*Muscles of abdomen*
Right shoulder (shrug)	*Back (arch)*
Left shoulder (shrug)	*Deep breath — hold — relax*
Right foot	*Neck (arch backward)*
Left foot	*Teeth (clench)*
Right calf	*Mouth (open wide)*
Left calf	*Eyebrows (pull together)*
Right thigh and buttock	*Eyebrows (lift)*
Left thigh and buttock	*Eyes (close very tightly)*

B. Mental Relaxation Through Coherency

1. *There is a point of maximum relaxation in the very center of your head. Imagine waves of relaxation spreading from that point throughout all your mind and body.*

2. *Imagine the point of relaxation beginning to move, carrying the feeling of letting go throughout all areas of your mind. Imagine it moving inside your head much like a tiny table tennis ball. You may imagine little flashes of light or sounds as unnecessary thoughts, questions, and memories are erased. Imagine those thoughts disappearing just as the reflection on the surface of a pool of water dissolves as a stone is thrown into it.*

3. *After a minute or so your mind will be partially or completely emptied of random thoughts. Return the relaxation point to the center of your head again, and give yourself the desired imagery suggestions. Let any thoughts that still wander into your mind be erased by the relaxation point.*

C. *Imagery: Tension-Spasm Relief*

1.   *Become aware of one of your hands. Imagine that the center of this hand is one of the most relaxed parts of your body.*

   Now slowly begin to roll your hand into a fist over the period of about one minute. Allow yourself to be completely aware of each change as it takes place in the hand and the connecting arm. Feel the movement of each muscle as it gradually contracts. Your mind is learning, in selective detail, what contracting is. (About one minute)

2.   *When you have a really tight fist, notice the discomfort in the hand and arm as you squeeze tighter. You may notice that this feels similar to the feeling in the muscle upon which you have chosen to focus. Tense this muscle until the two feel about equally tense. This will make it easier for the unconscious* mind *to transfer the process of relaxing in a few moments.* Squeeze it *tighter. Even though your hand and arm would like to relax, do not let them do so. This way you will be producing the same condition that is present in the target muscle. It too would like to completely relax, but your mind has not yet learned how to let the tension go. Keep all the rest of your body completely calm.* (About one minute)

3.   *Slowly begin to relax your arm and hand. Imagine your hand and arm superimposed over the muscle you have chosen to relax along with it. Let your hand become more and more relaxed. Notice each of the feelings of the arm and hand, such as any numbness, tingling, or throbbing. These are part of the process of relaxing a tension.* (About one minute)

4.   *You will find that when your hand is almost completely open, it will stop opening by itself and you will have a feeling of wanting to stretch your fingers out. Do not do this. Instead, imagine that there are little strings attached to the ends of your fingertips slowly pulling them open, much as the strings on a small parachute might pull it open. You may notice that as your hand opens the final 1½ or 2 inches, the movements begin to feel a bit jerky, like a cogwheel. This is a sign that little muscle spasms are* *being slowly released. Spasms such as these, which are now being released, are being released simultaneously in the target muscle. Now double the relaxation by opening and closing your eyes. Feel the doubled relaxation in your eyelids, take a deep breath, and draw the relaxation up from your arm and hand and into your chest. As you let your breath out, imagine it flowing right to the other muscle that you wish to relax and allow it to feel the same doubled relaxation. You may double the relaxation once or twice more by taking deep breaths.* (About one minute)

D. Returning to Your Usual State of Consciousness

Find the most pleasant, enjoyable, or energetic part of your body, and imagine the point of maximum energy at the very center of it. Imagine that as you count to yourself, from one to five, that the feeling from this point starts to flow throughout your body. Feel it spreading like ripples from a stone thrown in the water. Tell yourself that you are coming up feeling wide awake, relaxed, and refreshed. It is always a good idea, when "bringing yourself up," to tell yourself that you will feel fine when you "awaken." This will avoid any drowsy feeling you might otherwise experience. (About one minute)

As you open your eyes, imagine that you are now in that most perfect universe where you are exactly the kind of person you want to be—feeling just as you would like to feel. Make sure you are alert and wide awake before going about your next activities.

To Be Read After Listening to Software Two

You are now becoming aware of the remarkable ability of the mind to relax areas that have been in spasm for long periods of time. In fact, you may be experiencing the complete relief of a chronic headache or back pain that has been present for weeks or months. Or you may be noticing 75 percent, 50 percent, or 10 percent relief. The muscle may still be a bit sore because of the length of time the spasm has been present, or only part of the spasm may have been relieved. Generally you will find that experiencing this process several times in a row or perhaps once or twice a day for a while will be sufficient to completely eliminate any discomfort that remains. Let your own rate of improvement guide you in deciding how often to repeat the induction.

As with all skills you learn, the more openness with which you enter this state of deep relaxation, the more proficient you will become at achieving it. By this time you probably are just beginning to notice the way your mind can rapidly and automatically slip into this calm state. Each time that you apply this technique, you will be giving yourself an opportunity to learn, in a fundamental way, the mechanism whereby relaxation may be achieved in any tense muscle. Further, you will gain an increased ability to eliminate muscle tension rapidly in any place in the body.

The Lift-Drop Variation

Some people find it more effective to substitute the following imagery for Part C:

Imagery: Tension Relief

1. *Allow one hand and arm to lie next to you. Slowly begin to lift your hand and arm. Lift until you can feel a slight tension in the area that is doing the lifting. Stop lifting, and hold the arm and hand in this position while you allow your awareness to experientially explore this feeling.* (Thirty seconds)

2. *Notice how this sensation is similar to the feelings in the target muscle. Realize that the same process—contraction—is present in each, and mentally superimpose the feeling in your arm over that in the target muscle.*

3. *Release the tension in your hand and arm by suddenly letting them fall limp and loose. Picture the target muscle doing the same thing.*

4. *Repeat steps 1 and 2 with this hand and arm; then repeat the entire sequence on the other side. You may also repeat with one or both legs. The unconscious will recognize that the process of tensing and relaxing is the same in all these muscles and can now transform the target muscle.*

5. *All the preceding steps should be carried out with the utmost awareness, with the mind and body quiet.*

CHAPTER 7

Positive Imagery: Visualization and Projection

One of the most fascinating features of the unconscious mind is that we are usually unaware of its functioning. Even as you read these words, your unconscious mind is causing your breathing to proceed regularly, your heart to beat at a certain rate, and your eyes to blink frequently enough to keep them moist. Your blood pressure is remaining at a fixed, predetermined level; the lenses of your eyes are changing their focus continuously, and the black and white marks on which you are focusing are being transformed into words, meanings, and ideas. In fact, thousands of activities involving many different areas of the body are taking place continuously and automatically. Though you may become aware of some of these activities as they occur and may even know which stimuli cause them, there is a gap between these two observations. These processes take place in the unconscious mind. We refer to these processes as *reflexes* and *responses*.

Obviously, some of these reflexes, such as the heartbeat, were present even before birth. Some, such as respiration, have been present only since birth. And some have been present only since they have been learned through trial and error. Such activities as walking, dancing, counting money, sitting down, and reading are called *learned programs.* In order to carry them out, you merely decide on your goal—such as reading a particular poster—and the unconscious activities commence (moving the eyes from point to point, focusing, and translating) without having to pay too much attention to them. We are then free to interpret the results of their actions.

Because our awareness of most of our activities is limited to stimuli, both internal and external, and the responses of the unconscious mind to them, we would do well to learn the rules by which they are related. This can then lead to a better understanding of how the unconscious functions and can enable us to work in a more coordinated fashion with it. This is similar to learning the rules of touch typing so that we can increase our speed and accuracy. One of the simplest of these rules is the rule of positive programming.

Positive Programming

One of the newer scientific fields, cybernetics, is based upon the fact that learned patterns stored in the mind are handled much the same as programs that are processed in a human-made computer. These programs operate on data fed them and produce responses, or answers. Because of the similarity between learning (conditioning) and the reading of programs into a computer, I often refer to this process as *positive programming.* Many people, alarmed by what they see as a gradual dehumanizing of society by the use of today's technology may not wish to use the word *programming.* I wish in no way to demean the central nervous system. Usually I prefer to speak of patterns rather than programs. Here I am using the latter word simply because the analogy is useful for conceptual understanding.

When a child performs an activity, such as tying his or her shoes or feeding himself or herself correctly, we praise the child. Similarly, we all know how important it is to let our friends and co-workers know when they have done a good job by telling them so, and we understand, almost intuitively, that this will help them do a good job in the future. When training animals, we often give rewards in the form of food and caresses and often reward our friends and children with gifts when they have performed in a way that satisfies us or our ideals.

The most important feature of this type of learning, or conditioning, is that the desired activity becomes associated with something pleasant. The emotions that result from the reward are positive and are interpreted by the mind as being related to the activity. By rewarding, or reinforcing, the desired activity, we hope to make it more attractive to the mind. Exactly the same procedure may be followed when you are training yourself to do something. Your feeling of satisfaction as you learn each part of the task serves to reinforce the pattern.

Now let's move on from this intuitive understanding of positive programming to a laboratory experiment that will help us to better understand how it occurs. Though similar demonstrations may be carried out with human beings, I will describe how it is performed with a dog, because the results will be easier to interpret. These results will then serve as a useful model as we learn their application to ourselves.

The demonstration is simple, and could be carried out using your own pet. First of all, the dog is taken to a room where it can be observed; the stimuli and responses will be recorded. A bell is rung soon after the dog is placed in the room and a few seconds later it is given a dish of food. The dog begins to salivate, its tail begins to wag, and its stomach and intestines become activated and secrete digestive juices. Indeed, a whole host of changes begin to take place in its body as it prepares to accept food. As it eats, we note that it gradually becomes more calm. Although it may have been very active, even jumping about at first, by the time it finishes it may feel so relaxed that it may even curl up and go to sleep.

This procedure is now repeated several times a day for a few days. If we now bring the dog into the room and ring the bell, its body will prepare for food even if we give it none. It will salivate, its stomach and intestines will become more active, its tail will wag, and it will experience a decrease in tension.

This decrease in tension can be readily demonstrated if you have a dog who is excitedly and angrily barking at the mail carrier. If you call it to eat or rattle its food dish, it will rapidly forget its tension and prepare for food. It is this decrease in tension that is the most important response to the conditioned stimulus (bell).

Simply stated, the law of positive programming is that when a group of perceptions and physiological changes occur together repeatedly in an animal's life, and when they are associated with relaxation, the animal tends to become positively programmed. If stimuli are then presented to the animal so that one or more of these perceptions or physiological changes take place, the animal tends to reproduce the remaining changes. This response is an involuntary one.

The principle of positive programming is demonstrated when changes in the body (usually present only when the animal is eating) take place when a bell is rung. We could just as easily have conditioned the dog to respond to a gong, a flash of light, or a specific way of petting it. Because this is a dog who would not normally (in nature) respond in this fashion, this type of stimulus is sometimes called a *conditioned stimulus*. The food, on the other hand, is referred to as an *unconditioned stimulus*, because the responses of the mind-body complex to the presentation of food did not have to be learned. They were instinctual (or at least present before we began our experiment).

Food and the response to it are not the only rewards we can use. We could just as well let the dog go out for an hour each day as a reward and soon condition it to undergo certain bodily changes such as jumping about, barking, and wagging its tail in response to the ringing of a bell, the shaking of a doorknob, or the sight of its leash. When you train your dog to sit or lie down, you often reward it with food or with caresses so that it will respond in this way following the stimulus of your verbal command.

This kind of conditioning ensures that the dog will remember the shortest route to certain familiar places and situations, recall where food and water may be found, and remember the solution to familiar and frequently recurring problems. The dog does not consciously think, "Aha, the bell is ringing! Soon food will arrive; I'll start salivating," just as we do not consciously decide to salivate when we look at a picture of a delicious meal or hear someone speak of a visit to an excellent restaurant in Paris. This is evidence that the pattern is carried out by the unconscious mind relatively independent of conscious processes.

The table tennis player whose backhand flashes out and deftly returns a shot is also depending upon a conditioned pattern. Obviously, no one could consciously calculate the speed, direction, and spin of the ball and correlate that with the speed, direction, tilt, twist, and elasticity of the paddle with equal rapidity. Through the process of reinforcement learning, the player has trained the unconscious mind to respond automatically with far more speed, accuracy, and complexity than the conscious mind could.

Extinguishing Positive Programs

If all positively conditioned patterns lasted indefinitely throughout an animal's life, it might soon prove maladaptive in its natural environment. It might become so conditioned by repeating events that its behavior would actually interfere with desirable activities. For instance, if it had eaten near a tree on several occasions, it might find itself salivating for years afterward whenever it walked by that tree even though food never again appeared in that area. This would be contrary to nature's principle of economy of energy.

Because positive conditioning fades (is extinguished) if not reinforced, it would probably salivate the first few times it walked past the tree, but its mind would soon learn that this was to no avail and the salivation and other physiological responses to food would begin to diminish and would eventually become extinguished. If a conditioned stimulus is presented repeatedly to an animal without the occasional simultaneous presentation of the unconditioned stimulus as a reinforcement, the programmed response tends to become extinguished.

This means that if we continue ringing the bell in the presence of the dog each day, but move its feeding time to another part of the day, in a few days the dog will stop salivating. The decrease in tension that was present as a response to the ringing of the bell will also disappear. In nature, extinguishing ensures that an animal will not continue to go to a dried-up water hole to attempt to quench its thirst.

You can probably find many examples of extinguishing in your life. If you have not typed in some time or have stopped playing a musical instrument, you will find your skill markedly diminished. People often find that they have forgotten many things about a field of interest in which they were once quite proficient and from which they derived a great deal of pleasure. I have a friend, Burt, whose story illustrates this principle.

Every afternoon Burt would get the idea that he'd like to play tennis and, four or five times a week, following his day's studies, he could be found at the tennis court enjoying his favorite sport. Thus a conditioned response had been established: the finishing of his work in the afternoon would elicit the response of thinking about, and going to, the tennis courts, where he would play tennis and relax. One of the most important features of the positively conditioned pattern is apparent here. He was not forced to play tennis, for had there been a party he wished to attend, he would have been able to override this program. The presence of the learned pattern simply ensured that, in the absence of anything more pressing, he would tend to reproduce the same activity day after day.

The next few years, however, brought about certain changes in Burt's environment (stimulus complex). After receiving his bachelor's degree, he went on to graduate school, where his studies, his part-time job, and his family consumed most of his time. Though very often after finishing his studies in the afternoon he would think about how he would like to play tennis, his many commitments forced him to forgo this desired behavior. Now, several years later, Burt has a regular job and is finished working by four each day, with plenty of time to play. Actually, he plays tennis only once every month or so, although he would probably prefer to be playing tennis every day after work. If you were to ask him, he would tell you that playing tennis is more fun than the books he reads or the movies he sees, but somehow, the old urge just isn't there anymore.

The positive programming that had led to Burt's regular and frequent tennis game has become extinguished. My advice to Burt, or to anyone else in this situation, is to consider consciously reprogramming this activity. If he added tennis to his schedule each work day for only a couple of weeks, Burt would find that he could regain all of the love and skill he once had, and still find it a simple matter to play tennis after work each day.

Reprogramming

In a similar manner the dog who no longer salivates in response to the bell can be rapidly reprogrammed. One of the rules of reconditioning is that the number of trials necessary to reinstitute this response is far less than the number required to teach the pattern originally. In the same way you will find that your typing or musical skills will return quickly if you expend the necessary energy for a few days or weeks. The necessities of life may have separated your desire to perform these activities from the reward you received in doing them. As a result the unconscious mind has extinguished the stimulus-response bond and does not generate sufficient motivation to perform the work necessary to reach this desirable goal. It may take a little effort to get yourself back into the habit again, but if you repeat it enough times, the pattern will be reestablished.

EXPERIENCE EIGHTEEN

Close your eyes, and after a few moments of eliminating unnecessary thought patterns, drift back through your life and see how many positively conditioned activities (such as jogging, exercising regularly, collecting stamps, going to parties, and so on) were once a part of your life. You will probably find that most follow the pattern of being associated in some way with a general feeling of relaxation and pleasure. Verify this for yourself as you think about each. Spend a few moments with each one, and see how closely you can determine exactly what changes in your life caused them to become extinguished. At the same time decide whether you would like to resume these activities (if this is possible in your present environment), and if it would be desirable to reinterest yourself by putting them into your daily schedule.

Occasionally I will refer to conditioned activities as *habit patterns*. The word *habit* is used with its usual meaning, and it should be clear that positive programming leads to the development of a *positive habit pattern*. Therefore, we might well say that a dog is in the habit of salivating when the bell rings. We might also say that after salivation has been extinguished that the dog has gotten out of the habit.

Characteristics of Positive Programs

In summary, then, positively reinforced habits (positive programs):

1. Are the result of one or more reinforcements.

2. Are associated with a decrease in tension and viewed as pleasurable by the person.

3. Are usually termed desirable, or good, habits.

4. Are not compulsive; the person can always decide whether to carry out the activity.

5. Tend to fade if reinforcement is not given in the form of relaxation.

6. Can be rapidly reestablished after being extinguished.

Positive Programs and Image Rehearsal: Blueprints for Yourself

Visualization and image rehearsal are the means by which we will apply the principles of positive programming to obtain desirable patterns of emotions and performance. The fundamental technique is familiar to you. The little boy who pretends he is his favorite movie star fighting a battle among the planets in a distant galaxy is practicing a rudimentary form of visualization, as is the basketball player who sits in class thinking about the baskets she will score in a game that night or the vacationer who daydreams on her plane flight about what she will do when she arrives at her vacation spot.

Many of us, however, frequently practice image rehearsal in a negative manner. The person who has stage fright may continually imagine himself or herself making horrendous mistakes during his or her next speech. The worried student may fearfully imagine himself or herself forgetting the answers to important questions on the final exam and flunking out of school. Few people realize that this rehearsing of failure tends to create a mental program that may actually serve to produce exactly the unwanted response.

I was once in a radio station with a disc jockey who had to read a special announcement over the air. Although he spoke regularly on the radio and hardly ever made errors, he was nervous on this particular evening because the owner of the radio station was listening and evaluating his performance. Just before he went on the air he turned to me and said, "Well, here goes. Bet I'll make some stupid mistake." He did, and when he was off the air he complained he was so mad he could "kick himself." He didn't realize that he had actually *succeeded in performing in exactly the way he had programmed himself to perform*. How often have you set out to do something with the statement, "I'll probably blow it" or entered a new situation with the negative self talk "I'll try but I don't think I'm good enough."

Actually, we unconsciously use visualization and image rehearsal before carrying out any conscious activity. If you wish to do something as simple as turning off a light switch across the room, it is first necessary for you to briefly imagine getting up and walking. Whenever you decide to do anything, your mind always goes through an extremely rapid visualization of the major points of the activity, just as though you were planning to take a vacation trip and stop at many points; first you would map out a rough idea of how you will travel. The more familiar the activity, the less time needs to be spent on visualization. Just a rough idea is necessary and then the unconscious mind carries out the rest.

The visualization that you are about to learn is of a much more intense variety. It will be applied during the deeply relaxed state, and you will focus on the most minute details of a single desired activity. The remarkable effects that can be produced in this fashion are well demonstrated by one of the favorite stunts of the old time intinerant stage hypnotist. The day before his presentation he would arrive in town, locate a pianist and hypnotize her. He would then induce her to imagine that Johann Sebastian Bach would play tirelessly through her fingers. For the next twenty-four hours she would sit in a prominent store window playing, while a nearby sign announced "I am playing continuously, and effortlessly for twenty-four hours, under the hypnotic power of Mr. Mysto, who will give a public demonstration on Saturday . . . and so on, and so on," This would provide ample free advertisement for the charlatan.

Of course, we now recognize that he had no mysterious power. He merely possessed the knowledge of how to induce the subject to hypnotize herself and to form the necessary image.

Probably few of us desire to repeat this particular stunt, but you might be interested in learning how the power of this visualization technique can be used to overcome stage fright, simple phobias, habitual mistake patterns (as in a bad golf stroke), and lack of self-confidence. Let's start by learning a little more about how the nerves acquire and transmit information, because the secret lies in their function.

Reality and Your Image of Reality

As we have discussed before, most of our actions are based upon responses to the perception of stimuli in our environment. These stimuli enter your mind from your body through the five senses. When you place your hand upon an object, it appears to you that you can directly feel it, but this is actually not the case. If I touch a candle flame or table with my finger, the only contact made is between the outer layer of my skin, which is nonliving, and the object I have touched. The sensation of touch, pressure, or warmth that I feel is merely the result of the activity generated in certain nerve receptors located many layers of skin below the surface. These nerve endings, then, register changes occurring within the body. They do not register any information about the actual point of contact.

The electrical discharges from these specialized receptors are now carried toward the spinal cord by afferent neurons. When the neurons reach the spinal cord, they end. The impulse must now be transmitted to another nerve. The electrical discharge cannot, however, cross over the space between the ending of one nerve cell and the beginning of another. Instead, a small amount of a chemical is released from the end of the first nerve. Ordinarily, the chemical is stored in little packets in the end of the nerve, but when a discharge comes down the fiber, the little packet releases into the synapse (the space between the nerve cell endings), and its material travels across to the receiving nerve cell.

The end of the other nerve has special receptors for this chemical, and electrical discharge is set up in the receiving nerve. This discharge is now carried up the spinal cord and into the brain. When it reaches the brain, other chemical packets are released to carry the information across another synapse to still another nerve cell. Another electrical discharge occurs across the membrane of this cortical neuron and the process is repeated a certain number of times (depending upon whether touch, heat, cold, or another sensation is being transmitted) until finally the area of the brain that receives and interprets the information (in this case, touch) is reached. If the impulse were blocked anywhere along the pathway (by a nerve injury, surgical interference, or anesthetic, for example), we would have no awareness of the sensation of touch, even though we might be pressing heavily on the object.

Generally speaking, we can use this as a model by which information is relayed to the brain from any sensory receptor. Our awareness is not of the actual object that we have touched, but of a particular pattern of neural discharges at the end of a long pathway consisting of nervous tissue, synaptic spaces, and chemicals. As a result of nervous discharges and the associated chemical packets, we perceive that something is happening at the level of the finger.

The *efferent nervous system* (motor nerves) operate similarly, but information is carried in the other direction—from the brain *to* the effector organ. The part of the mind that decides to bring about a particular action (for example, a muscle contraction or glandular secretion), transmits this decision by means of little packets of chemicals to another chain of neurons and chemicals down to the organ (for example, a muscle or gland) that is to function. Analogous to what we said about the efferent system, then, we might say that we don't really move the arm, we merely send neural discharges toward certain synapses in the brain. The chemicals liberated there then initiate a further series of discharges, activating lower conduction systems, which finally results in muscular action

You'll gain an even clearer picture if you imagine the conscious mind operating like a person sitting at the controls of a giant robot. Bring to mind one of those huge robots used in an atomic energy research laboratory to move radioactive materials. A person sits in a control room, shielded from the dangerous material by leaded glass, with various controls attached to the arms and legs. As he or she moves a finger, the robot moves its finger in the other room. If you were to try to locate your conscious mind within your body, you would probably choose a place near the center of the brain. When you feel something or desire to move something, you interact not with the actual organ that carries out the action, but with a set of controls in the form of nerve endings in this "conscious" area of your brain. In a very real sense, it can be said that no human being has actually experienced the world directly. Your actual experience of the outer world is, in a sense, as indirect as that of the operator of the robot.

You can probably discover other examples of this "servo-mechanismlike" feature of the mind and body by scanning the past for some of your own experiences. If you have ever fallen asleep on your arm, you may have awakened very aware of the absence of feeling in the area where you usually perceive neural impulses coming from your arm. Because the nerve conduction has been cut off temporarily, there are no signals coming to the nervous system from your arm. You may have the eerie impression of your arm being there, but not there. There is a mental image of an arm, especially when you look at it, but no incoming tactile or proprioceptive stimuli to ratify its existence.

Those who have lost a hand or foot often experience what is called phantom limb pain. The amputee feels as though the foot or hand is still there although it has been removed. Even though visually he or she is aware that it does not exist, he or she can still "sense" the minute details of the nails, the webs between the toes, and so on.

Through the activity of unconscious processes the mind, through its natural functioning, has the ability to alter or even eliminate the perception of activities and sensations from the periphery. If you have ever sustained a minor injury, such as a cut, scrape, or bruise, while playing a game, you may have noticed that your interest in the game completely blocked the reception of pain from that area. Indeed, your first awareness that you had been injured may have been when a friend noticed blood on your clothes or a bruise and asked you what happened. Later that evening, after the game was over, you may have been kept awake by pain in that same area. Had you not been so involved in such an interesting activity when you were injured, you would have felt this discomfort immediately.

Athletes have been known to play an entire football game in ignorance of the fact that they had fractured a rib during the first quarter. Even though there are nerves from the injured area carrying the appropriate pain impulses, this information never reaches the conscious mind in its little control room because the excitement of the activity has decreed (at an unconscious level) that this information will be blocked.

Have you ever had the experience of frantically searching for something for five or ten minutes, only to discover at the end of this time that you have been holding it in your hand all the while? Or that it has been sitting directly in front of you? This situation is analogous to the one in which you were unaware of an injury. Though you were not conscious that you had been hurt, your unconscious mind was quite aware, had begun to stop the bleeding, had initiated swelling, and had begun to isolate the area. The first mechanisms of healing had been instituted.

EXPERIENCE NINETEEN

A clear awareness of these principles is most valuable in developing the ability to synchronize with, and influence activity at, the mind–body interaction. Induce a state of relaxation through the use of one of the processes you have learned. (Five minutes) *Then let your mind drift back and discover some examples in your own experience in which your conscious perception has differed markedly from the actual situation. Experiences with psychoactive substances may be included.* (Five to ten minutes)

Your Self-Image

These simple examples should serve to demonstrate that your conscious image may differ considerably from reality. We now need a functional manner in which to view this curious property of the mind so that we may use it to our advantage (rather than our disadvantage) to contact and alter our psychological and physical aspects as we desire. Obviously, your images of your emotional and physical makeup are based on many different sensations, memories, and interpretations. You conceive of your skin as feeling a certain way, you conceive of your taste as being of a certain quality at this moment, and you also have an image of yourself and your environment in terms of smell, touch, body position, temperature, and the amount of mental activity that is going on. You can also perceive your general emotional state and have some vague impressions of the condition of your internal organs.

In a more general sense, you are aware of certain beliefs concerning your abilities. You are aware that you can or cannot play the violin, run one hundred yards at top speed, or feel comfortable speaking to an audience of five hundred people.

The image you are receiving and manipulating on the screen in your little control room is, then, a complicated one. You are aware that you are not a flat creature like an image drawn on a sheet of paper. You have depth, a three-dimensional quality. This image of yourself seems to be suspended in your mind, where you conceive of it as either sitting, standing, or walking in a certain environment. You might think of it as a miniature, detailed puppet of yourself, which you may sense and manipulate. By manipulating this little marionette, your "real" body "down below" will respond and give you the required information about your sensations, provided all the connections are functioning properly.

Recall the illusion of seeing your reflection or that of someone else in a mirror. Your eye is fooled into believing there is actually someone on the other side of the mirror, though you know that looking behind the glass would prove that your perception is inaccurate. (The ease with which your perceptions can be tricked is used to create merriment in the hall of mirrors at carnivals.) Like the image in the mirror, your body usually carries out all the detailed activities you mentally perform on your mental image.

What we have demonstrated is that we have a mental image that corresponds, more or less, to the actual stimuli impinging on our bodies. Even the most significant sensory information, however, may be altered or blocked before reaching consciousness. Moreover, the image you are consciously aware of may differ from the one present in your unconscious. This, of course, can lead to a rather "schizophrenic" situation, in which a person behaves one way when he or she is consciously paying attention and the opposite when he or she is not paying attention. This is because a different image is being used as a reference.

Aspects of your self-image that are more abstract types of self-awareness are also subject to these limitations and misinterpretations. How often have you been convinced that you did poorly on an exam and then been congratulated for your excellent performance? How many times have you met people who believe that they are unattractive, stupid, or weak, but it was obvious to you and everyone else that the opposite was the case? And, of course, some believe they are the best at everything, although few agree with their self-assessment.

Generally speaking, the more the image we have of ourselves and of the world corresponds to reality, the more effective we will be at whatever we do. If your image of the empty milk carton you are about to lift is incorrect, you may jerk the carton into the air because you expected it to be heavy with milk. The man who is convinced he will make mistakes in his speech often fails, although most around him may feel he was capable of doing much better had he a better image of himself. It is the self-image that has generated the birth of so many schools and techniques for sales representatives and executives to improve their self-image and self-confidence. Often people with low self-esteem don't even try to obtain positions and promotions they could easily have had, because they feel incapable of succeeding.

EXPERIENCE TWENTY
SOFTWARE THREE

The following Experience will help you find an objective space in your mind. When you reach the guided imagery you will be invited to explore the various aspects of your personal image.

The relaxation induction is based upon the image of our physical reality and our mental reality as being composed of concentric spheres, much like the layers of an onion. The induction is excellent for centering as we begin by relaxing the outermost portion and then move in toward the center.

A. Physical Relaxation: Centering

1. *Think about some people, places, and things outside the range of your immediate vision, hearing, and touch. You may become aware of various countries, places you have lived, the place you were born, people you have met, the place you went to school, items you may have stored in your parents' attic, and so on.* (Fifteen to thirty seconds)

2. *Become aware of things that are just outside the room you are in; cars going by, airplanes, voices, and so on.* (Fifteen seconds)

3. *Become aware of things in your immediate environment, within the room you are in; furniture, lights, ceiling, and so on. Let the thoughts of what is outside your room recede from your awareness.* (Fifteen seconds)

4. *Become aware of those things that are in direct contact with your skin; clothes, the surface beneath you, the air around you, air currents, your hair.* (Fifteen seconds)

5. *Become aware of your skin, from the top of your head to the tips of your toes (think of it as being like an envelope.) Let the thoughts of things in the room fade away. You may let your eyes close at any point from here on.* (Fifteen seconds)

6. *Become aware of the muscles beneath your skin, beginning with those closest to the surface, such as your eyelid muscles, forehead muscles, and so on. Become aware of them, but do not move them. Let go of any tensions you find. Focus on every area of your body, out to your fingers and your toes. Let thoughts of things not on the inside of your body disappear.* (Thirty seconds)

7. *Focus on the deepest levels of your physical body. Be aware of your heart beating and your breathing. Then let all thoughts of more superficial things fade away as you become aware of your innermost feelings.* (Thirty seconds)

B. Mental Relaxation: Spiraling Inward

1. *Become aware of your thoughts as though they were layers of an onion. On the surface are thoughts about sensations and actions and thoughts about thinking. These are little, inconsequential thoughts, such as, "What is that noise?" "What did I just do?" "What will I do next?" Focus in deeper than these thoughts.* (Fifteen seconds)

2. *At the next level are thoughts based on preconceived images. "Should I?" "Can I?" Drift deeper than this layer of thoughts.* (Fifteen seconds)

3. *Gradually you will reach a more subtle, abstract level of thought. These are amorphous ideas often accompanied by a physical sensation that can entice you into developing ideas and explanations for them. As you notice their presence, notice also that it is easy to avoid developing ideas by thinking deeper within even that layer.* (Thirty seconds)

4. *At one level you will probably encounter thoughts that strain to define your being or to relate it to the outside world. "Who am I?" "Where am I going?" Focus in deeper than these thoughts too, and continue focusing inward in this direction.* (One minute)

C. Imagery: Your Self-Image

Explore your self-image. Take a close evaluative look at yourself. Are you the kind of person who bounces out of bed in the morning, happily greeting the day, or would you rather stay beneath the blankets? Do you spend most of your day smiling, or are you burdened with responsibilities? Do you stand tall and speak confidently, or are you shy and retiring? How are you around members of the opposite sex (including your partner)? The same sex? Are you satisfied with your job performance, your emotional makeup, your mental abilities? Are you sure in your actions or halting? Do you make many mistakes, are you capable of making important decisions quickly, are you usually on time? Do you see yourself as a leader or a follower; are you happy with your position? Is your body weak, attractive, ugly, repulsive, too fat, too thin? Rather than answering each of these questions directly, just let them serve as rough guidelines, and formulate as clearly as possible your own thoughts from your experiences of the recent and distant past. Follow yourself through a few days in the past or project into the future. In other words, allow an image to form in response to the question "How do I see myself?" Continue with this investigation until you are aware of the complete image, even if it takes some time. (Ten to thirty minutes)

D. Returning to Your Usual State of Consciousness

Return, by gradually adding on new layers of awareness, beginning with mental awareness and finishing with physical awareness of the body extending outward until you become aware of your location and position in respect to the outside world.

Try, as you retrace in reverse order the steps of mental and physical relaxation, to add on each new layer in a way that feels right, so as to avoid investing yourself in images you no longer desire. Thus, if you were annoyed about something when you began your relaxation, it is possible to return being not annoyed. Similarly, negative feelings about yourself or your environment can be replaced with more positive feelings. If you are familiar with affirmation or autogenic suggestions this is a very appropriate point at which to make these statements to yourself.

Remember at the very end to remind yourself that upon returning you will be wide awake, comfortable, and refreshed. I stress the importance of these final self-statements, because they help ensure full wakefulness and the continuing desire to use these valuable states of awareness.

Positive Image Projection (Positive Programming)

Up until this time you have been envisioning yourself in a more or less familiar way. It is also possible to imagine yourself with a completely different image, in much the same manner that an actor learns to portray a character.

EXPERIENCE TWENTY-ONE

Close your eyes a moment and imagine that you are someone you have thought it might be nice to be for a while; a movie star, a king or queen, a great thinker or religious leader; a farmer or a sailor; a character you have read about in a novel or one you have invented. Repeat this until you find one that is really satisfying to you.

This was probably an experience that you have had quite often. You may have thought of it as daydreaming. Let us now see what techniques can be used to develop this so that it can be used as a tool for self-development.

EXPERIENCE TWENTY-TWO

Relax yourself by using the concentric spheres induction (Experience Twenty) over a five-minute period. This time, when you reach part C (imagery), focus more closely on the most attractive and satisfactory character you discovered in Experience Twenty-One. Spend two to ten minutes bringing in as many details as you can.

If you chose to be a fisher, see and feel the fishing rod, smell the fish and the water, and hear the birds and the waves. If you chose to imagine yourself a race car driver, experience the crowd, the noise, and the smell.

Allow all the feelings and emotions to develop along with the sensations. Do more than "see" this internal movie, experience playing the part—how do you walk, speak, see other people, hear sounds, smell smells, feel movement, sense temperature.

You have just performed a simple experiment in temporarily altering your mental image. If you recall the emotional quality of this experience, you may discover it to be a good deal different from the way you felt just before the exercise. If you selected a calm, peaceful character, you probably had a relaxed, comfortable feeling. If you chose an active, excited character, you probably felt an acceleration in your breathing, heart rate, and other factors related to movement.

This simple altering of mental image is believed by many to be possible for no animals except humans. Perhaps humans are the only ones who can create such a mental image, thereby producing information that the unconscious mind can respond to by filling in an emotion and other details. If you did not know what an astronaut was, you would have had difficulty producing the emotion consistent with being an astronaut. Your memories, brought to life through purposeful imagination, then, were of the utmost importance in producing the quality of this experience.

Though the vast majority of your daily activities are run almost entirely by the unconscious mind, it bases most of its decisions and actions on the mental images that you customarily possess. If you are riding a roller coaster and imagine yourself to be riding on that roller coaster, your unconscious mind will respond accordingly. If you are watching a movie about a roller coaster ride, you will probably ignore the reality of sitting in a movie theater and imagine the roller coaster ride to be real. Your heartbeat and pulse rate will probably speed up, and you might find yourself gripping the armrest, breathing excitedly—proof that the unconscious is responding to your imagination rather than reality.

Now if someone shouts "Fire!," your image will become one in which you are sitting in a theater that has just begun to burn, the responses of your unconscious mind will be correspondingly altered, and you will feel fear. *Again, your image will be at odds with external reality if the shout has come from a practical joker.* In other words, the unconscious mind uses your mental image as the raw material (stimulus) from which it determines the emotions (response) that you experience. These emotions are the driving force (motivation) that causes other portions of the unconscious to begin the appropriate action (speeding up the heartbeat, gripping the chair, running out of the theater). Herein lies the greatest power of the human mind. We can suspend external reality (for example, the theater) and create a mental image (a real roller coaster) to which the deeper levels of the mind will respond. In fact the very basis for all design, planning, and creativity is the producton of an internal image of things that are not physically present.

In the theater or the movies, we usually choose to "trick" the unconscious in this manner because we enjoy the emotions it produces; it entertains us. Sometimes, however, the mental image you are holding may produce an unwanted (maladaptive) response—undesirable actions and emotions. For instance, an image of yourself as an uninteresting public speaker might produce fear and mistakes rather than confidence and accuracy. The resulting failure then *reinforces* the unwanted image (program). Fortunately, it is possible to alter this unwanted image, thereby creating a new reality for the unconscious mind—one in which your responses are more acceptable to yourself.

Writing Your Own Script

Imagery, or imagination, is also used in the production of your state of mind when you are experiencing induction. The sounds coming from your tape recorder are simply vibrations and compressions of the air molecules, which you perceive as messages. When guiding yourself into relaxation, using one of the processes you have learned, your mind is scanning memory traces. Any state of mind you reach is achieved by allowing yourself to create a mental image corresponding to the message or memory you perceive. Therefore the more you are able to follow the suggestions and images presented, keeping out any extraneous thoughts, the more profound will be the alteration of your state of consciousness to one of greater and greater relaxation. As you allow yourself, through practice, further freedom to drift into this state of mind, you will obtain the ability to experience all the phenomena usually associated with auto-hypnosis.

This includes the ability to tap your hidden resources of strength, endurance, and accurate recall and to alter your self-image to produce greater self-confidence and banish undesirable patterns. Images suggested while you are in this state of mind tend to be accepted uncritically by your unconscious as reality, and it begins to function according to the new reality. A simple way to view the difference between images offered in this state and the usual state of consciousness is demonstrated by the following story.

Lydia was a twenty-five-year-old woman who came to see me because of an intense fear of the water. Her husband and children were good swimmers, and an Olympic-size pool had just been constructed in their backyard. Though she had simply avoided going near the water most of her life, she now felt silly, because she was afraid to even wade into the water up to her knees. When I asked her why she was so afraid of water, she stated that she had been afraid for a long time and that she could recall being told, when very young, that it was possible to drown "in a teaspoon of water."

"Sometimes I walk to the pool and really would like to overcome my fear and swim, but I stop myself, fearing I would lose control and become hysterical. I know it's ridiculous for me to feel this way—even my two-year-old son can swim."

In other words, whenever she mentally pictured herself jumping into the water and swimming, this image always evoked fear and doubt from her unconscious mind. Her unconscious mind would not believe that such a thing could happen without disaster following.

After teaching her one of the methods of relaxation you have already learned, I suggested that she continue to remain relaxed and eliminate questions and unnecessary thoughts while she produced a mental image of going to the pool and stepping into the shallow water. She imagined herself walking out in the water until she was up to her chest, where she met her swimming teacher, someone she trusted. She then imagined him teaching her to swim in the manner she had become familiar with through reading books on learning how to swim—an effort she'd made in an attempt to overcome her phobia. Through my assistance in maintaining the deeply relaxed state as she produced this sequence of images step by step, her unconscious was not stimulated to produce the usual doubt and fear and she was able to visualize this clearly. Whenever doubt or fear arose, she erased it from her mind. She decided to imagine a series of events taking place later the same day.

That evening I received a phone call from Lydia. She said, "It happened just as I imagined, and I've already learned to swim the length of the pool. I know that I'll never again be afraid of the water."

My experience has been that, generally speaking, she really never will feel that same fear of the water, because she carried her image into reality and found that it was accurate. No difficulties were experienced; her image of herself as a swimmer was further *reinforced* by reality. Now her desired mental image and reality correspond.

This use of deep relaxation followed by suggestions and image rehearsal is a high-speed form of positive programming. The deep relaxation allows the pattern to be transformed from a mental image to a usable program. In conditioning a dog, we find it necessary to present stimuli and reward repeatedly in order to produce the desired pattern. This is necessary because an animal is not able to visualize an entire image, no matter how great the reward. Its mental capacity is too limited. Humans, however, can use the Selective Awareness capability of the mind to choose the desired image. This shortcut often permits the desired response to be programmed using one (or a few) session of visualizaton of the desired image. Lydia's desire to overcome an obviously irrational pattern produced the driving force to program in a new image. When she actually swam, this led to a further reward (the pleasure of swimming), and each time she swam, the reward served to strengthen the new pattern.

Sometimes, in other cases, a more gradual approach is needed, and image rehearsal sessions may extend over several weeks. (See the cassette, "Freeing Yourself from Fear," Appendix p. 286.)

Choosing Specific Patterns

In the usual phobic patient/client the offending stimulus, the unwanted behavior (overt *and* emotional) and its consequences are generally obvious. Most unwanted emotional responses that people would like to change are not, however, so clearly linked to stimulus precursors. Our next goal is to develop a clear image of the emotions and behaviors associated with a given unwanted response. The meaning of terms such as *general anxiety, confidence,* or *insecurity* is too sophisticated and complicated for the simplistic unconscious mind. To make these vague terms more concrete, we can select memories that bring our present undesirable patterns out clearly. A young sales representative who suffered from a lack of confidence recalled the following concrete examples:

"Last week, while making a sale, I felt that I could have sold more and written a larger contract, but I settled for less. I knew that a little pressure would have turned a mediocre sale into a real triumph, but I didn't have the courage to try."

"A few days ago my parents said I'd been going out too often in the evenings, and should stay home. I wanted to discuss the fact that I needed a little more freedom so that I could get out of my unhappy rut, but I've never been able to face up to my parents."

"Gladys asked the other night if I minded if she had a date with Charlie. I wanted to tell her my true feelings, and I knew that it was theoretically possible to express them while still remaining open to her thoughts, but I was afraid I might say the wrong thing and mess things up. I just felt terrible as I told her that I didn't mind."

EXPERIENCE TWENTY-THREE

Select an aspect of your performance or self-image you would like to change. It may be a physical activity, such as tennis, skiing, or bowling; a mental activity, such as reading, studying, or procrastinating; or an emotional response, such as lack of confidence, fear, frustration, depression, or rejection. Do not choose too complicated a pattern for your first goal. Enter the Selective Awareness state through one of the relaxation inductions you have learned. Recall a set of memories that give a rounded picture of the response you wish to change. Think selectively, imagining as clearly as possible each event, from start to finish. Then erase it and relax before going on to the next memory. Remain relaxed and objective. Emotional reaction to each should be minimal. Spend three to ten minutes with this self-diagnostic experience.

The next step is to develop a set of new ways of behaving and responding that you would like your unconscious mind to learn based on Experience Twenty-Three. Then after reaching the deeply relaxed Selective Awareness state, mentally rehearse the new pattern by imagining and reliving these situations, changing the story a little. Rewrite the script your unconscious followed, see yourself responding in a new, more desirable way. Imagine yourself responding in the way you consciously know is possible.

The sales representative would see and feel himself in each of these past situations. He would alter them, giving himself courage to assert himself and speak up. The memory and pain of failure is selectively excluded (by erasing these thoughts and emotions as they come up using the mental relaxation techniques you have learned). The entire situation is imagined as vividly and as clearly as possible, including the room, the clothes that people are wearing, the time of day, where the people are sitting in the room, and so on. In other words, all the stimuli of the original situation are reproduced for the unconscious mind to see. This time, however, the relaxed unconscious mind is allowed to see that there is a different way of handling that set of stimuli. As it sees this new way of handling things, it will become aware of the powerful feeling of triumph that you experience as you respond in the desired manner.

This emotion of satisfacton is a most important aspect of the programming. It is the reward. The stronger you can feel the emotion of success, happiness, and security, the more your unconscious mind will accept this new, better way of dealing with the situation.

This same procedure can then be repeated with several more of the memories you have found in which the unwanted response arose. This new pattern of responding will tend to be accepted by your unconscious mind as desirable, because it feels a reward in response to that behavior (as when a dog is rewarded for sitting on command), and because fears or doubts about this response are eliminated through selective attention relaxation. The elimination of fears, doubts, and nonessential ideas is almost as important as feeling the strength of the pleasant emotion.

Next, after reliving and restructuring the past in this deeply relaxed and selective state, you project to the future, creating the image of a similar situation that could arise. For instance, in the example of the sales representative, he knows that if his girlfriend tells him she's been invited to visit with friends on the night of their next date and asks him if he minds, he would like to say, "As a matter of fact, I *do* mind. I've been looking forward to this date for a long time. I think I'm being quite fair; after all, I've allowed you to break our dates several times in the past without saying a word about it. I'd really prefer that we went out this night."

He knows that if he has an important client who suggests he is thinking of shifting to a competitor, he would like to have the confidence to request that his client give him the opportunity to compare his product with that of the other company and show its advantages, rather than following his previous pattern of backing down and leaving empty-handed. He then imagines himself expressing this clearly and directly.

So, while still deeply relaxed, he imagines himself acting in this new way. Along with this new pattern, he experiences powerful feelings of confidence, pride, and exhilaration. He sees and feels himself successfully leaving this meeting with a new sales contract in his hand, whistling to himself on the way home.

On the other hand, your goal must be kept realistic. The sales representative knows that no matter how perfectly one performs, there are bound to be some failures. After visualizing a few positive victories he must also imagine how to handle setbacks. Remember, *his* appropriate behavior is the one to be rewarded. He thus imagines another future time in which the client, in spite of his following exactly the right behavioral pattern, still won't budge. Nevertheless, he is proud of his ability to have really tried, he is happy that he now has the self-confidence he needs to try all possibilities before writing off the sale, he has the good feeling of having done his best. He is still whistling on his way home, because he knows that his perseverance will soon pay off. In your imagery it is important to visualize the confident response *even in the face of a temporary setback.*

Of course no activity in our lives takes place in a vaccum. Every event interconnects with others. The unconscious mind knows this, so it's a good idea to include peripherally related events in your repatterning. The sales repesentative sees himself returning to work, where his boss congratulates him on his new techniques (indeed, so enthusiastic has he been that he has actually developed new sales techniques). He pictures his fellow sales representatives beginning to talk about him in an admiring way. He becomes the one selected to train new sales representatives. Even his mother and father notice the change and begin to show more respect for him.

Yes . . . But

You might be thinking at this point, Aren't there many people who daydream of success but remain failures? Isn't this just creating an unrealistic fantasy world?

Although there are some similarities to this kind of imagination, there are critical differences. The daydreamer daydreams to escape reality, not to alter it. He or she imagines a perfect world but doesn't really believe, consciously, that it is possible any more than we believe a science fiction movie is real. Furthermore, he has no real commitment to the outcome, and he doesn't develop ways to handle adverse challenges that might arise. The daydreamer's goal is to escape reality; yours is to develop and maintain an internal attitude (confidence, courage, relaxation) in relation to reality. The daydreamer dares not imagine losing a sale, but the previously mentioned sales representative will take care to include some projections in which the sale is lost, in spite of his best efforts. He will

see himself remaining confident and realistic, not letting disappoint-
ment creep in and prevent him from recognizing that there is much
to be learned from temporary setbacks. He realizes that it may take
some real work to get where he wants to go, and he feels realisti-
cally confident of his capabilities. The daydreamer clings to the self-
defeating thought "If only I could." It's the difference between
hoping and anticipating. To use these techniques properly you must
hold the image of success in your mind and confidence in your heart
through whatever adverse conditions may develop. Remember, you
are using a specialized state of mind designed to transform your
behavior and your environment, not escape them.

"Suppose I do my part," you ask, "but reality doesn't cooper-
ate? Suppose the boss or my parents don't respond as I imagine?"
This should present no real problem. Remember, your goal is not
to program the responses of the rest of the world—only your own.
Imagining others praising you or marveling at your success has the
function of reinforcing the pattern you are programming. It tends
to work because visualizing ourselves being the focus of positive
attention is a powerful reward for the unconscious. The goal is to
alter your behavior pattern; once this is done, you have succeeded
and can feel justifiably proud of your progress.

If, however, the rest of the world doesn't respond as you had
imagined:

1. Perhaps you are not listening carefully; perhaps it is just a more
   subtle response than you expected.

2. More time may be required. People are sometimes slow to
   change an opinion (image) that they've held for a long time.

3. More improvement may trigger the desired response.

4. Your expectations of the world may have been a bit unrealistic
   at first, but now you can bring them more into line with the
   new reality.

5. Your actual goal was to alter your patterns. Beware of trying to
   change just to impress or please others. Standing on your own
   feet is much more important.

6. Do not let anyone's reaction or lack of reaction lead to discouragement or a setback to the same old maladaptive response patterns.

In such cases as these, perhaps your next goal will be to write a script to handle any reaction appropriately.

How to Rewrite Your Past

How will you rewrite the past for the items you chose? If you are trying to improve your tennis backhand, you might recall a time or several times in which your stroke was perfect even if it was by accident. As you relive the sloppy game of yesterday, you would then simply insert this remembered stroke for the actual ones. Or you might get a book or a video on tennis with descriptions and pictures and, in reliving yesterday's game, let yourself perform the movements pictured. Transfer those images to your own mental body. Perhaps you have seen someone who has the stroke you would like. Give yourself that person's grace and coordination and see how much more you enjoy the game. In other words, it is essential that you know, consciously, how to act in the situation you wish to correct. Trying to visualize the proper image without knowing what it is would be equivalent to attempting to train a dog to sit without knowing what a sitting dog looked like!

Similarly, whatever the pattern you would like to change, figure out what an appropriate response would look like. The human brain is a goal-directed organ and needs a clear goal. Reading suggestions from others who have been successful in the way you would like is helpful. Simply include their ideas and attitudes in your program. The image you develop to serve as a model is called your "image ideal." (See the cassette "Powervision," Appendix p. 286.)

After daily rehearsing and projecting ahead his desired work performance for a week or so, the sales representative might decide to begin focusing on another area of his life, perhaps his relationship with his girlfriend. He would then perform exactly the same maneuvers, this time rewriting past incidents with her and projecting ahead to future desired responses. Still later, he might decide to work on his relationships at home. Once he had spent a few sessions on each of these areas, it would then be possible to cover several of them in the same sitting. Generally speaking, during each session, it is best to deal with three to five past memories and two or three future projections. Because of the tremendous focusing of energy, the nervous system can become overloaded if one attempts to stretch this process beyond fifteen or twenty minutes. The overload (sometimes experienced as fatigue or boredom) might tend to destroy the positive feelings. As a rule of thumb, you should continue to correct old situations and project new ones only as long as you can maintain the feeling of pleasure and excitement at the point where you perform correctly in your mind.

In summary, then, image visualization and projections require:

1. A clear, concise image of the desired behavior and responses.

2. Strong positive emotions, even to the point where you can feel your breath quicken, your heart pound, and your body tingle. When you feel really good, you might even feel yourself smile in happiness.

3. Imagining the activity in context, connecting it to the rest of your life.

4. Imagining others commenting on it or noticing how these good feelings can carry over to other things you do.

In the case of more complicated goals or those that are part of many areas of your life, the method of image reinforcement must be used. In addition to the preceding, this requires:

5. Repeated sessions of the preceding type. Attempt to cover all aspects of the desired behavior. You might wish to use day-to-day experiences to help you modify your script. For instance, if you find that in spite of several days of image rehearsal you still have trouble in a situation of the type you have been working on, then your next session might include this recent failure while the stimuli are still clear in your mind. Or, alternatively, you might concentrate on a different aspect that is more fundamental.

6. Similar maladaptive behavior may be found in circumstances from early childhood, such as the inability to answer questions in school because of a fear of being incorrect. These situations may also be relived.

EXPERIENCE TWENTY-FOUR
SOFTWARE FOUR: "THE WHOLE IS GREATER..."

Now experience the relaxation and imagery that follow, or another of your choice, and remember, strong positive feelings are your reward. The stronger the reward, the quicker the results. The tape "Writing Your Own Script" is an excellent guide to learning this technique. (See the list of tapes on page 285.)

This Experience allows mental and physical relaxation to proceed simultaneously and is especially good for those whose relaxation is often marred by "mind chatter," the continual need to question every little thing that occurs. It also helps us avoid those obsessive mental patterns that try to get us to carefully scrutinize every detail of awareness. The object is to give this constant questioner, or backseat driver, so much work to do that it simply gives up and allows the inner self full use of the mind and body. If you like, you can add a few suggestions for relaxation as you go along.

A. & B. Physical and Mental Relaxation

1. *Start by letting your body be seated or recumbent in a comfortable position. Let your eyes roll gently upward as you allow your eyelids to close. You may wish to imagine that you are looking at a point on the inside of your forehead, the word* Relax, *or a little scene or a pleasant object of focus suspended on the inside of the forehead (where the third eye would be). Even if all you can imagine seeing on the inside of the forehead is darkness, imagine that the darkness means* Relax.

2. *Go through your body from top to bottom or bottom to top, and imagine that you are receiving a gentle massage to each area.*

Imagine the massage is relaxing muscles. If at any point you become distracted and your awareness goes to another part of your body or an unrelated idea, use the following procedure:

a. *Become aware that your mind has wandered to another subject.*

b. *Notice the new focus of your mind.*

c. *Do not attempt to solve the problem or answer the question it has raised. Imagine the unnecessary thought is like a bus stopping at your corner, but it's not the bus for which you're waiting. Then just as a bus continues on its way, let the idea leave without your having to climb aboard and actively pursue that thought. Or you may imagine the thoughts are like clouds that slowly appear at one horizon, move across the sky, then disappear beyond the other horizon, without your doing anything.*

d. *As you let go of a thought, transfer your mental energy to the spot on the inside of your forehead, the word* Relax, *or the darkness on the inside of your forehead. Reward yourself with a good feeling for having let go of the unnecessary thought.*

e. *Do not scold yourself or feel frustrated or defeated because your mind wandered. You should reward the act of discovering the wandering and returning to relax. Punishing your mind for wandering will invite failure.*

f. *After focusing on the inside of your forehead, return to the part of your body you are in the process of relaxing.*

3. *When your body has become relaxed and your mind has become relatively clear of unnecessary thoughts, proceed to part C.*

C. Imagery

1. *One by one, review past experiences of the pattern you wish to change. As you go back through each experience, change it. Feel yourself going through it with success. Feel your mind and body working perfectly. Use as many ways as you can think of to imagine yourself performing flawlessly. Perhaps you have a photograph of someone who is an expert at this. Imagine yourself in*

his or her place, and feel the feeling that is appropriate to what
you are doing. Spend about one or two minutes on each of these
memories.

2.   After you have rewritten three or four memories, realize that you
     have been looking at the past. Feel within yourself that you are
     no longer forced to behave or respond as before. Feel yourself
     moving toward the future, more in control of your own life.
     (One minute)

3.   Now project ahead, looking forward a few hours, days, weeks. See
     yourself in a situation that before would have been difficult or
     impossible to handle. This time allow yourself time to go through
     it without experiencing unwanted (maladaptive) responses. Feel
     yourself able to function perfectly in mind and body.
           If the events to which you are projecting ahead are those that
     other people might be observing, allow yourself to note surprise
     and pleasure on their faces when they see how well you are able
     to do things. (For instance, if you are visualizing yourself with
     confidence on stage, feel yourself speaking or performing impecca-
     bly, and let the powerfully positive response of your audience
     produce a feeling of satisfaction within.) Spend about thirty
     seconds to one minute on each of the two or three "future
     memories."

D. Returning to Your Usual State of Consciousness

Picture yourself in a place you would like to visit, perhaps on a
beach, or skiing, or taking a walk. Imagine yourself looking and feeling the way you would like to, doing something you'd like to be
doing, really enjoying yourself, far from anything that could disturb
you. Enter this picture and experience it with all your senses and
emotions. Become this person. See, hear, feel, smell, and taste all the
things around you that help you to feel good. Tell yourself that each
time you picture yourself in this positive way, you become more and
more the person you want to be. Then let yourself slowly come back
to physical reality. Remember to remind yourself to feel, upon awakening, relaxed, refreshed, and alert.

Once you have chosen a behavior or other response pattern that you would like to change, repeat this experience several times. The end point that will tell you you are successful is when you feel confident in your ability to handle things in this new way, and when your actual behavior demonstrates the new pattern.

CHAPTER 8

Maladaptive Patterns (Negative Programs)

People have employed the power of the imagination to make desirable changes for centuries. Though the exact techniques have varied considerably, nearly every self-improvement method has employed visualization in some way. Imagination is central to the work of shamans in all cultures.

Imagining yourself the way you want to be while in a state of deep relaxation such as the one you have learned seems to produce more rapid changes than imagining it while in your usual state of consciousness.

Still a large group of problems seems to resist even the most determined efforts of this type. The reasons for this will become clear as we discuss the other major way the mind records and stores learned patterns of response. We will call this *negative conditioning, negative patterning,* or *negative programming.*

Negative Conditioning

As you read the section entitled "Positive Programming" in Chapter 7, you probably realized that not all the behavior patterns we learn are taught to us by offering us rewards for the proper behavior. The child who has his knuckles rapped for rudeness, the adolescent who is punished for staying out late, and the woman who receives a huge fine for driving too rapidly on the highway may thereby be induced to behave in a certain way (that is, to be polite, to come home on time, or to drive more slowly) because of the unpleasant emotions evoked in these situations. On the other hand, the business executive with a tension headache at the end of each work day, the child who develops an asthmatic attack whenever separated from his mother, and the teenage boy who has been afraid of water ever since falling out of a motorboat during a storm are also experiencing the effects of negative programming. Thus, a negative program is not harmful in and of itself. Both adaptive as well as maladaptive traits and habits may be learned through this kind of conditioning. Although the term *negative* is often used to imply "bad," when we use the word *negative* here it will simply refer to the fact that the means used to train the person are not relaxing but rather *tension producing or painful*.

To see how this works let's set up an experiment using a dog, which will show some of the similarities and differences between positive and negative programming.

Once again we start with an untrained dog. We ring a bell, as in the first demonstration, but in this case we follow it not with food, but with a painful shock, lasting about one-tenth of a second.

If the dog has been eating, sleeping, or engaging in sexual activity, this activity stops immediately. The surprised animal usually jumps into the air and howls. It begins to run around the room and may urinate or defecate. The hair on its back stands up and its pulse and blood pressure increase. Indeed, all the observations we make on the dog show that its mind and body are using the nervous mechanisms reserved for the fight or flight response. The scientist recognizes this response as an overall discharge of the sympathetic nervous system. Anyone who has been unlucky enough to receive a shock from an electrical socket or the back of a television set would probably agree that the dog is experiencing fear, panic, and a marked increase in tension.

As time passes, the frightened animal begins to calm down because it is no longer being shocked, and because the shock was not large enough to cause permanent physical damage, it would soon appear normal.

Escape Behavior

Now let's change the experimental condition slightly, by leaving an open window at the other end of the room. The dog's response to the bell and shock is as before, except that after a few moments it discovers the open window and jumps through it. This is called *escape behavior.*

Now you and I know that the shock lasted only one-tenth of a second, and because we have only one conditioning trial per day, the dog hasn't really escaped. It would not have received any further pain even if it had chosen to stay in the room. Still, the inborn reflexes that serve the function of taking it out of danger have led it to get out as soon as possible. Think of the panic that occurs when someone yells "Fire!" in a crowded ballroom or theater, even though this may be a false alarm. Like the dog, the people are so frightened by this conditioned stimulus, they react automatically–even though they see no smoke or fire.

As you can imagine, the dog learns the negatively conditioned pattern quickly; only a few trials are necessary to condition it.

Now when we ring the bell, the dog behaves as though it has received a shock. It jumps and howls as before. Its physiological responses are similar: it urinates or defecates and its blood pressure rises. In its terror, it runs for the open window.

At this point you notice something surprising. The dog seems to be even more excited and to run more vigorously than on the previous trial, when the actual shock was present! You can check this out by attaching a leash to the dog's collar and measuring the strength with which it pulls to get away. When you then unhook the leash and let it run out, then repeat the trial, you find a harder pull each time you ring the bell. Its response to the bell does not fade away as you might have expected from your knowledge of positive conditioning, even though the reflex is no longer being reinforced by shocks. We can understand this better if we take a closer look at the mechanism of escape behavior.

Self-Reinforcement of Negative Patterns

As discussed in the section entitled "Positive Programming" in Chapter 7, an animal will tend to repeat behavior that is associated in its mind with an increase in relaxation, or a relief of tension. If Rover runs to the kitchen when its name is called, it expends this energy because of the motivation generated by previous conditioning. The greater the decrease in tension and the more often this occurs, the greater the motivation.

In the present case the state of high tension induced by the bell has been associated repeatedly with escaping through the window, which is associated with relief in the dog's mind. So now in addition to the motivation to respond with panic to the bell—the negatively programmed response—there is the motivation to run as rapidly as possible toward the window—a positively programmed response. Thus there are two forces acting on the dog. It is like an iron object being repelled by one magnet and attracted by another.

If we continue to repeat this procedure and measure the strength with which the dog pulls on the leash prior to our letting go, we will find the leash tension grows greater with each trial. As with all events regularly associated with tension release, the motivation and subsequent tug on the leash will be greater the more often it occurs.

Thus the subtle, often overlooked, but critically important feature that makes negative programming and escape behavior so hard to deprogram is that *the escape behavior itself becomes more positively programmed each time it is utilized.*

The level to which the tension can be elevated can be demonstrated if we continue to strengthen the reflex in this fashion day after day, then board up the window and ring the bell continuously. The dog will continue running around and around the room; its tension level will rise higher. Soon it will fall on the floor, quivering in a state of shock. It will be unresponsive if its name is called, and it will not respond to food, pin pricks, or even electrical shocks.

The dog will have experienced a physiological collapse, which has many features in common with what is called a nervous breakdown in human beings.

It is obvious that such a simple demonstration works reliably with the dog because it cannot figure out the rules of the game, and its psychological response mechanism is unable to distinguish between the ringing of the bell and the associated fear of pain. Its tension grows greater, as do its other responses, because its mind presses it harder and harder to seek what it thinks is the escape route.

We have become a society filled with people suffering from stress overload. Their tension has not been produced by immediate threats to physical survival, the kinds of threats that this stress response was originally evolved to deal with. Instead it is the day-by-day accumulation of stress due to vague social threats against which the physical responses of fear and tension are not helpful. Instead they build up within, producing an intolerable state, which then leads to the familiar escape routes in our culture: suicide, cigarettes, overeating, drugs, alcohol, or bizarre behavior patterns. Our hospitals are filled with the consequences—cigarettes cause more than 50 percent of cancer, alcohol 80 percent of auto accidents, drugs 90 percent of crime, and overweight is a major factor in a large percentage of hospitalized people. Yet the pain we are trying to escape from is inside, and if it were not for our reaction to them the triggering events in our environment would cause no more tension than the ringing of a bell!

Negative Programming and Maladaptive Behavior Patterns in Human Beings

What about experimental evidence of the same type of response in human beings? Such experiments as the preceding one can be performed easily with animals, because they cannot figure out that they're being fooled. Their conditioning has rendered them unable to distinguish between the bell and the shock insofar as their responses are concerned. They are tricked into thinking that the open window is actually an escape, and the compulsion to use it increases because it has invariably seemed to be part of decreasing the tension. (Simple observations can often show strikingly similar patterns in people. Watch someone expecting a crucial phone call. Whenever the bell rings he or she will respond to the bell with tension although the call might not be for him or her. Many people experience a slight feeling of anxiety whenever the phone rings, even in someone else's home, because of the many times they have received bad news by phone.)

Experiments (of a less dramatic nature) have been performed using human beings instead of animals. The results indicate that we all will respond, as does the dog, provided the conditions are right. One of the most important conditions is that the subject of the experiment must not be allowed to figure out the rules of the game, so it is usually necessary to make the experiments much more elaborate than the one with the dog.

One research paper I read described the plight of an infant who, during a long hospital stay, which included a number of painful minor surgical procedures, was noted to become cranky whenever he heard the distinctive clicking sound of surgical instruments. It so happens that the child also had a furry stuffed mouse that he enjoyed caressing. As an experiment, on several occasions while he was playing with his toy, the surgical instruments were rattled. Although the instruments were not used on him during this period, he would stop playing and fidgit. Gradually, during this time he began to lose interest in his toy and pretty soon would cry whenever it was given to him. Not only did this reaction remain, it was soon noted that he became upset whenever any furry toys were given to him.

This demonstrates another feature of negative conditioning, stimulus generalization. Because the sound of surgical instruments is not itself painful, this was probably a response to conditioning at an earlier date, perhaps at the time of circumcision or a minor surgery. In addition, the *avoidance* response to the mouse began to transfer itself to other furry things. This spread of negative conditioning to include other stimuli is common and troublesome. Eventually the child could not tolerate even fuzzy blankets.

The persistence of negative conditioning tends to maintain unwanted symptoms. Tension headaches and ulcer pains do not vanish when daily problems become more numerous and more insoluble, whereas positive responses such as salivating and looking for food extinguish if they aren't followed by a reward, at least some of the time. Higher and more frequent doses of medicine are often required for ulcers, colitis, and high blood pressure. The doctor's repeating to the patient that his or her health will improve as soon as he or she stops responding to emotional situations with muscle spasm seldom suffices to disconnect the physical reflex from the emotional or environmental stimuli. The anxious child continues to have asthma attacks and the business executive to worry, even though these responses are not rewarded.

Negatively conditioned, maladaptive emotional patterns are also quite resistant to confrontation with reality. The boy with a fear of water will not be helped by dragging him to the end of the diving board and pushing him in. The fact that he manages to splash his way to the edge of the pool and get out does not convince him that he need have no further fear of the water. He would simply develop a new habit; not going near a pool when you're around. You would have made his fear worse. Likewise, the Surgeon General's warning or that of the smoker's doctor seldom produces behavioral change. In fact, if the doctor keeps it up the patient will probably escape by finding another doctor.

Persons with claustrophobia, who at first are able to ride elevators by grasping the handrail tightly and closing their eyes, often reach the point where they will not ride at all, choosing instead to walk ten or twelve flights up a dark city stairway rather than take the lift to their apartment. Explaining that there is nothing to fear or demonstrating your own confidence in the elevator seldom disconnects the tension from the stimulus for them. The little girl with a fear of snakes is not helped by her brother who holds her while a friend holds a garter snake next to the little girl's stomach so she can see it doesn't bite.

A maladaptive habit pattern is the dog's jumping out a window or a young woman's chewing her fingernails while awaiting a job interview. The woman is relieving her tensions in an irrational fashion. Although she feels even worse for the way these habits make her look, her unconscious pushes her continually toward this escape route.

When he goes on a diet, the overweight man forces himself to stay away from food. His unconscious mind pulls him toward it, but he keeps a constant hold on his dietetic leash. He is usually slightly depressed, in a bad mood, or may have rapid and unexplainable surges of emotion at this time. This represents the same kind of tension the dog feels when it is held by its leash and prevented from racing for the window. Finally, something really upsetting happens in the man's life and, diet or not, he walks into the kitchen, opens the refrigerator, and proceeds to stuff himself, taking his old escape route. In doing so, he has just strengthened his maladaptive pattern. Now when he goes on another diet, he will, like the dog who has run through the window, develop even greater tension and will have even more trouble maintaining it. Verify this for yourself. How many overweight people do you know who have been on only one diet? How many have been on five diets? How do they feel while trying not to take that extra nibble of food? Notice how their tension is customarily relieved only by their escape (eating).

The tyranny of escape behavior is pointed up in the following example:

Imagine two male roommates in college with identical grades, each studying for the same final examination in a difficult course. One is a heavy smoker (cigarettes are his escape), and the other does not smoke. On this particular night neither has any cigarettes. Who do you think will appear the most nervous? Of course it will be the one who has an escape route. As the hours pass and his tension grows, he will lose valuable study time searching ashtrays for old butts or visiting his friends to borrow smokes. He may even drive forty-five minutes to an all-night gas station to feed his habit. He leaves his car, places his money in the machine,and carries his cigarettes back to the car. Sitting in the front seat, he now opens the package and lights one, leaning back and closing his eyes as though he were finally receiving relief from the tension he had had all evening. His compulsive escape route has forced him to neglect the more adaptive solution to his tension—that of simply studying more instead of wasting so much time.

The cigarette smoker also demonstrates well the tendency for negatively conditioned patterns to become stronger with time. After the first, second, or third cigarette of his life, he certainly did not have a habit. Yet he continued to smoke occasionally, including during tense situations. After a while, his mind began to link the cigarette with the tense situation and he did, in fact, have a habit. In the beginning he may have smoked only five or six cigarettes a day and then only during the most tense periods.

Soon even minor tensions caused him to light a cigarette, and then he began smoking regularly throughout the day. Now he is up to two packs per day and he has "nicotine fits" if there are no smokes around. (Of course habits such as cigarette smoking, habitual alcohol usage, and drug or medication dependence have a feature not shared by simpler habits such as stage fright or nail-biting. Here there is also a *physiological dependence* on the chemical. This means that even when the environment is not tension producing, even when the person is relaxed, a craving will develop. This is because these chemicals act on the nervous system by filling the receptors of certain nerves and preventing them from responding to stimulation. As the drug is eliminated from the body, these nerves undergo a transient increase in discharge, which is interpreted by the person as a craving for the chemical. Fortunately, the physiological dependence disappears in just a few days if the person stops the habit. If he or she should begin to use this escape route after this time, it is because of a purely psychological motivaton.)

Another interesting feature of negative programming is the *stereotyped response pattern.* If the dog takes a particular path to the escape window during the very first trial, when it is receiving a shock, it will continue to use the same route later, when the bell is rung but no shock is administered. Even though there may be a shorter way to get to the window, the conditioning is so powerful that the rational processes are halted and it continues to take the long route.

Human habit patterns are usually stereotyped also. Some persons with habitual alcohol consumption drink only when alone. Others drink only with friends and still others drink only in taverns or at parties. People who overeat find that there is a particular food, such as bread or chocolate, toward which they are continually drawn; others may note that their specific habit consists only of taking extra helpings or snacking between meals.

Imagine the cigarette smoker who receives a phone call and the voice of the caller says, "Hello, Ed? I've got some bad news for you." At this point Ed says, "Wait a minute till I light a cigarette." Ed searches through his pockets, finds a cigarette and a match, strikes the match, lights the cigarette, and takes a puff in his habitual fashion before he faces the upcoming problem. Obviously, we are dealing with an ineffectual stereotyped attempt of the unconscious mind to escape. Ed may think he has consciously decided to smoke, but we can see this is not true. Although Ed might realize that the time taken in preparing to listen might well have been spent more efficiently by actually listening and beginning to get to work on the problem, he is unable to do so. Like the tricked dog, he is unable to view the situation rationally. He must take the stereotyped pattern.

Ed may view his habit as a minor or major annoyance, depending upon whether he has chronic bronchitis, how high his blood pressure is, and how much his doctor has been trying to convince him to stop smoking. But his unconscious mind is seemingly unaware of these facts. It merely knows that a painful situation appears to be imminent and, like the dog running from the bell, is avoiding it as much as possible, even if only for the few seconds' relief he obtains while his attention is concentrated on the ritualistic tasks of preparing for, and taking, his first puff.

Many people find the quality of their lives diminished by the frequent occurrence of angry outbursts that go beyond the healthy expression of feelings. Explosive anger, a mechanism designed to allow a primitive person to attack anything that physically threatened that person or his or her family and that could not be avoided in any other manner, follows the same pattern. The female bear, who will attack anything that comes near her cub, demonstrates this kind of response. On the other hand, probably all of us have, at one time or another, found ourselves becoming unreasonably angry with someone we are close to, only to realize later (and even sometimes while we are raging) that this loss of temper was an inappropriate reaction. We may feel guilty and sorry about this and it might have been obvious at the time how silly our behavior was, but we were nevertheless temporarily incapable of making that rational judgment and transforming our response into an adaptive one.

Tensions arose that caused the triggering of an automatic escape behavior mechanism, and we escaped from the internal state of tension through the pathway of anger. The anger that was meant to be vented against huge boulders that blocked our way, attacking animals, or invaders from other tribes is instead displaced onto those whom we love the most (our husbands, wives, children, or friends). Obviously, the more often this type of tension comes up the more often our anger will be triggered, and the more unstable our interpersonal relationships will become. If we do nothing to extinguish this reflex, the more often this occurs, the more tension we will develop in similar circumstances in the future. In such cases, the angry outburst is merely the reaction of a person who has allowed himself or herself to feel so frustrated that he or she cannot find a rational solution to a problem. The person attacks because he or she feels impotent in the face of frustration. The pain and fear of helplessness is so great that the person responds irrationally.

Even the condition that can cause the dog to collapse is sometimes produced in human beings. Once, while working in an alcoholism clinic, I asked a number of people with severe, chronic alcohol habits what would happen if someone locked them in a room without a drink. Their replies were the same: "I'd go crazy, Doc." In other words, they had the inner awareness that the rise in tension attendant upon not having their habitual escape route would reach an intolerable level. This is also the basis of much of the heroin addict's cold turkey withdrawal experience.

In my medical practice I have seen people who have had pain from surgery or some other physical problem that has lasted for several weeks. In order to keep such patients free of acute pain, they are medicated with narcotics. Soon, of course, they are quite addicted. When the medical problem is no longer present, however, it becomes necessary to withdraw them from the medication. It is dangerous to stop the medication all at once, so the dose is decreased daily, and over the period of a few days, the patients are completely off the medication. During this time there are signs of withdrawal experienced by the patients in the form of mild headaches, nausea, itching, and sweatiness. But because their addiction is only physical, and not emotional and mental, they do not have the craving that the street addict has. Nor is there any further request for the drug by the patients after they have been withdrawn.

The person who has been using narcotics as a way to escape from emotional pain presents a very different picture. The symptoms he has been avoiding are not merely the physical ones, and it is those symptoms that keeps him or her addicted. When an addict attempts to withdraw from drugs he or she focuses on these symptoms, and because the addict has been so accustomed to escaping "through the window," they produce a physiological hell and his or her tension rises. This, of course, increases these minor symptoms even more and we have the classic picture of the addict sweating profusely and shouting while undergoing cold turkey withdrawal. It is not uncommon to find that those who have made good use of relaxation and positive self-imagery while withdrawing describe withdrawal as being like a case of the flu, when relaxation and positive programming have been used.

When we examine the familiar problems of indigestion, colitis, ulcers, or other symptoms that are often caused or exacerbated by emotional stress, we see how the human body may react to various stimuli by the development of changes in the functioning of the *autonomic nervous system*, or *visceral nervous system*. In this case it is the gastrointestinal tract that becomes symptomatic. We are reminded of the dog who, at the ringing of the bell, experienced hyperfunctioning of the bowels and defecated on the floor, as it did when the shock was originally given. This occurs partly because the output from the *sympathetic nervous system* interferes with the normal *parasympathetic* functioning. In human beings similar mechanisms can cause spasm, hypersecretion, and diminished blood flow to other areas of the body, accounting for an astounding array of problems, from headaches to gangrenous toes.

Sometimes these kinds of problems show an internal self-reinforcing cycle, as in the case of the heroin addict. The woman who has been told by her physician, "If you don't change your way of living and eliminate your symptom, you will need hospitalization for surgery, or you will surely die," may thereby have a negative avoidance program initiated by the warning. As she notices the appearance of a headache or stomach pain, she recalls the doctor's warning. This very thought begins to produce more fear and, of course, makes the symptoms even worse. At this point she is past the stage at which she could have eliminated her problem by relaxing, and must turn again to medication for relief.

Anyone who has worked psychologically with patients with chronic diseases can present numerous similar examples. Of course each person's conditioning is individual and has its own characteristics. Thus not all cases of maladaptive patterns will be in the pure form as in the illustrative examples I present here. These examples should not be used to evaluate yourself or any other person. They are included to give you a general sense of how negative conditioning and maladaptive responses develop and operate. As we go on, the discussion will become more specific, and you will be able to identify the details of negative conditioning in yourself and in others more accurately.

The Eight Hallmarks of Negatively Programmed Maladaptive Patterns

1. *The person usually experiences some degree of tension, anxiety, or fear.* Sometimes this may be described as an inability to relax. The person may become aware of this early, such as while the person is raging at another, or this may not become obvious until later in the pattern—as in the case of the person who feels happy while overeating and then later feels guilty and depressed.

2. *Unwanted symptoms or habits tend to occur.* These often occur in specific combinations with emotions, for example, depression and headaches, worry and ulcers, anger and high blood pressure, anxiety and overeating.

3. *The response patterns are compulsive.* You may be a good typist or have the ability to open a window, yet you don't have the compulsive urge to do this fifteen or twenty times a day even when it is inappropriate or unhealthy. With negative conditioning the person is not in control of his or her patterns, and feels forced to smoke, eat, or have stomachaches compulsively all day, although these patterns are regarded by the person as unpleasant.

4. *The person himself or herself usually considers these patterns maladaptive*, and if given a choice would probably desire another way to deal with stress and tension.

5. *The patterns are self-reinforcing*, tending to remain even if they are not reinforced by further physical shocks. They are not automatically extinguished, as are positively conditioned responses; though irrational, they tend to become stronger. This is because the unconscious mind thinks it is escaping from a physically dangerous situation.

6. *The pattern is persistent.* The negative response is usually still present even though years may have passed during which it was not elicited. Fear of heights may not disappear even after five years of living in the flatlands. This is in contrast to positively conditioned patterns, such as typing or dancing. One's ability to respond to the typewriter would be severely compromised after five years of not typing.

7. *The awareness and functioning of the organism is limited* because of the maladaptive pattern. For instance, the man with a fear of elevators may never see the view from the Empire State Building; the angry wife cannot have a happy marriage.

8. When carried to its extreme, *severe mental disorders,* such as nervous breakdowns, or *life-threatening diseases,* such as hypertension, bleeding ulcer, or heart attack may occur. It would almost seem that the unconscious would rather extinguish its own (and the patient's) life rather than face the "bell."

EXPERIENCE TWENTY-FIVE

How many of the traits in the preceding list can you find in each of the negatively conditioned patterns you have identified in yourself? Be as objective as possible. Look at your problems as you would examine those of someone you have never met before.

Also, see how many other negatively conditioned, maladaptive patterns you can find, now that you understand the process better. Choose a few of the most important ones that you've identified, and link the symptoms, emotions, and habits that fit. Even if you are feeling fine at this moment, list those patterns that you have from time to time, or have had at some time in the past. Now is a good time to begin exploring them.

If you are in the health or helping professions you may also call upon the experiences you have had with your patients or clients as an additional exercise during this and other Experiences.

CHAPTER 9

Deprogramming: Eliminating Maladaptive Patterns

First, let's go back to the dog who was programmed to panic at the sound of a bell. (With the exception of phobias, most of our negative responses are much less violent than those of this dog. Our symptoms and escape habits are usually far more subtle, but the analogy will help your understanding.) We would like to bring it home from the laboratory, but every time the doorbell rings when it is at home, it smashes through the plate glass window. In addition to being an unhappy situation for the dog and the broken windows, it is also not pleasant for us. Of course we could disconnect the bell, pump the dog full of tranquilizers, or have it placed in a hospital for emotionally disturbed dogs; but there is a much better solution. It is called *deprogramming,* or *deconditioning.*

First of all, with a tape recorder, we record the sound of the bell on a magnetic tape. Next we place a large dish of tasty food in front of the dog. Then as it is eating (and therefore its tension is decreasing) we turn on the tape and play it at a very low volume level, so low that the ringing is just barely perceived by the dog. We notice that the dog's ears perk up a bit, and it may glance nervously about, but it is hungry and the bell does not sound quite so frightening, so it continues to eat. Perhaps you have seen a dog eating when the doorbell rings. Ordinarily, it would run to the door, barking, but when it is eating, it will merely growl or whimper into its plate and stay with the food. The same sort of thing happens here, and the dog continues to eat *even though it hears the sound of the bell*. When it stops eating we turn off the tape.

The following day we turn the tape recorder on after it has begun to eat, and we find we can turn the volume up a tiny bit without disturbing it any more than on the previous day. This process is continued daily, each time increasing the volume of the bell, and, depending upon the breed of dog, the strength of its conditioning, and other factors, in one or two weeks we will be able to play the bell back at full volume and the dog will not seem to notice it at all. It will simply eat its food, as though it had never been conditioned.

If we now repeat one of the original trials by bringing the dog back into the laboratory and ringing the bell at full volume without giving it food, we will find that it will salivate, wag its tail, and look about for food. Its tension level will go down and it will behave as any dog who expects food. *It now experiences a tension decrease instead of fear.*

In other words, by gradually reexposing the dog to a negative stimulus while it is undergoing a decrease in tension, we have eliminated the programmed responses of fear, bodily disorganizaton, and escape behavior. Instead, the stimulus induces relaxation. The tension level goes down instead of up, because a new response has been conditioned. Defecation and urination do not occur. Running and barking have disappeared, as has its escape behavior. In the absence of tension, there is no need for it.

So the ringing of the bell, which may previously have caused complete neurophysiological collapse, now produces no fear, but instead an increase in relaxation and an expectancy of a pleasant event. Technically, this is called deconditioning by *reciprocal inhibition* because relaxation inhibits the usual negative response.

Though our stimuli are not always bells, and though we might not wish to trade our unwanted habit for the response of expecting food, as does the dog, we can still make use of these principles of deconditioning. Because our maladaptive responses are also negatively conditioned, all we really need is a means of producing a markedly decreased tension level and a way of gradually reintroducing the negative stimuli. In this way the old pattern may be deprogrammed.

Actually, this process is not unfamiliar to us in our daily lives. The upset man whom you calm down and encourage to tell you his story often feels better after getting it off his chest. This is the "shoulder to cry on" principle. He has reexposed himself to the painful thoughts in the relaxing atmosphere of your understanding attention.

It is even more obvious in the case of a child who has had a fear of being in automobiles since falling out of a car window when very small. To help with her problem you would certainly not merely lock her in the car and drive away (the "sink or swim" method). You might, instead, begin by playing tag or "hide the ball" around and under the car. The next day you might play hide and seek, sometimes hiding in the car. After a few afternoons of playing tea party in the back seat of the car, you might begin to play rocket ship pilot in the front seat. If you followed this with a game of "stop and go," letting the car roll short distances, you might soon be able to get her to travel with you comfortably for short rides (preferably to the ice cream shop). Soon, in this fashion, her fear of riding in cars would become deprogrammed, and she might actually begin to find auto trips pleasurable.

The three main factors necessary for deprogramming are:

1. The stimulus, or trigger must be identified.

2. A means must be available to reliably produce a state of relaxation and decreased tension.

3. The offending stimuli (most of the time the original stimulus has generalized and there is more than one) must be presented to the mind gradually, in increasing amounts, over a period of time. This is a most critical factor: had we rung the bell at full volume the first day, while he was eating, we would simply have added indigestion to the frightened dog's list of problems.

The induction techniques you have learned are an effective form of relaxation that can be used to decondition. The image projection (positive image rehearsal) technique can serve as a way to gradually reintroduce stimuli by means of the memory, because reexperienced memories, like the bell, tend to elicit the same responses. A difficult problem remains, however, how to discover exactly which stimuli to use in the deconditioning process. The inability to properly identify the stimuli for maladaptive patterns seems to be the most common stumbling block in the successful use of the simple image rehearsal technique you learned in Experience twenty-four. An example may help demonstrate why.

Edgar was a concert violinist who came to my office to investigate the fear he experienced whenever he was on stage. He had used image visualization and self-hypnosis in the past to picture himself playing the violin on stage without fear. He had had some degree of success, but there was still a stubborn knot of discomfort that he had been unable to dispel.

We explored the problem using the techniques you will learn in the next chapter and discovered, quite to his surprise, that the stimulus responsible was not the *playing* of the violin in front of the audience but the act of walking out onto the stage in front of an audience carrying the violin.

In reliving his memories of several times in which he had felt this fear, he noted that the fear began at exactly the moment he stepped from behind the curtain and in front of the audience. It turned out that this fear had been present even during his first violin concert although it had not been nearly as great as it had grown to be in recent years. We went back further into his childhood and discovered the event mainly responsible for this fear (the sensitizing event). It had occurred several years before his first concert, while he was on his way to violin practice. That day he was set upon by the tough guys in the neighborhood, who saw him carrying his violin case. They called him a sissy and told him that if they ever saw him again, they would beat him up. From that time onward frightened Edgar took only rarely used back streets to get to his violin lesson, in order not to be seen by the other children. Thus the act of being seen with his violin was the stimulus for fear in front of the audience.

Though all of his memories had been available to his conscious mind before he came to see me, he had never connected them in this fashion. Because he could now relive these early childhood events with a feeling of calm and equanimity, the first step in deconditioning had been taken.

When he left my office I gave him a tape recording, consisting of a five-minute induction to produce a deeply relaxed state, followed by imagery suggestions that he relive several incidents in which he had experienced fear of appearing in front of people. He listened to the tape and followed its instructions several times a day and on his next concert tour, one and a half weeks later, found that he played more calmly in front of the audience than he had in years. (This case, like many others in this book, describes a rapid resolution of a problem. Of course all negative patterns do not respond this rapidly. Numerous factors influence this, including basic personality strength, motivation, commitment to change, belief in the technique, and skill of the therapist, if there is one.)

Why Is Negative Programming So Persistent?

Because the theory of evolution dictates that only reactions that have survival value persist, it makes sense to ask what value is it to have negative conditioning be so hard to undo. Why is it so tenacious? Why does it not respond to simple conscious alteration, as does positive conditioning? Why is it these basic connections cannot be made by all of us, resulting in a simple means of deconditioning?

Consider the prehistoric environment in which our body and unconscious mind developed. Let's imagine a primitive man has located water some distance from the entrance to his cave. To reach the water he walks along a certain path, around a certain tree and to a particular clump of bushes, and then over a small hill, where he finds his drinking water each day. Because he does not have maps or diagrams, he must depend upon his conditioned reflexes to relocate the water each day. Those of us who develop the habit of stopping at a particular shop for coffee each morning know how strongly ingrained this reflex can become. If we go to work on a Sunday,

when the coffee shop is closed, we might find ourselves automatically stopping the car in front of it.

Suppose a change in the weather led to a drying up of the primitive man's water hole. It would not take long before he discovered
there was no water left. He might wander back to his cave, and
later on that day begin to feel thirsty. His reflex would lead him
to follow the same pathway, not understanding the mechanics of
change in the weather and the drying of the water hole. Once again
he would be surprised to find the pond dry. Because of the tendency of positive programming to fade if it is not rewarded, a few
trials such as this would lead to the rapid disappearance of the
response, and he would cease his trips to that place.

This course of events is reasonable, because the habit, if continued (as it would be in the case of a negatively conditioned pattern) would cause the primitive man to die of dehydration while
walking continuously back and forth to his dry water hole. Instead,
the tension of thirst and the fading of his positively conditioned
response would soon develop a *motivation* to seek water in other
areas, and he would begin to search about (exploratory, or problem-
solving behavior).

Now let's take a look at the primitive man's negative programming. We begin with a primitive boy who, at the age of three years,
climbs to the top of a two-foot-high rock. Because he has never had
experience with height, he is not aware that walking over the edge
of the rock will cause pain and discomfort as he falls down. (Many
of us have seen babies walk off beds, chairs, and steps, because
they do not understand the principles of gravity, falling, and hurt-
ing themselves.)

As our primitive boy walks off the rock and strikes his head,
a situation of pain and increased physical tension occurs, and all
the criteria for negative conditioning exist. It is unlikely that he will
have to fall off many rocks before he gets the idea. Within the next
six months, he will know quite well to be careful of high places.

Because this is negative conditioning, it will tend to remain,
even though for the next ten or fifteen years he may live with his
family in the desert flatlands and never again see a high rock. As
soon as he moves to the mountains again, when he walks to the
edge of a cliff, he will immediately feel the same tendency to refrain
from stepping over the edge of the cliff—just as he had felt when

a young child. His escape behavior consists of backing up a few safe inches. If his negative conditioning had faded, as positive conditioning does, then he would have had to learn this lesson over and over again, perhaps with disastrous consequences. The accident rate for primitive people would have been extraordinarily high indeed.

It is reasonable that negative programming would be provided for us by nature to help with such problems as high places, thorny bushes, deep water, predatory animals, and other potentially dangerous situations that primitive people might encounter during daily life. Because there was no adequate language or books, nature could not trust the conscious mind to learn these things, and instead developed automatic processes for learning.

Nature also saw to it that deconditioning could be used at the proper times. If the primitive man has learned to avoid cacti because of their sharp thorns, he may continue with this behavior for many years. Yet if there happens to be a drought in the desert, and if his water hole has dried up, he might find that his old aversion to cacti rapidly fades as he discovers that he is able to obtain moisture by breaking them open. Of course he will do all in his power to avoid becoming impaled by the thorns as he works to extract the fluid, but he will almost certainly receive many thorn pricks. Here the positive reward of water partially deconditions the fear of cactus. Like the dog who has been deconditioned to the bell, the primitive man who used to take special paths to avoid these cacti now runs happily toward them to seek their precious liquid.

Generally speaking, however, it is difficult to alter negative programming, because the survival of an animal depends primarily on its ability to defend itself against the threats to its life. These defenses are present in the form of fight or flight mechanisms, which require increased levels of tension, so they are negative programs. Positively programmed behavior, on the other hand, is useful for exploring the environment and for obtaining food, shelter, and other comforts. An excellent example of the supremacy of negative response over positive response can be seen by watching a group of deer or squirrels browsing about for food. Although they may have traveled a long distance to reach the meadow and may have gone for days without food, the sudden appearance of a wolf or lion (or you!) at the edge of the meadow will cause them to stop their positive program of eating and launch into headlong flight (negative program), because the negative program to ensure survival is much more compelling.

In our present world these primitive responses can cause quite a problem. There are few wolves, lions, or cacti about. Instead, humans have been trained to fear stimuli that pose no actual immediate physical threat. We stutter when making an important speech, our bodies responding with fear although we are aware that regardless of how poorly we do, we will not be physically attacked. Headaches prevent us from studying for a test, our neck muscles tightening as though the test were a lion coming closer. Anger alienates us from our families and friends, because this strong emotion was originally a reaction to a life-threatening situation. Our alcohol, nicotine, tranquilizer, and heroin escape routes are slowly killing us because we know no way to deprogram our irrational fears, and so we try to simply drug the unconscious mind beyond the point of fear. Will we soon be extinct, like the dinosaurs? Will our highly developed minds, like the bodies of the dinosaurs, prove to be our own undoing?

I think not. Dinosaurs had no means for self-alteration as the environment changed, but along with the development of the society that has produced our problems, humans have produced the understanding and tools to deprogram unwanted responses of the mind. Perhaps nature has foreseen this, even as a scientist knows that a monkey will eventually figure out the way to pile up boxes to reach bananas suspended from the ceiling. The fact that not everyone will choose to put this knowledge into practice is probably just another of evolution's selective mechanisms to ensure survival of the fittest, or, as Dr. Jonas Salk describes it, "survival of the wisest."

How do we begin to update our primitive programming to fit the twentieth-century world? How do we decondition ourselves? First, we must uncover the stimuli (items, thoughts, or situations) that set off our fears.

Uncovering the Stimulus: Fine-Tuning Your Awareness

Sometimes the resolution of a maladaptive response pattern involves the discovery of an event hidden in childhood, followed by a cure. This happens in some, but not all, cases. Sometimes, especially in phobic situations, which are characterized by high levels of fear and anxiety, the discovery of the true stimulus involves the sudden recollection of a childhood (or even an adult) memory that has not been brought to consciousness for years. This memory may then make clear to the conscious mind and unconscious mind the actual stimuli involved, and desensitization can be instituted.

Sam came to see me because he became carsick whenever he traveled any distance in the backseat of an automobile. Curiously, he had no difficulty when he rode in the front seat. During the course of our work, we discovered a memory dating back to just before his first birthday. At this time his mother had had to go to the hospital for surgery. He had been with his mother day and night since birth, and because she had had to leave him in the care of his aunt and uncle while she had gone to the hospital, he had become extremely frightened. As his uncle had driven away from the hospital, his aunt had attempted to humor him by playing games in the backseat with him. She had been unable to stop him from crying, though, and as he had seen his mother fade into the distance out of the back window of the car, he had had a sinking, lonely, upset feeling. For the rest of his life, this program was remembered by the unconscious mind each time he got in the backseat of a car. Had he remembered it consciously, he would have been able to go through it with an adult understanding, but because it had never been deconditioned, the unconscious mind treated the backseat of all cars as the ringing of a particularly frightening bell. His emotional tension was converted into dizziness, nausea, and a feeling of being trapped. Sam relived this memory with an adult understanding, and was able to decondition himself by going through other memories of times when he had experienced fear while riding in the backseat of cars. His maladaptive response pattern faded rapidly.

Some of my patients can recall in detail events that occured before the first year of life; their parents verify their recollections. How can this be?

When you think about it, it's not unreasonable that these early memories of events and even words exist, albeit initially without understanding. I learned the words to "Frere Jacques" and "Alouette" in school long before I knew what they meant. Later, when I studied

French, I could recall the songs and translate them. Indeed, many people find themselves unwilling to sing "Alouette" after they learn they are singing a song about the cruel mutilation of a bird!

In a similar fashion the mind recalls each event as a movie camera might. One of my patients, Doreen, ate too much because she felt ugly. Her sensitizing event had been at birth, hearing her mother cry as the doctor handed her the newborn baby, "Oh my God, she's ugly!" Doreen called her mother and asked if she'd said those words. Her mother answered, "Dr. Wilson promised me he'd never tell anybody that!"

Doreen's mind was capable of storing every detail of her birth. The motivaton to store it was provided by the trauma of birth itself (increased tension). She did not know at that time, however, what her mother's words meant. She hadn't yet learned English!

But a few years later her mind had learned the meaning of all the words and translated them. It was then believed that Mother was right (Mother always seemed right), and the belief that she was ugly became a program related to eating (Mother had put her to the breast right after birth).

This translation and decision took place only in the unconscious, without it being brought up for conscious review. Therefore there was no way for her unconscious to learn that the reasons for that remark were her mother's fear, the dulling of her mind with anesthesia, and her unpreparedness for the sight of a child with a large head and covered with blood. Doreen had never consciously experienced this event and the meaning of the words simultaneously. Thus, no matter how hard she might search consciously, this connection could never be discovered. We had to let her unconscious mind present it by letting the scene gradually appear in her mind during a state of deep relaxation.

Are you doubtful that a newborn could be capable of such mental activity? Consider the premature baby, born after seven months in the womb. By the time it has lived two more months, it has learned to smile, focus its eyes, and understand words, yet its brain is the same as that of the newborn of nine months' gestational age. So the thinking mechanism is obviously developed long before birth. The last few months in utero seem to be devoted almost exclusively to the development of muscle and fatty tissue, to cope with the physical environment. The brain is ready to receive programming even before birth!

Actually, such early memories arise rarely, and perhaps only one-fiftieth of the memories useful in Explorations are of this type. In a large pecentage of the cases of successful deconditioning, the memories were familiar, having been previously recalled by the person. The important factor in these cases was the reexperiencing of the emotion that was present during the memories, even if the person was unaware of it, or only slightly aware of it, at the time. This emotion provides a means by which seemingly unrelated events are connected in the unconscious mind, thereby giving rise to a deep insight and the discovery of the mechanism of the maladaptive pattern by the unconscious, which may then (through deprogramming) be instructed to eliminate it.

Jeanne came to see me because her attempts to maintain her proper weight were continually thwarted by a compulsive need to eat too much at meals. She always felt guilty and thought the guilt was because she ate too much. As she relived memories one by one, she noted that although there was pressure to eat, there was no real hunger. She felt, instead, powerful emotions of guilt as she overate. When this emotion of guilt associated with eating was traced back further, several memories were reviewed in which Jeanne was reprimanded by her parents for not finishing her food. She was embarrassed in front of her family and friends and felt guilty. In one of her earliest recollections she recalled a memory in which her mother said, "You should be ashamed of yourself, leaving food on your plate while little babies are starving to death in India!" She had an intense feeling of guilt. Somehow, she felt, her not eating was causing others to suffer. She responded by cleaning off her plate. Of course her parents had been attempting to accomplish what they felt to be a positive outcome by using guilt to force her to eat what they felt was a proper meal. The unfortunate result was, however, that this same association of being forced to eat and feeling guilty had continued as a negatively conditioned response into her adult life. Her unconscious mind still compulsively reproduced the guilt and compulsion to eat whenever food was around. The adult conscious mind, in an attempt to rationalize the association of these factors concluded that the guilt was the result of the eating.

By reliving, in a state of relaxation, these and many other memories from her childhood and adult life in which similar stimuli and emotions were present, and projecting forward appropriate eating patterns her unconscious was able to allow her to stop eating as soon as real hunger was satisfied. Her weight subsequently fell to normal. (See the cassette, "Imagine Yourself Slim" Appendix p. 285.)

It is common for us to choose the wrong explanation for unpleasant emotions. The woman who has had a particularly difficult day at work will be more sensitive when she comes home. Her husband may talk to her in the same way he does every other day, but on this day she will feel attacked. Though her frustrations are at her office, she may treat him as though he is the cause of her bad feelings, and an argument is likely to ensue, an argument in which she cannot understand why he is picking on her. He, in turn, cannot understand why she is so short-tempered. This is an example of the dangers caused by the tendency of negative programming to become associated with other stimuli. One's problems are often compounded. The woman now has a tense situation at home *and* at work!

As in the preceding example, some maladaptive patterns can be understood following a detailed reliving of recent events, using the extreme sensitivity of Selective Awareness to refocus attention within each memory.

There are many other ways in which the proper investigation of one's memories can lead to an identification of the items truly responsible for unwanted responses. No two individuals respond to exactly the same stimuli or have the same emotion. Each person's story is different, and must be discovered individually by him or her. Generalizations such as "people who have a fear of height or water are simply reacting to their own strong death wish," or "men with impotence have a problem dating back to their relationships with their domineering mothers," are, at best, oversimplifications, and at worst disastrously misleading.

If it is true that the correction of our maladaptive patterns requires only the discovery of stimuli and then deconditioning, and if these can be found from examining our memories, why is it that we cannot simply run through our recollections while in our usual state of consciousness and discover them? Why is the unconscious mind so unwilling to pinpoint the actual causes of our problems? Perhaps one more experiment with the dog will help us understand this.

Fred came out of his house one morning to find one of the neighborhood dogs busily unearthing the flower bulbs he had just planted. He yelled at the dog but the digging continued. The dog had never learned to respond to Fred's words. Fred picked up his garden hose and turned it full force upon the dog, who retreated down the street.

The next day the dog was back but still refused to leave when Fred yelled at him. When Fred picked up the hose, however, the dog didn't wait for the water—it ran immediately. Two days later Fred found that the dog would leave when he simply yelled, "Get out!"

About a week later the dog was back, but upon seeing Fred come out of the house it ran away, and ever since that time the dog has carfully avoided going near Fred's garden. This demonstrates the tendency of negative conditioning to generalize!

Here we see a pure form of negative conditioning with the elements of spreading—as in the case of the baby who disliked surgical instruments. The dog had not learned to understand English, and its continued digging in other gardens on the street showed it didn't comprehend that gardens are not for digging. Its mind had simply been programmed to avoid a certain plot of ground; it did not understand the reason why it should. Now, whenever it begins to walk toward that piece of ground, it will find tension growing within. As it goes closer and closer to it, the conditioned response of turning and leaving will become more and more dominant and it will, because of its internal programs, be *unable* to reenter the garden. Its going in another direction represents the same avoidance behavior as seen in the dog who ran through the window to escape the bell. This time, however, the stimulus is much more complicated. It consists of the image of the garden, its smells, its surroundings, and so on.

Similar responses can be seen in human beings. A person with a fear of heights avoids windows when in tall buildings; the smoker desires a cigarette when the phone rings, as the smoker's mind temporarily "runs" from the possible threat posed by the phone. In other words, there are certain groups of stimuli that the unconscious mind has learned to avoid or delay in one way or another.

In Chapter 1 it was noted that in addition to recalling the physical (objective) aspects of a situation, the emotional (subjective) feelings may also be evoked if desired. You may have noticed that people will often resist recalling painful events ("I get sad just thinking about it").

The unconscious mind may make a similar decision if it feels the memory may cause discomfort. It will "forget" just as surely as it will "lose" a set of keys. The memory of the event is stored in the memory centers of the mind, but the amount of fear associated with recalling it deflects the memory beam whenever the conscious mind begins to think in its direction. In other cases the unconscious mind simply refuses to recall all the aspects of the situation we are remembering because of the fear that would arise.

Although Jeanne experienced feelings of guilt every time she overate, when she looked back at her habit in her normal waking state, the unconscious mind simply did not allow her to see the guilt stretching back into her childhood. Because it was so accustomed to running from this feeling, the mind would not let her realize the childhood feelings and the true cause of her problem. As a result, Jeanne thought the guilt was because of each individual act of overeating, and because the childhood guilt remained unresolved, the blocked emotional energy maintained the pattern.

Sometimes this forgetting results in the blurring of the details of a situation. The violinist knew that his fear had something to do with being on stage, but to identify the fear as beginning at the very instant in which he stepped from behind the curtain was too painful an experience for his mind to access *under ordinary conditions*.

Although we might wish, consciously, to become aware of these items, the unconscious mind may resist us strongly, as in the case of the five-year-old with a water phobia who resists our attempts to coax him off the end of the diving board. No amount of rational thinking can overcome the fear response. No matter how important we might feel our positive goals to be, the fear response is programmed by nature to overcome this. Therefore when we seek to figure out our problems, we often fail. All that we are aware of consciously is that we can't seem to figure it out; our minds refuse to reexperience the frightening memory, just as the dog avoids the garden.

Sometimes our emotional memory may fail us also. Perhaps you have discussed with a friend an event that occurred a long time ago. One of you might remember quite clearly that the other was depressed, angry, or afraid, whereas the person himself or herself simply doesn't recall that emotion. Sometimes you might see photographs taken on a day you had always remembered as happy, only to discover that your face looked sad indeed. When it comes to the emotional memory of those events responsible for our present maladaptive programs, special methods, such as the Exploration in the next chapter, may help our recollection considerably.

CHAPTER 10

A Look at Yourself: The Exploration

The Exploration

A s mentioned in Chapter 2, my first experiences with deep relaxation and imagery involved the elimination of physical pain. I had experienced their effectiveness over the months in which I had used them in the emergency room. I then reasoned that the temporary relief of unwanted emotions could take place in the same way as the elimination of unwanted physical pain. Indeed, usually the most important factor in helping people become free from pain in the emergency room was the reduction of the fear that they were experiencing. Once fear was subdued, pain was easier to control.

My next efforts were directed toward studying something long known in the field of hypnosis, the phenomenon called age regression. In age regression a person becomes very relaxed and can choose to relive earlier situations in his or her life. During this process the person may remain as consciously aware as you have been during the relaxation experiences and is capable of terminating any experience by projecting it on a mental blackboard and erasing it.

I vividly remember my first experience with age regression. One day I was waiting for a friend at his house. While waiting, I engaged in a discussion of hypnotherapy with his sister. She expressed a desire to experience an induction and said she would like to relive some events from her early childhood.

After helping guide her to a relaxed state of mind and body, I asked if she would like to go back to the first day she ever walked. (Most of us in our early experiences with hypnosis are attracted by the novelty and drama inherent in the recovery of such memories, and the ease with which this is often possible. Soon, however, we learn, as I have mentioned, that only a minority of therapeutically useful memories date back to the first few years.) She indicated that she would, and I began to suggest to her unconscious mind that it reproduce that experience for her. Soon she was able to picture the living room of the house in which she had grown up, and was able to describe her mother, father, and grandmother in detail, even down to the clothes they were wearing. She described the room, and as she went through the experience, could recall walking toward her mother, who was sitting on the sofa. She felt great satisfaction because she could now walk about, as did her sisters and brothers and parents.

After returning her to her usual state of consciousness, she felt comfortable and pleased with the memory, especially the vivid quality of her visual experiences. (Only about 30 percent to 40 percent of people are able to clearly visualize in their first attempts. The others, who "sense" memories rather than see them, seem to be able to use these methods just as effectively, perhaps even more so in some cases. Eventually, with practice, a person can perceive with all five senses.)

Because this was the first time I had worked with age regression, I was skeptical about the various details she had recovered. She assured me they seemed very real, but there was one confusing item—the couch upon which her mother was sitting. She recalled the house quite well in her usual state of consciousness, because she had spent the first fourteen years of her life there, but never before had she recalled seeing this couch. She described it in detail, the shape of its arms and the small tufts of material on its surface. She could see its color and the pattern printed on it.

Her confusion was ended when her brother arrived. She described the couch to him. He was as amazed as we were, but for quite a different reason. He was several years older than she, and was surprised that she had described a couch that had been sold before her second birthday to make way for a new couch. She had been correct in her description, even down to the tufts on the cushions.

As I used age regressoin with more and more people, the belief shared by many neurophysiologists, that the mind retains every perception and every experience, seemed to be borne out. It seemed that almost any event an individual was truly motivated to recall could be reached through the use of deep relaxation and selective awareness. Slowly, a remarkable series of thoughts began to develop in my mind.

We are not born with most of our maladaptive habit patterns. Babies don't smoke, have a fear of playing musical instruments in front of people, or have problems with procrastination. There must be some point in our lives at which the negative conditioning is begun.

As adults we continually respond with fear to stimuli that are only symbolic and cannot really harm us (for example, we fear being alone or speaking in front of people), but—if the rules of negative conditioning are correct—there must be some time between our unconditioned infant state and our present patterns, a time in which these stimuli were associated with an event of fear and tension, as the dog's negative pattern was originally produced by linking the bell and the shock.

I then reasoned that perhaps maladaptive symptoms, emotions and habit patterns could be traced, using the amazing recall potential of humans, the very first conditioning events. The ability of the adult conscious mind to understand the events that had been so confusing to the child, and that had continued to operate in the unconscious, could lead to a deeper understanding and a significant insight into the difficulty and, at the same time, provide the raw material for deconditioning.

Describing an analogous situation might help to show how this can happen.

I was once called to the hospital to give emergency treatment to one of my patients, who had attempted to kill herself by ingesting a large quantity of pills. After emptying her stomach of the drugs, I asked her why she had tried to kill herself. She proceeded to tell me, very tearfully, about an argument she had had with her husband the previous day.

He had stormed out of the house, saying that he didn't know how to handle the situation. When he had not come home that night, she had become afraid that he had left for good and that he had found another woman. The following day, while she was grocery shopping, she saw him walking toward his car in the parking lot, with his arm around the shoulder of a woman in a green dress. She did not see the woman's face, but she feared the worst— she'd lost her husband. So great was her shock and fear that she went home and attempted to take her life. As she told me the story, she still seemed determined to kill heself.

As I began to discuss the inadvisability of suicide with her, her husband came into the treatment room. At his side was the woman in the green dress. My patient was dumbfounded; she recognized the woman. It was his sister. He had been so confused and upset by their argument that he had driven that night to a distant town, where he had spent several hours talking with his sister. She had driven back with him, intending to help, and when they were seen by his wife, he and his sister had just eaten breakfast and were on their way to the couple's home to try and patch things up.

My patient cried again, but this time for a different reason: she was happy to find she had been wrong. There was no further thought in her mind of taking her life. It had taken but a few moments of seeing things in the right perspective to completely change her emotional state.

In the same way, when a person reviews some of the actual events responsible for his or her maladaptive patterns, the understanding that arises may go a long way, in itself, to change the responses (this is a form of "insight therapy"). In addition, the careful examination of these events will reveal the stimuli, which can then be used to decondition the unwanted response in the way we have discussed.

Actually, methods of personal change similar to this have been used for many years with varying degrees of success. What I had difficulty in understanding was why principles so simple, specific, and easy to apply were not used universally, with more significant results. I decided to investigate this problem more fully. Perhaps I would discover, as did the Wright brothers, that all the necessary information and materials were present, but no one had put them together in the right fashion.

In setting out to stitch together the fabric for a coronation gown for a queen, a designer would never dream of beginning without a pattern. No engineer would attempt to move the pillars of a suspension bridge without a careful, detailed appraisal of the structure. No architect would start construction on a house until he or she had drawn a plan of it. Similarly, no one would dream of building or repairing a computer, especially one as complicated as the human mind, without having a "diagnostic program," a program that is inserted into the computer whenever it breaks down. The computer can then analyze itself according to this program and point out the circuits and areas that need to be examined. In the belief that the intelligence responsible for designing the human nervous system must have allowed for the use of such a program, I attempted to follow a mathematically consistent pattern for identifying the kind of information that would be required by the mind in order to perform this same operation. In my work I gradually altered my approach and my theory as these principles were revealed to me, using my gradually improving results as feedback.

One of the most useful approximation to a self-diagnosing, self-correcting process is that of the Exploration. A basic outline for how I might proceed to guide a person in an exploration follows.

First, the person with the maladaptive pattern explains his or her goal: the elimination of a particular symptom, emotion, or habit. Because I am a therapist working on a one-to-one basis, the level of relaxation is often much greater than that which a person will reach without a guide present. A guide can help eliminate nonessential thoughts and ideas through suggesting further relaxation. In addition, observations of the person's movement, tone of voice, rate of speech, and so on, can be used to help guide the process.

When the body is relaxed and the mind clear, I give instructions that lead to the recollection of a recent event, occurring perhaps within the past few weeks, during which the person experienced the maladaptive pattern. Because the event was so recent, it could have been recalled prior to the person being in a state of deep relaxation. The scene is not, however, chosen *consciously* by the person. He or she simply takes the very first memory presented by the unconscious, just as you earlier experienced spontaneous thoughts. He or she then relives the memory and the emotions associated with it, recalling also the way he or she got out of the difficult situation (escape route). Following this, I suggest that the person clear the mind completely in preparation for the next memory.

I then suggest that the unconscious choose a memory which occurred at an earlier time, in which the same pattern (symptom, habit, or emotion) was present. Again, the person relives it as vividly as possible, and primary attention is paid to the emotion or feeling state associated with it.

As more and more memories are recalled, we go back to earlier and earlier periods of the person's life. Because the emotional response is the aspect most responsible for the development and maintenance of the problem, attention is focused on it. The serial reliving of the memories tends to accentuate the emotion's strength and quality, and by the time the childhood memories are reached, the emotions are often quite strong. Following the recall of each event (which lasts a minute or two) I instructed the unconscious to erase it and all previous memories temporarily, as was done with the numbers in the deep relaxation inductions. This begins to build up confidence within the unconscious that any memory that it recalls can be handled consciously by erasing it if necessary. (It is important to erase unneeded thoughts. Unerased memories keep negative stimuli within the field of consciousness and cause the unconscious to avoid the "garden," where important discoveries are buried.) A series of memories with hitherto undiscovered relationships and emotions may thus be traced.

I then suggest that the person go back to the very first time when this particular emotion and habit pattern were present (the sensitizing event). It is here that people may recall events from their early infancy and, in reviewing them, can comprehend, on a deep level, the irrationality of their previous response patterns. Even when only recent or previously recalled events are reviewed, new connections and meanings are discovered. The resulting insight is most valuable for the deconditioning.

By observing the patterns present in the memories elicited, a list of the stimuli responsible for the unwanted response can be drawn up. While still in a deeply relaxed state, the person reviews all of these memories with his or her new understanding. On the person's leaving, I give him or her a tape recording of the relaxation procedure, followed by instructions to continue to review and relive other memories that fit the same pattern, but only while completely relaxed. I suggest that the person start with the easiest ones to understand and gradually work up to more difficult ones, especially those in his or her current life. The process of deconditioning continues for a week or two, or until another visit to my office, at which time other patterns may be investigated or further work done on the original response pattern.

To complete the deconditoning, image rehearsal (positive image projection) is used to project imagined future events, replacing the old habit with the desired behavior and feelings, rewriting the script and the outcome.

Exploring Early Memories

Several questions often arise when people face the prospect of exploring their memories. The most common is, "Will I be able to remember the necessary events?"

Because nothing is ever forgotten, and because your mind is running a maladaptive program learned in the past, then not only must the important memories (conditioning events) be available, but your mind must know exactly which ones they are and where they are stored. Simply being ready to explore the process and allowing the memories to arise is sufficient in most cases.

Of course there is still a part of you that is aware of your actual physical location, although you need not remain constantly aware of it. If you were to go to a movie that was frightening, you might allow yourself to feel the fear, but you would always be partially aware that if you were to become too uncomfortable, you could close your eyes or walk out of the theater.

"Suppose I have had an easy life and a happy childhood with no trauma. Is there any need to explore my earlier years?"

Events that cause our negative programming might not be terrifying or confusing to an adult mind, but because of our age when they occurred, they might have caused a fear reaction and initiated negative programming at that time. An example here might help.

Let's imagine a baby soon after his birth. At first he simply lies in his crib, but after a few weeks he is able to follow things about the room with his eyes. He can wiggle his arms and legs and may smile at his mother and father, but he has few other ways to respond to his environment.

One day he discovers that the thing he often sees waving in front of his face moves in response to something he is doing in his mind. He has discovered that his hand is *his* hand! (You may have observed a baby who has just discovered his or her hand and noticed how fascinated he or she was with it.)

Soon his discovery is noticed and someone puts a rattle in the hand. He now finds that his hand can manipulate an object in his environment, and he soon learns that he can bring objects to his mouth. He does this with every object he touches.

Within a few weeks he has learned that he can toss objects out of his crib and his parents will happily return them to him. He probably considers his hands a most wonderful tool.

As the weeks continue to pass, he learns to stand and walk about in his playpen. His playpen is filled with toys, and he is allowed to touch everything within his reach. His mind considers the world "a place where you can touch anything you want to and where everything is fun to touch."

At about this time he is allowed out of his playpen and permitted to crawl about on the floor. At first he is a bit surprised that it is possible to move in places other than his playpen, but he soon becomes accustomed to doing so.

His next goal is the shiny object on the coffee table. For months now he has been able to see it and has wondered what it was, how it felt, and what it tasted like, but he had never thought he would actually have a chance to experience it. He starts crawling directly toward the coffee table. As he nears the shiny object he grows more and more attracted to it, when suddenly a voice booms out, "No!" He pauses for a moment. He is confused. He realizes the sound of the voice is negative, but can't relate it to the present experience. Never has he been restricted from touching anything within his reach. He decides to continue to investigate this wonderful shiny object and he grabs it.

The parent who has been watching realizes that the shiny object is a crystal vase and that it can be broken by the child. Suddenly the baby finds the shiny object taken from his hands, and he begins to cry in frustration.

Frustration ends quickly for a child, however, and in a few moments we find him reaching for the object again. This time the parent decides more vehemence is necessary, so he or she gives the baby several slaps on the hand. The parent then places the vase high on a shelf.

The child begins to cry helplessly. The look on his face tells you that he is extremely confused and very unhappy about what is happening.

This reaction may continue for only a minute or two, and we, as adults, know that no serious harm has been done. We may therefore pay it little attention.

We might better understand the situation if we look at it through the eyes of the child. We must remember that the child's perception of the situation and his general perception of time is very different from ours. To us the vase is an insignificant part of the child's entire world, but this is not the case to the child's mind.

While he is reaching for the vase, he is not aware of his playpen—full of toys—in the other room. He is not aware of his baby carriage, the long rides in the stroller, or the fact that Daddy brings home presents every night. He is not aware that he is loved by his parents. He does not have friends with whom he can discuss his confusions and pains.

His mind has only one focus, the shiny object he wishes to touch. He wishes to explore his environment and get involved with new activity. As he is interrupted in this, his perceptual world is suddenly and meaninglessly shattered. There is no way for his little biocomputer to analyze the situation. Suddenly everything is topsy-turvy. He feels as though all the good things in his life have suddenly come to an end.

Imagine you are a business owner who has been out of town on business. On your way home from the airport, your car smashes

into a tree and you awaken in the hospital to find yourself para-
lyzed from the waist down. On opening your eyes, you find someone there who informs you that during your absence your best
friend and business partner, together with your husband have taken
all your personal and business savings out of the bank, sold all your
worldly goods, burned your house to the ground, and left the country. In a sense the baby experiences a shock like this.

Actually, in a way the business owner is better off than the child.
At least she has heard stories of people suffering setbacks and then
reestablishing themselves. At least she can talk to psychiatrists or
friends. The child has none of these resources. For that thirty
seconds in which he cries helplessly, his world is shattered.

As a parent who has raised several children I am certain that
most other parents will agree that it is impossible to avoid situations in which a child is forced to do something that he doesn't want
to do and reacts in helpless, heart-rending tears. Leaving the zoo
at closing time or going to bed are familiar examples in my house-
hold.

But even if by extraordinary patience and the use of clever distraction and bargaining parents manage to avoid such unpleasant
events, others in the child's environment may react in this way when
the parents are not present and the parents may never learn about
it. The child cannot tell them and within a few minutes after the
event he has stopped crying and appears to be comfortable. Recall
now the experience of the dog who was conditioned to have fear
of the ringing bell. Within a few minutes after each conditioning
trial, he too seemed perfectly normal. At any rate, most children
have repeated experiences of this sort that serve to strengthen the
associations. Thus the parents may see nothing except the apparently (and actually) normal reactions of a child to the limits of the
"real world." Meanwhile, the basis for a maladaptive pattern is being
established.

Let's look at the conditioned response, the program that may
be instilled in the mind of the baby each time such an event takes
place. If we could convert it into words, it might be something like
the following:

"The world is a beautiful place and hands are really great things
to have. There are many things you can touch with your hands and
enjoy freely, but there are some things that are dangerous to touch.

If you should touch them, something really bad will happen. You may be yelled at or spanked. Worse, there is no way to tell beforehand whether you can touch a particular thing. In general, it seems that those things that are new, unusual, or the most beautiful (that is, things such as shiny vases, which you might really want to touch) are the ones most likely to be dangerous to touch."

Of course the child eventually grows older and learns which objects must be avoided and why. The basic unconscious program however, may remain unless the program happens to be deconditioned by the environment as he grows up.

These first experiences in childhood may be reinforced through the years. Time and time again there are those things that the child wants to have but are forbidden. This continues through the teenage years. Adolescents often demonstrate their dissatisfaction with restrictions they feel are unreasonable, making this period one of the most painful of maturation experiences.

Is it any wonder that a child with many such experiences may grow up with a lack of confidence? If such experiences have happened over and over again in our life, it seems reasonable that we would have an inability to reach out and touch new and beautiful things. By the time we have grown up, the program of being able to reach out and touch new things, the ability to leave the routine everyday patterns and try something new, may have been trained out of us.

How many people are caught in a rut and do nothing about it? Isn't that rut an awful lot like the child's playpen—full of allowed but boring toys? Why do we complain about our rut and how beautiful things are elsewhere? Why don't we just get out of it? Don't we seem to be afraid of some imagined block that might prevent us from reaching our goal? How many of us have stated, "I'm my own worst enemy?" Procrastination may also have its roots here.

We are afraid to reach out; we lack confidence. The emotional pain and dissatisfaction we feel with ourselves because of this pattern only serves to strengthen it further.

In other words, it is usually not a traumatic event that underlies our problem, but the day-to-day frustrations, dating back to childhood times, when we did not have enough information stored in our memory to adequately comprehend what was going on. In order to protect us from further discomfort, the mind has developed a program in which an emotion, symptom, or habit "saves" us from this type of situation. The Exploration, then, is simply a way of tracing events through our life while keeping our mind relaxed so that it will not run from the important facts.

Obviously, no one can avoid this happening during childhood. Further, with love, patience, quality time, and sympathetic support from parents all along, negative programs are for the most part eliminated as the child goes through each successive stage of growth. Yet for many of us in our culture where the industrial age has shattered families and communities such support was unavailable. Most of us are indeed the "adult children of dysfunctional families." Alcoholism, divorce, stress, and social alienation have deprived us of the opportunity to recover and intensified the negative patterns.

EXPERIENCE TWENTY-SIX

1. *Think about some of the things you'd really like to do but somehow haven't gotten around to doing. Would you like to get a better job? Travel? Would you like to begin a new hobby? Move to another neighborhood? Another city, state, or country? Is there some person or group of people you'd like to get better acquainted with but haven't the courage to approach? Is there a habit you'd like to break but haven't been able to overcome? Would you like to be more assertive? More expressive? More able to relax?*

    Now close your eyes for a few moments and become aware of the emotions you feel when you think about your inability to respond the way you really want to. You might describe them as frustration, lack of self-confidence, fear of the unknown, or expectations of failure. Don't let words suffice—feel the emotions associated with them. Perhaps a short induction will help prepare you to experience this.

2. *Now look back over similar difficulties you've experienced during the past ten or fifteen years. The exact problems you have now may not have existed then, but you will probably find several times when you experienced similar emotions. Perhaps you can remember a fear of speaking in front of a group of people. Perhaps*

a lack of confidence led you to fail in phoning an important person. Maybe you kept a job you really didn't like or want because you felt insecure about changing. Perhaps you tried repeatedly to eliminate some habit pattern, only to fail.

3. *Look back to the time when you were a teenager or perhaps just before then. Can you remember some of the things you really wanted but were not allowed to have? You might remember a car, bicycle, football, or vacation that was denied you merely because an adult decided it should be that way. Perhaps you can remember intense frustrations leading to arguments with your parents. Do you remember all the forbidden fruits you dreamed about and discussed with your close friends but that you dared not attempt to reach? Experience again the emotions you felt when your inclinations were thwarted.*

4. *As you look further back, you may continue to find it was always the adult world that didn't seem to understand how nice it would be for you to have a few extra pieces of candy, go to the movies whenever you wished, or stay out late. As you recall these events, allow yourself to experience the emotions you felt at that time, almost as though you are empathizing with another person. Do not let your present understanding of the situation substitute for the emotions you can still feel within.*

The purpose of this experience was to show how easily the mind can recall for you emotions associated with a given event when you give it the freedom to do so. You also saw how the same emotions recur through the years.

These memories and many others have been collected by the mind and used to create certain programs. These programs run over and over in your mind, telling you that you are not successful, questioning your successes, causing you to slow down and fail when you should be moving forward and succeeding.

Like an angry tiger, this program crouches invisibly in the unconscious mind, waiting for the slightest faltering, the least pause, the smallest imperfection, to begin convincing you that what you have noticed is a sign that you are going to fail.

You then begin to feel fear, uncertainty, and doubt about what you are trying. The increased tension now causes further mistakes, mistakes in what you say, what you do, and what you think. These further mistakes seem to justify the previous doubts and they grow stronger. Finally, the problem snowballs to the point where you actually fail. Then you feel disappointed, depressed, and angry with yourself. The pattern grows stronger.

The Exploration is a means of gaining an emotional understanding of such maladaptive programs so they can be eliminated. The process is similar to the memory exercise in Experience Twenty-four.

The Exploration Differs from Just Remembering

In Experience Twenty-six, when asked to recall several times when you felt a lack of self-confidence or frustration, you began to sift through a number of events that came to mind. After looking at several possibilities, you chose one that seemed appropriate. As you looked back to earlier and earlier periods of your life, other memories came up, some of which did not have anything to do with a lack of self-confidence or frustration, and you thought no more about them.

This means that in addition to selecting from among the many memories that came up from your unconscious, you compared each memory to the ones you had already listed to see if it really fit.

You may have also found your mind wandering into unrelated areas. You may have remembered friends or other events, which distracted you momentarily from continuing with your search for appropriate memories.

In the Exploration you use an induction to free your mind from pursuing extraneous things. Generally it is best to focus on only one memory at a time, and usually the first memory that occurs to you is the best one.

You begin by thinking, "Now I will go back to a memory in which I experienced the symptom, emotion, or habit pattern on which I wish to work." Pretty soon an event will occur to you, exactly as it would have were you not deeply relaxed. This time, however, instead of just proceeding on to another event, focus your attention upon that memory. Then allow yourself to relive the memory in your imagination, experiencing as much of the original emotion as possible, and preventing yourself from getting sidetracked on other events.

When you have revivified this memory from start to finish, allow it to fade from your consciousness; erase it. Then relax and let your mind drift back to an even earlier event. Your unconscious will make sure that you go back to one with similar emotional content. Keep your mind as clear as possible of interfering thoughts by continually erasing them if they should arise.

You may think, "This memory doesn't seem to be related to the subject of this exploration," but if this thought occurs to you, simply erase it. The unconscious knows exactly which memories you need to see, and it will bring up those memories. This is precisely the point of the Exploration; you wish to learn the unconscious connections between what you do and why you do it.

In short, the conscious mind merely observes the productions of the unconscious mind and eliminates all unnecessary ideas. Allow your unconscious to make the decisions while you are in as completely relaxed a state as possible. As your unconscious finds that you are not pressuring it, not judging it, and not trying to guide it, it will begin to review memories of greater and greater significance. These memories will include the emotion being traced by the unconscious, and the connections will become clear to you *following the Exploration.*

Because the unconscious is sometimes unwilling to go into a painful area, allow it to go back to just a few moments before the unpleasant emotion being traced arises in the memory. This way you will be completely relaxed as it begins. For example, you may find yourself sitting comfortably in a classroom. The thought might even occur to you that this memory is not relevant. Erase this thought immediately and allow yourself to bring the scene in more clearly. Then go through it. You may suddenly realize that on this day you opened a letter with bad news in it. As you realize what is happening, you can allow the emotion to come on suddenly, exactly as it did during the actual event.

Although you release your analytical control over the memory, maintain a continual awareness of the emotions you are feeling.

When a painful emotion comes up during a memory, allow it to grow strong. You may even exaggerate the emotion until it feels much stronger than it seemed in the original event. When the unpleasant feeling becomes as strong as you can handle, or when you reach the part of the memory in which the unpleasant situation has passed, use your relaxation techniques to eliminate the unpleasant feeling, along with the memory. It is most important to both accentuate and then obliterate the emotions.

Important: If the recollection of any event in this fashion produces intense fear or panic, severe physical symptoms, or feelings of being out of control, or if you think the feelings may become hard for you to handle, then erase all memories of, and emotions about, them and return to a relaxing image. In a few minutes you will be calm again. It is best to seek professional psychological help if you experience emotions of such overwhelming magnitude. This situation is very rare and is mentioned only for the sake of completeness.

Remember, the Exploration is not a cure, nor does it attempt to find the cause of a problem. It is merely a key that helps you see a pattern of stimuli and responses that was not clear to you before. Because the unconscious mind has made all the decisions during the Exploration and because the only goal was to seek this pattern, you are seeing your computer's own analysis of its problem. Its conclusions may seem a bit strange, but you were tracing a problem using only the unconscious and therefore did not have the conscious knowledge for solving it. It is only reasonable that the results are sometimes unexpected.

For twenty-four to thirty-six hours following your Exploration, you may find additional memories coming to you, provided that you allow yourself to be open to them. These memories will fit the pattern you have uncovered and, if you continue to write them down, they will help you to understand yourself better. The final bits of the jigsaw puzzle will be added by any dreams you have and by flashes of understanding that occur during the days that follow the Exploration.

The function of the Exploration as described to this point is to

1. Better define the physical/mental/emotional/behavioral problem to be changed

2. Aid in understanding the roots of the situation

3. Help you develop control of the emotions associated with the problem

4. Help you "write a new script," that is, develop a new strategy for approaching the situation

All that is needed now is a way of precisely defining for the unconscious the new behavior (new script) you want to use. For this you turn to visualization, which was explored in Chapter 7. One to three times each day, enter a deep state of relaxation and review past memories, rewriting them so that you visualize yourself carrying out a new, more adaptive set of behaviors and responses. Then project forward into the future and rehearse, through visualization, being successful in the kind of situation that once might have caused failure. In effect, you create a new past, and a new future that goes along with it.

Sound simple? It is! And almost unbelievable until you try it. I suggest that at first you work with one of the items from the bottom or middle of the list of things you would like to change about yorself. Your ability to use this technique effectively will increase with your experience. Don't be in a hurry to get to the most important or the most emotionally charged patterns in your life.

Experiencing an Exploration

A number of ideas seem to be important in carrying out an effective Exploration. Any deviation from them may produce difficulties and your results may be less profound. After you have experienced several Explorations, however, the instructions will become automatic and your Explorations will become more powerful because you will have less thinking to do. *You may then feel free to change them* in any way you feel the process can be improved.

1. Decide on the emotion, habit, or symptom you wish to investigate. The first few explorations may prove easier if you use an emotional problem rather than a symptom or habit pattern as your goal. The following are indicators of whether an emotion is really maladaptive:

a. The feeling is unpleasant.

b. The feeling is not useful (that is, you could handle the situation as well or better without this emotion).

c. Sometimes the feeling is harmful; it decreases your ability to handle things.

Choose something that is important to you at this point in time and that is a pattern that originated in the past. Don't attempt to remember specific events just yet. Once you have chosen the maladaptive response pattern you wish to investigate, shift it out of your awareness. You don't need to continue thinking about it anymore. Commit to memory the following instructions *before* beginning the deep relaxation process. (Examples of proper guidance for an Exploration appear on cassettes #12, "Headache Relief," and #03, "Down with High Blood Pressure," Appendix p. 287.)

1. Choose a place where you may remain comfortably relaxed, sitting or lying down, for twenty to forty minutes. Make sure you are neither hungry nor have to go to the bathroom. Make sure the phones are off the hooks and there is a sign on the door to keep visitors away. A quiet place is always preferable, because interruptions during the Exploration can interfere with the flow of memories. The Exploration should be done from start to finish without stopping, in order to reap the full benefits.

2. Allow yourself to become completely relaxed. If you wish you may utilize any techniques you know for completely eliminating bodily tensions and for erasing all unnecessary thoughts.

3. Your mind is now almost completely blank. Now imagine yourself in a movie theater, waiting for a scene to emerge from your memory. Your only knowledge at this point is that you are going back to just a few moments prior to a particular response, preferably sometime within the past few weeks.

As the first memory comes along, use your five senses to make the memory as vivid as possible. Do not allow the thought *in my bedroom* to suffice. Imagine your bedroom clearly. Be aware of the window and its position in the room, the bed, the dresser, and the lamp. Is there a rug on the floor? In which area of the room are you? Are you seated or standing? Is it day or night? Are you alone or with someone? What smells are present? What sounds do you hear? What can you taste? What can you feel? Slowly, allow these details to come in clearly before going through the memory. Do not question whether this is a good enough memory. Merely bring in that instant as clearly as you can.

4. Make sure that you feel completely relaxed—pretend you don't know what is to happen next in the memory. Then begin to allow time to pass. What happens next? What do you say or do? What does the other person say or do? Become aware of the change in your feelings as you relive the memory. Notice exactly what is happening at the moment you experience the uncomfortable feeling within that accompanies the maladaptive response pattern.

5. Allow this emotion to grow strong, until you can feel it intensely throughout your body. Become aware of the tensions in your body that develop along with the emotion, and the symptoms that accompany it (noise and a feeling of tightness in the stomach, dry mouth, sweaty palms, and so on). Allow this emotion to become as strong as you can comfortably bear. Then continue through the memory.

6. See what kind of escape behavior you use to diminish the tension. Do you become angry to force the offending agent away from you? Do you become lonely or depressed and begin eating, drinking, or smoking? Do you turn to someone else to help you out of your jam? Does a bodily symptom become so bad that you are forced to direct your attention to it rather than the problem? Continue through the memory, allowing your tension to be relieved just as it was after the actual event. Finally, use

your five senses to perceive the results or consequences of this sequence of stimuli and behaviors. Let this scene fade away and then relax.

7. Spend about thirty seconds completely relaxing any areas in your body that may have become tense. If you find that little areas have become tense without your knowledge or that part of your body has been wanting to move, make sure that this tension is calmed down before proceeding. This is most important, because tension will inhibit further exploration.

8. Your mind is blank once again and you are now drifting back to an earlier time, perhaps months or years earlier, to just before you felt that emotion on another occasion. Do not think of what the emotion is, and erase any fragments of the previous memory that might still remain in your mind. Imagine that you are sitting in a movie passively awaiting the next scene.

9. As you begin to sense the place your mind is suggesting, begin to intensify the scene and continue with steps 4 through 8. Repeat this until five to ten memories have been evoked. Make sure you do not try to figure anything out, make decisions, or link patterns together as you go through them. See each memory as though it were not connected to the others. The analysis will come following your Exploration. Each memory relived in this way should last about one to four minutes, although it may cover a period of hours, days, or even weeks.

10. If more than one memory comes up simultaneously, then choose the memory that is most clear. After reviewing that memory, you may go on to the other one before permitting any other memories to come to mind. When possible, choose the memory in which you are older to review first.

By the time you are experiencing events from your childhood, the type of event may have changed considerably. Obviously, problems of a complex social or sexual nature will change considerably as you go back earlier and earlier in your life. Generally speaking, the emotions felt become more primitive and the events and problems are seen from a more childish view.

Though it might seem like a trivial event, it could well be an important one. And by allowing yourself to relive it you will be able to reexperience the emotion in the same way you can empathize with a young child who is crying because her dog has been run over. You can empathize with yourself in going through the memories and experiencing these feelings. Often, seemingly unrelated scenes will have a strong symbolic relationship when you look back after the exploration is completed.

11. Do not criticize your progress during the exploration. Criticism creates negative emotions and the process may be limited. Erase criticisms and accept whatever happens.

    You may find that your memories don't proceed in an orderly chronological fashion. Your mind may jump around. Accept this; you will be able to put the memories in order later.

    Scenes of which you have had no conscious recollection may come to mind. Some of these will be memories that simply have not reached your consciousness before. Others will be fantasies. Some of them, especially those that seem irrational, may be dreams that you have never before recalled. All of these scenes are useful.

    Similarly, don't reject familiar scenes. Only a minority of your initial explorations will trace problems back very far. Some may go back only a few months or years, depending upon how long the pattern has existed.

    Rather than trying to classify scenes as worthwhile or worthless, simply allow yourself to go through them. Even fantasies are stories synthesized from many events in your life and the lives of people you have read about or seen in movies. Such experiences can be even *more* important to review than something that actually occurred, because they may be the condensation of many of your individual experiences.

12. As soon as you have relived five or ten memories, clear your mind and allow yourself to become completely relaxed. This is of critical importance, because you are demonstrating to your unconscious that you can have the confidence to go back into its areas of confusion and that you will always calm it completely afterward. Your next Exploration will then be even more effective.

Now "step outside yourself" and, while maintaining this complete state of relaxation, gradually begin to review the memories that have gone through your mind. Do not allow other memories to come to you. Look at these thoughts only, as though they were all you knew about yourself. By keeping yourself extremely calm, you will be able to look at the person in the memories as though he or she were someone else. Realize that you are looking at mere recorded impressions, as unreal now as a movie or book, and that you need not feel any unpleasant emotion whatsoever. Allow yourself to analyze these memories. Which stimuli are common to several of them? Are you always about to go on a trip or begin a new project? Are you always outdoors or indoors? What are the similarities in emotions, symptoms, or habits? Do you drink or smoke in most of them? Do they cause you to retreat from people? Does panic or anger "save" you from the difficulty? How do you feel at the very end? Frustrated? Cheated? Lonely? Helpless? Angry? Guilty?

13. Now pretend that this is all you know of a person and you must give him or her advice on how to handle such situations. What kind of advice would you give that person? How would you explain to him or her that the emotion he or she felt at that time, on each occasion, was not adaptive, that it only served to strengthen the unwanted pattern? What should the person do instead of carrying out the usual escape behavior? What insight can you give him or her on the situation from your special vantage point of relaxation? How do you want to rewrite the script of these scenes?

14. Now go back through each one of the memories. This time begin with the one in which you were youngest and work toward the present date. Make sure that you are completely calm as you relive each one of them—just as though you were there to whisper in your own ear what you needed to know. Inform yourself that although the problem looks gigantic and insoluble, a solution does exist. Let yourself see that being patient another five, ten, or fifteen minutes is all that is necesary, in most cases, to avoid feeling the unpleasant emotion or strengthening an unwanted pattern.

Understand that the first time you went through the events you did not have this advice, and it was reasonable, given your programming, that you responded as you did. Should this event ever come up again, know that you would not need to experience that unpleasant emotion. Notice that there is a way to handle that situation and that had you been relaxed and clear, as you are now, you would have been able to see it.

Relive the memory, behaving in a different fashion, demonstrating to your unconscious that such events need not be handled in the old way. Remember, the existence of the maladaptive pattern means that the unconscious has never been able to perceive a more adaptive solution.

After you have reviewed, in order, each memory in a calm fashion, ending up with the most recent (and therefore the most unpleasant) memory, completely clear your mind and project into the future.

15. Visualize yourself in several future situations where the old pattern might have been expected to occur. Using all five senses, perceive yourself living these future events with a new personality, a new pattern of responding to the world. Feel yourself comfortable, confident, alert, intelligent, and healthy. Give yourself the understanding and intellect you wish to have. Imagine responding in the way that the person you really want to be would respond.

16. Finally, clear the mind and give yourself a few suggestions so that, as you return to your usual state of consciousness, you will be much more confident and much more relaxed than before. Then allow yourself to return to your usual state of consciousness by counting from one to five. As soon as you have returned to your usual state of awareness, recall again or, better still, record in writing or on a tape, each of the memories and impressions that you had *during the Exploration.*

After you do this you can put in other comments, but make sure that each of the memories recalled is recorded in your waking state. Although they are clear at this moment, if you do not record them they may, like dreams, suddenly slip from your grasp.

Throughout the next week or two, or as long as you are working on this particular pattern, carry a small notebook with you in which to record all memories related to this pattern that occur to you at various times during the day or night. Each day use two or three periods for rewriting your script. This can be done by relaxing deeply and reviewing three or four memories from the past, reliving them without any unpleasant emotion, and projecting ahead to three times in the future. As soon as you can go through a memory completely relaxed and calm and with a clear understanding of it (and can visualize yourself performing the way you would like), cross it off your list.

There is no need to think of this pattern or how you are changing it at any time other than these. Attempting to further figure things out while in your usual state of consciousness may confuse matters.

As you finish with all the memories on your list, you may undertake another Exploration if there are any remnants of the pattern left. (It is not unusual to collect fifty or sixty memories on your list during the process of desensitization.) Make sure that you have completely desensitized any feelings in the memories brought out in the Exploration. If this has not been done, the unconscious may refuse to bring up any more memories.

17. From day to day you may find that some traces of the old habit pattern are still around. This is perfectly all right and should not upset you. It will provide further material for rewriting your script. If you worked on your problem of eating because of feeling lonely, and if you have just done that again this morning, do not allow yourself to feel guilty or defeated. Merely relive this recent situation several times, feeling completely relaxed, and you will make more progress in eliminating the maladaptive feeling and habit.

We have seen how important it is to reward positively conditioned behavior if we wish for it to persist and how easily negative emotions can grow. Thus, be certain to continually praise yourself for whatever progress you make during and after the Exploration. Treat all of your discoveries as major and important ones. If you treat the Exploration and its effects as significant, the deconditioning will be much more effective and the next Exploration will lead you to even more important discoveries.

18. You can consider the desensitization process complete when you have reviewed each of the memories that have come up during the Exploration and those that have arisen following it, provided you have relived them while feeling quite calm and can imagine a more satisfactory way to handle the situation—one that would have avoided the maladaptive emotion, symptom, or habit. One week is usually sufficient, although it may take longer, or you may decide you need to experience an additional Exploration. If in doubt, spend a few more days rewriting your script before exploring the same or another problem.

After a few days you will get the knack of the process. You will find that only three to five minutes is necessary to become completely relaxed, review several memories in the past, and make several projections into the future.

19. As I have emphasized throughout this book, *experience* is the key factor, not *intellectualization*. The experience of the Exploration allows you to see your script so that you may rewrite it. The experience of the desensitization gives rise to the experience of having the maladaptive pattern become less compulsive. Of course you can always overeat, drink alcohol, or smoke cigarettes *if you choose to do so,* in the same way in which you could have opened your eyes by unrelaxing them. Rewriting doesn't *prevent* you from being able to respond in the old way. It merely gives you the choice of being able to respond in a new way. In order to have this choice, you must spend this time letting your unconscious experience positive alternatives to the unwanted patterns.

EXPERIENCE TWENTY-SEVEN:
WRITING YOUR OWN SCRIPT

Familiarize yourself with the instructions that follow by memorizing them or by recording them on tape, and carry out an Exploration and deconditioning. The following suggestions, given to yourself after an induction of physical and mental relaxation, are excellent for bringing about desired changes. Apply this procedure several times a day following the Exploration, and remember to suggest to yourself that upon returning to your usual state of consciousness you will feel alert and comfortable. The most effective way to learn how to experience an Exploration is by following the suggestions on tape 202 "Writing Your Own Script," or part 3 on tape 10, "Tools for Taking Charge."

Begin by relaxing, mentally and physically, using any process you choose. The suggestions will involve your tracing back through two or three events in the past in which you found yourself acting or responding in a maladaptive way, a way that you would like to change.

1. *Relive two or three situations in which you felt the unwanted emotion or noted a maladaptive symptom or habit, seeing these situations as though you were reading a chapter in a book that you know well and no longer need to respond to emotionally. Feel yourself able to go through each memory in a relaxed manner. Let your mind know that you are simply reviewing a memory and that therefore there is no need for you to feel the tension that was present the first time. Realize that although the feelings you had at the time were natural and, in fact, important to you, you no longer need to feel them.*

2. *Now rewrite those memories. Change things around so that you respond perfectly—mentally, physically, and emotionally. Imagine that you are rewriting a script. Show your unconscious exactly the way you would have handled things if you were there with the knowledge you now have. Fully live these scenes through, experiencing all the emotions appropriate to your new, more successful, behavior. Thirty to ninety seconds per memory should be adequate.*

3. *After you have reviewed the memories, take a moment to realize that you have been looking at the past. Feel within yourself that you are no longer constrained to behave or respond as before. Feel yourself moving toward the future more in control of your life.*

4. *Now project ahead, looking forward a few hours, days, or weeks. See yourself in a situation that would have been difficult to handle before. This time go through it without experiencing a maladaptive emotion, symptom, or habit. Feel yourself able to function perfectly in mind, body, and emotion.*

As you perceive yourself being just the way you would like to be, allow yourself to have a very pleasant feeling inside. Feel confident and relaxed and yet very aware of the feelings of those around you, without being controlled by them. Spend about one or two minutes on each of the two or three "future memories."

5. *Bring yourself back to full waking consciousness, leaving yourself with the clear thought, "This is the person I really want to be, and this is how I will handle myself in the future."*

CHAPTER 11

The Coherency Theory

Now that we have explored the concepts of negative and positive programming and have discussed how stress can produce diseases brought on by muscle spasm, we can look for ways to broaden the principles so as to examine the psychophysiological underpinnings of other diseases.

The scientific way to do this is to develop a theory. A theory is simply a tool that provides a framework for our cognitive processes, and it also guides us toward new discoveries. Thus a theory is never "right" or "wrong" or "true" or "false"; it is only useful or not useful.

The time-honored rules for developing or choosing a scientific theory are: (1) it must be built upon the basic assumptions of science; (2) it must adequately describe all observed phenomena (e.g. experiments within its scope; (3) it must be internally consistent; (4) it must lead to new discoveries; (5) it should be as simple as possible, consistent with the foregoing ("Occam's razor").

The Coherency Theory is a framework to help us deal with an age-old issue: how does the mind, which is nonphysical, have an effect on the brain and body, which are physical? We need a way of conceptualizing how the mind, through its response to stressors, produces stress and, ultimately, physical disease. Many commonly used theoretical constructs fail us in this regard. The Freudian id, ego, and superego give rise to interactions that are so abstract that it's hard to connect them with physical expressions (for example, a bleeding ulcer or gangrene of the toes.) The neurophysiological description of the brain and bodily processes, involving the hypothalamus, the hypophysis, and the pituitary-adrenal axis, doesn't give us much of a direction for exploring what kind of self-image and what kinds of relationships will serve to keep us most healthy.

In Chapter 1 we discussed the fact that with every breath, with every movement and thought, we exercise at a cellular level precise control of molecular processes through involuntary mental processes. In the chapters that followed we explored various aspects of the imagination and its capacity to alter responses to the internal and external environment. We shall now explore ways that this ability may be extended beyond simple emotional, behavioral, and muscle tension control to include normally involuntary processes and the wide spectrum of human disease.

Making the Involuntary Voluntary

For many years Western scientists accepted the idea that it was impossible or at least extremely difficult to bring the autonomic nervous system under voluntary control. They seemed to be unaware of the serene Indian who rose from a bed of nails without shedding a drop of blood or developing an infection, or of the yogis who withstood being buried alive for hours, surviving on the oxygen that would ordinarily be consumed in minutes by an untrained person.

I was taught this doctrine in medical school; this blind spot was tacitly accepted. Although emotions were sometimes given credit for causing some diseases and making others worse, no attempt was made to explore the *mechanism* by which this occurred, to develop a unifying theory, or to find a means to reverse the process. We learned that back pain, asthma, and migraine often developed in an atmosphere of psychological tension, but the treatment was still chemical suppression of the symptoms. We were taught that allergies, arthritis, and dysmenorrhea could be triggered by anxiety; that high blood pressure, ulcerative colitis, Cushing's disease, and Graves' disease had emotional overtones. We were then simply told that reassurance should be given to the patient; selected cases should be referred to a psychiatrist (but few of them ever made it to a psychiatrist's office).

For most people in our culture, being sent to a psychiatrist is taken as a form of insult—no one wants to be known as emotionally disturbed, or as having a mental illness. In our world it is much more acceptable to be in the hospital with a bleeding ulcer than to take several days off from work because of emotional instability. Try listing several episodes of being mentally overwhelmed the next time you apply for employment.

And even if the referred patient *were* to see a psychiatrist, the psychiatrist would usually be at a loss as to what should be done to bring the patient relief from the symptoms.

Self-Induced Programs in the Autonomic Nervous System

A new day is dawning. The vastly increased speed and effectiveness of communications means that orthodox western physicians must find an ivory tower that is high indeed if they wish to avoid learning that human beings *can* and *do* learn to control autonomic processes. In other words, the "autonomic nervous system" is not *really* autonomic, not really independent of our conscious thoughts, images, and actions.

One simple way of demonstrating this is to sit in a dimly lighted room, facing an extinguished twenty-watt light bulb. Say the word *constrict* and as you do, turn on the bulb for ten seconds. Then say the word *dilate* as you turn it off again. Repeat this several times a day for a week, and presto! You become the first on your block to be able to dilate or constrict the pupils of your eyes by an act of will. You will now be able to get your pupils to respond to the words "constrict" and "dilate" without the light bulb. Simple? Yes. But don't you think most people would bet that you couldn't constrict your pupils on command?

With slightly more sophisticated equipment you can acquire skills that are even more useful and interesting. Get an electronic thermometer and tape its sensor (a thermocouple) to your finger, toe, or any other part of your body. Watch the meter while you imagine warm days, warm water, and a beach in Hawaii. You will soon see a rise in the temperature. Imagine falling into a cold snowbank and the temperature will fall. And the more you practice, with this simple device to give you accurate information on the state of your body, the more proficient you will become. The temperature rises because you are teaching the mind to dilate, at your command, the blood vessels in that part of your body, so as to increase blood flow and thereby raise the body temperature.

Experimenters in the field of biofeedback have developed still more refined devices for gaining control over bodily processes. They have even developed a capsule that contains a tiny transmitter. The capsule is swallowed and it transmits to a small receiver information that reflects the concentration of acid in a person's stomach. Thus the normally involuntary decision as to when to secrete digestive fluids can be made a voluntary one. Persons in deep states of meditation demonstrate a lowered metabolic rate, a different rate of oxygen consumption, and alterations in other autonomic processes.

That people who have learned such autogenic control report improvement in disease processes is not surprising. Nor should it be surprising that some people who participated in medical experiments with mind-altering chemicals such as LSD reported marked changes in long-standing physical conditions, in conjunction with powerful emotional changes, while experiencing the chemical and afterward. Further, it is not uncommon for a psychologist or psychiatrist to note the disappearance of chronic physical problems when an emotional difficulty becomes resolved.

As noted earlier, surgeons who include a deep relaxation and image rehearsal process in the preparation of the patient for surgery report a speeded-up healing of wounds. Dentists who include one use little or no novocaine and remark that there is an absence of bleeding or swelling. And obstetricians show babies to smiling mothers, who have prepared themselves by learning to work with, and not against, the delivery. (See cassette #203, "Successful Surgery and Recovery," Appendix p. 288, and #30, "Great Expectations," Appendix p. 287.)

Inducing Health and Inducing Disease

Why can't we just command a disease to get better, order our gums to stop bleeding? How can our thoughts and emotions produce that wide spectrum of physical disorders to which the human being alone is heir?

If a knife is placed to a man's throat and he is ordered to "Relax, or I'll kill you," he will probably fail. You have learned why: relaxation is a process that must take place gradually and as a response to the neural (perceived) environment. The presence of the knife, however, does not make for a relaxing environment. Though the motivation of the man to relax may be high, and though he may know techniques for relaxing, his autonomic nervous system will respond, instead, to his perceived environment, and he will feel fear and tension. In the development of a psychophysiological disease, the environment is also of primary importance. Just as in an induction the physical state and the autonomic state are *induced* by the environment, a disease state may be induced by the environment.

Life Changes and Disease

Thomas Holmes, M.D., a psychiatrist at the University of Washington, is one of the many scientists who have studied the capacity of one's environment to induce disease states. He has developed a point system for rating the impact of major life changes on health by collecting data from many people on the changes in their lives in the period prior to the development of disease.

His findings indicate that welcome changes, as well as unwelcome ones, place a stress on the individual. Further, the ill effects of life stressors add up and may not be apparent for months or years. A few of the point values from the scale are as follows:

Death of spouse...100
Divorce...73
Personal injury or illness..............................53
Marriage..50

Mortgage over $10,000.....................................31
Begin or end school..26
Change in eating habits..................................15
Christmas 12
Minor violation of the law.............................11

Of course in any individual case this can be only a rough guide, but in several studies he found that the people who experience changes totaling more than 300 points in a single year have a 79 percent chance of being laid up with a major disease within the following two-year period. Those with a score of 200 to 299 points have a 51 percent chance of developing a major disease.

Moreover, he found a close link between life changes and minor health problems, such as headaches, upset stomachs, and so on.

One study of one hundred college football players showed that 50 percent of those who had high scores became injured during play but only 9 percent of those with low scores did.

The "Type A" Personality

Two physicians, Meyers and Friedman have published intriguing evidence that persons with what they call a Type A personality have a statistically much greater chance of developing heart disease early in life. This type of personality is characterized by traits of feeling highly pressured by time, a tendency to focus intently on deadlines and job pressures, feelings of hostility beneath a calm surface, and a tendency to take on considerable responsibility, including responsibility for others. This relationship is quite interesting, especially in view of the fact that heart disease is one of the major killers nationwide.

Emotions and Your Blood

Other scientists have demonstrated that the composition of one's blood may be altered by what one experiences, perhaps with the ultimate development of manifest disease. It was found, for example, that the blood sugar level of diabetics went up during stressful interviews but not during unstressful ones. This is presumably because of alterations in the production of, or response to, insulin (or both).

Another study measured a factor called achievement orientation, the tendency to engage in multiple activities and push oneself to achieve. This investigation looked at the relationship of this type of activity to serum uric acid. A very close correlation was found. Those who have higher scores in achievement orientation have much higher levels of uric acid. We also know that people who develop an excess of the uric acid molecule in their bloodstream tend to develop gout, a form of arthritis.

A study by the National Aeronautics and Space Administration (NASA) found that when job pressures were increased, subjects experienced an increase in heart rate, which is a measure of stress. More important, they also detected a significant elevation in serum cholesterol, a molecular substance which, when it is elevated, predisposes a person to cardiovascular disease.

The evidence continues to accumulate daily that the way an individual perceives the environment can help determine his or her state of health, susceptibility to accidents, and ability to heal. It can also help determine the molecular constituents of the bloodstream. In the preceding chapters we have seen how the environment may induce mental programs that are either beneficial or harmful and how certain techniques can restore internal balance and alter the harmful programs. We will now attempt to design the final piece of the puzzle—a logically consistent means of conceptualizing the link between mind and body that fits with all other accepted principles of medicine and with experimental findings such as those just noted, and that gives us a means for preventing and curing diseases.

Let's start back at the one-cell stage of growth and observe the development of the cell's internal environment and external environment and the connection between them. The awareness that each one of us has traveled the continuum from fertilized egg cell to complete individual may help our understanding of how the perceived environment of the individual may induce the cellular change responsible for producing disease. Ultimately, it is cellular change that produces such varied processes as arthritis, hypothyroidism, hay fever, and cancer.

Back to Basics: One Plus One Equals One

Scientists have examined the nuclei of all the different cells in the human body. Their examination indicates a startling fact: each nucleus contains exactly the same number and kind of chromosomes and genes as every other nucleus. This is true whether we examine a cell of the pancreas or a cell of a fingernail. Obviously, not all the genes are used by any one cell. The cells of each organ select certain genes to use, much as you might select a certain volume of an encyclopedia to study.

The color of your eyes, your intelligence, and your height are largely dependent upon the genes present when you were a single fertilized cell. In many ways, then, you represent the projection of this information through time, much as the image on a screen is a projection of its slide. We might imagine that we have shone time through this single cell as though time were a light.

Each cell, then, though specialized, is a sibling cell. The function of each is to support the existence of the organism as a whole, even if some, such as skin cells and white blood cells, must regularly sacrifice themselves to this cause.

Linking all these cells together are the cells of the nervous system, itself composed of sibling cells, each with the same genetic image, arranged and functioning according to instructions contained in this image. As it develops, through time and learning, the nervous system acquires the motivation and means to cope with the problems of the external world as well as the problems within the confines of the body. Done coherently, this coping leads to health and satisfaction. Done incoherently, it can produce failure, fear, tension, or disease.

We talked earlier about visualization and the fact that each person has a complete image of himself or herself at every moment, although it is an extremely complicated one. You have images of feeling as well as of sight; you have images of the interior of your body; you have images of your emotions; and you have images of your images. Moreover, throughout your entire life, your mind has been taking a complete, stereophonic, full-color movie of each instant, complete with vision, hearing, touch, smell, taste, emotions, and so on. You can imagine your memory, then, as a long string of visualizations extending back into your past. The similarity becomes more obvious if you trace the origins of your physical image and mental image of yourself.

Biologists and geneticists are fond of the phrase "Ontogeny recapitulates phylogeny." This means that the development of a human being from a single fertilized egg is parallel to the way in which the human race developed from the very first forms of life. The fertilized ovum is one cell present after the union of the female's egg and the male's sperm. The further development of the cell is governed primarily by the genes present on the chromosomes within the cell's nucleus.

Soon after the fertilized ovum is produced, it begins to divide. Its division, however, is not simple, like an apple or a piece of wood splitting in half (see Figure 1). First, all the genetic material forms into long strands of deoxyribonucleic acid (DNA). DNA is a long strand of molecules linked together in a pattern that gives the cell information, similar to the way in which a magnetic tape gives information to a tape recorder or an electronic computer. Then each of these strands forms a duplicate of itself. They then line up in the middle of the cell, much like kindergarten students line up side by side to go back to class after recess. Each strand is identical to its partner.

As the cell divides, these partners split up, granting each of the two cells (daughter cells) exactly the same genetic complement. Thereafter, each division proceeds in exactly the same fashion. Thus even today each normal cell of your body has exactly the same genetic informaton that was present in your very first cell.

The cell divisions become more and more numerous, and then a clump of cells results (see Figure 2). One of the first signs of cellular organization is a line that appears down the middle of this clump. This line is called the *notochord*, and soon a primitive spinal cord forms along its axis.

The spinal cord is then used as an axis of symmetry. Alongside the developing spinal cord, groups of cells begin to cluster in an orderly fashion. These clusters are called "somites."

As the cells in each of these somites divide, they travel out from the cord in an orderly fashion. They form the buds of what will eventually be the arms, legs, chest, and so on. In watching the process under the microscope, it looks as though the early spinal

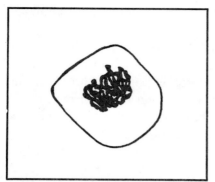

A. The cell prepares to divide.

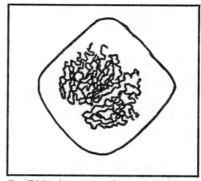

B. DNA forms into long strands and duplicates.

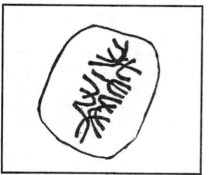

C. Strands line up in the middle of the cell, each strand identical to its partner.

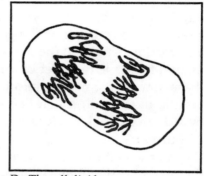

D. The cell divides.

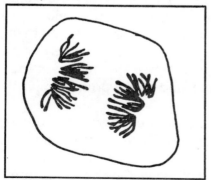

E. Each daughter cell has exactly the same genetic complement.

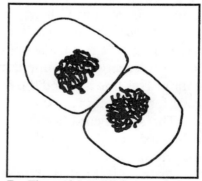

F. The nuclei reorganizes.

FIGURE 1

cord is already directing and coordinating the development of the embryo. The cord itself even sends out special cells to the developing buds, so that once the organs are formed, there will be nerves going to each. These will eventually form the channels of communication through which the different organs of the body will talk to each other.

Before long the end of the spinal cord, corresponding to the head of the embryo, begins to enlarge rapidly. As did primitive animals developing on the Earth, it is forming a brain. The difference here is that at this early stage of development, the brain is not being used to obtain food or to move the body. When the higher centers are added to the developing brain, they also are not immediately put to their ultimate use. The normal course of embryonic life requires that the brain do little at first in the way of learning or imagining.

Nevertheless, the brain is capable of functioning in this manner as early as the third to sixth month of embryonic life, but the comfortable intrauterine environment usually renders it unnecessary to begin this high level function until around the time of birth.

In a certain sense even at this early stage a nervous system self-image is present, mostly that contained in the fertilized egg. The image is, of course, primitive, but the infant brain does "know" that sucking and swallowing will one day satisfy its hunger, that certain processes will stimulate the bladder or bowel to evacuate, and so on.

When the infant passes through the birth canal, his or her world changes permanently. No longer does the baby float passively, obtaining oxygen, food, and protection from the uterine environment. The portions of the self-image responsible for feeding, breathing, and so on, must now be activated or the baby will perish. The baby enters a world in which learning is all-important. The infant must learn to signal hunger to his or her mother (the primitive woman did not feed according to the clock), and must eventually learn to use the hands, use the legs, and think of himself or herself as a unique entity with the goal of surviving.

The genetic programs present in the fertilized egg still continue to operate; the individual will grow at a certain rate and have certain

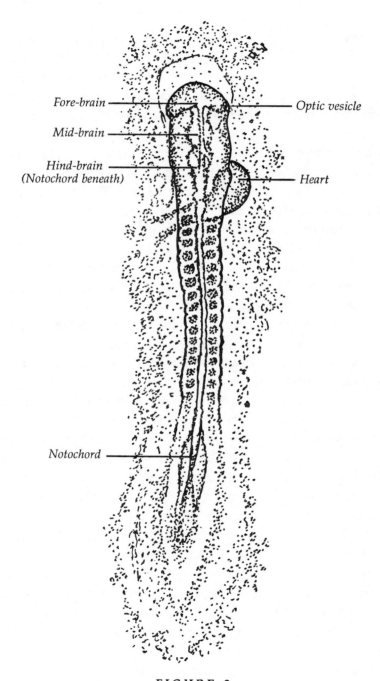

Fore-brain

Mid-brain

Hind-brain
(Notochord beneath)

Optic vesicle

Heart

Notochord

FIGURE 2

characteristics of development that depend upon his or her lineage, but no longer is this the only factor. Experiences in the world now begin to affect the individual's image.

Nature has given the infant legs and muscles, but his or her experiences in the world (e.g. proper nutrition, polio, exposure to others who walk, and so on) will determine whether he or she ever walks. Genetic programs are responsible for causing the fingers to stop growing at a certain length and to have a certain thickness of skin on their tips, but conditioned reflexes will determine whether those fingers learn to touch-type. The information in the fertilized egg provides the capacity for gastric contraction and acid secretion. The individual's life experiences will determine whether he or she gets an ulcer and needs an operation.

Superimposed, then, on the genetic image is the learned (programmed, or conditioned) image. Dissection of the brain will not show either of these images, but we know they are present and it is with them that we have been working up until now.

Become aware of your hand. Your awareness is merely of electrical signals being delivered by the nerves of your arm; the idea of *hand* is part of your conscious image. If you move your hand, you are actually moving the image within your mind. The hand obeys because of the nerves that connect it to this image.

Recall the point in the center of your head, which you found during the relaxation induction. Picture that point as a sender and receiver of information. Your self-image is much like a photographic slide insofar as it corresponds to this image, and you can direct your body and your feelings according to the image that you have. This information is present in the form of patterns of neural activity.

Certain patterns are useful and rewarding to perceive; others help us function in a coordinated fashion. Let's call these patterns coherent. They help the group of cells called "me" survive together.

The unpleasant, maladaptive aspects of your mind, body, and emotions are the incoherent aspects. *Incoherent* is a good word to describe the state of mind and symptoms, emotions, or habits that we have but would rather not have. We will now see how the coherent energy radiating out from the point in the center of the head through a distorted image can produce incoherency and disease in specific body organs.

Incoherency: Internal Distortion

The fearful violinist knows his violin playing patterns quite well (coherent), but when faced with an audience, an irrational image is formed. He has been programmed to feel afraid of this audience, as though they would physically attack him if he made a mistake. The information perceived by his brain is, therefore, incoherent—determined by his programming. As he attempts to play, the information relayed through this same image (afraid he will make a mistake) emerges distorted, and the coherent neural patterns responsible for playing properly are disordered. He makes a mistake. His fingers function incoherently.

The employee views the angry boss as though she were a saber-toothed tiger. Her neural image is of an actual physical threat to her body. This is irrational, because her employer will not physically attack her. The normal, coherent information that would be going to her stomach and digesting her breakfast is now interfered with by the incoherent (in this situation) response of fight or flight and spasm; abnormal secretions and an ulcer begin to develop.

We can see the same process in a more detailed way if we actually measure the discharges flowing through a given group of nerves. Up until now you may have thought of a neural connection as being similar to the connection between a switch and a light. When the current flows, the organ is activated, and when it stops, the organ is inactivated. It would be more accurate to view the connection between the central nervous system and an organ of the body as being similar to a telephone line or closed circuit television cable. Even when an organ is not actively being used (for example, the bowel for digestion or the feet for walking) continuous information is being sent to maintain its health.

These impulses function to maintain the organ in a healthy, ready state. They ensure that the skin of the hands remains at a certain thickness, that the cells of the liver receive sufficient blood to nourish them, and that the lens of the eye receives enough oxygen to prevent cataracts from forming. If the nerve to an organ is cut, that organ can no longer be nurtured and kept in a healthy, balanced state by the mind, and it rapidly deteriorates (atrophies). Simply hooking a battery to the end of the nerve to the organ will not maintain the organ in a state of readiness. A specific, coherent pattern must flow down this nerve cell in order to achieve the desired effect. In order to stay healthy, a group of cells must receive exactly the right nutrients and be in the right chemical environment. Its wastes must be removed and worn-out cells must be replaced. And the neural discharges to it must be exactly the right ones.

Anyone can pick up a guitar, place the fingers on the frets, and produce a sound. But if this is not done according to a precise pattern or if the guitar is not accurately tuned, a pleasant sound will not be produced. Coherent neural patterns appear to the cell much like a pleasing guitar chord sounds to the ear. A tonal discord causes pain and displeasure to our musical sense. Discordant neural patterns cause poor blood flow, inadequate nutrition and waste removal, spasm, susceptiblility to infection, and inadequate functioning of an organ.

Measuring Incoherent Patterns

An interesting study was performed in which electrical recordings were taken of nervous impulses going to muscles (electromyography). If a person with a normal hip muscle is told to move it, the discharges going to the muscle at this time form a curve, increasing and decreasing smoothly.

When a group of people with sore, tense muscles and abnormal walking patterns (which had been present for years with no apparent cause) were tested in this same fashion, the recordings of the discharges going to the muscle from the spinal cord appeared erratic and irregular.

Following deep muscle massage (e.g., Rolfing) and the experience of certain emotional memories that arise during these treatments, these muscles were retested with an electromyograph. The reading now appeared normal. In addition, comfort and mode of walking had improved considerably. The nervous impulses to the muscle had been made coherent. The abnormal state of the muscle had been maintained for years by incoherent impulses from the nervous system.

One of the most interesting electronic devices developed in recent years is the Psychological Stress Evaluator. This device consists of a tape recorder that replays spoken words at a very slow speed. The information present on the tape recorder, in the form of magnetic waves, is plotted out on a strip of paper. What is seen is an electrical tracing that corresponds to the vibrations of the person's vocal chords.

If a man speaks in his normal fashion about unemotional topics, such as the weather, the room in which he is sitting, and so on, you can obtain a pretty good tracing of the manner in which his vocal chords usually move.

Now we ask him questions. As long as he answers the questions truthfully, this same pattern is reflected on the paper. If, however, he answers a question untruthfully, a change is apparent in the tracing. This change will be noticed even if the lie is as insignificant as saying that his watch is on his right wrist when it is on his left wrist. The change in pattern is remarkably similar to the difference between the normal and abnormal tracings from the nerve to the hip muscle.

Even more remarkable, if the man begins to talk about his recent life and memories, certain words will appear very different from others. If he has had an argument with his wife, the words *wife* and *fight* will show a disordered pattern. If a brother was killed in an automobile accident years ago, the word *brother* may still show a disordered pattern.

In other words, whenever an image is brought to mind and spoken about, the instructions from the central point in the head to the vocal chords must pass through that image. To the degree that there is an anxiety associated with the image there will be a disordered neural discharge to the vocal chords, resulting in abnormal vibrations during speech.

If you listen to someone speaking, you might notice that when he or she describes a particularly unpleasant event, the voice begins to waver or crack. This is usually more obvious with the female voice, because the differences in pitch are more obvious at higher frequencies. So sensitive is the psychological stress evaluator to incoherent vibrations, however, that through changes undetectable to the ear, a person's words may be shown to reflect tension although he or she may be unaware of the tension or the reason for it. Sometimes the reason can be found through reviewing the person's experience with the objects, people, or events associated with these words.

Other, even more obvious examples of incoherent patterns of neural response will occur to you. Discharges to the stomach become disordered when the person experiences fear soon after eating. The discordant pattern is reflected by muscles that contract too forcefully and in the wrong rhythm, cells that secrete acid uninhibited by the usual controls, and a failure to replace injured cells. A woman's hands begin to shake as she reaches for the steering wheel the day after driving her car into a telephone pole. The normally fine cortical control is overpowered by gross, purposeless discharges generated by fear. As a man looks at something that makes him angry, his anger may rise to the point that his vision actually blurs. The tension is too great to permit precise focusing.

When we discussed the plight of the negatively programmed dog we saw that a stereotyped escape behavior, a specific tension, and a physiological state were programmed. Incoherent physiological states can also be programmed into the human being by the environment. These states lead to increased susceptibility to malfunction and disease.

We can distingush two main categories of disease. In the first category are those diseases that are initiated and sustained by factors external to the subject. Included in this category are gunshot wounds, snake bite, amputation of extremities, the failure of a blister on the foot to heal because a person continues to run on it, and the diseases produced when the body is attacked by an organism with which it is not genetically prepared to cope (for example, the plague or tetanus germs, which the body cannot fight off).

The second category includes those diseases that are caused, exacerbated, or maintained by programs recorded in the unconscious. These programs are destructive physiological processes that occur repeatedly in response to internal or external stimuli with which they have been linked through negative conditioning. Common ones are high blood pressure, asthma, tension headache, and TMJ (temporo-mandibular joint) problems. As you might expect, these problems are often eliminated or notably improved through the use of deep relaxation, positive visualization, and exploration, which serve to substitute relaxation for tension, thereby breaking these unwanted links between stimuli and the mind-body.

What is most surprising, however, is the large number of diseases you might have thought belonged to the first category that turn out to be in the second category. Even diseases that have a decidedly nonpsychological origin may be strongly affected by psychological and emotional events. Diabetes, for instance, depends upon the presence of a certain gene. But whether the person's blood sugar is easily stabilized or not is often dependent upon their state of mind and the amount of stress in their lives.

CHAPTER 12

Emotions and the Diseases They Cause and Cure

"What the World Really Needs Is a Cure for the Common Cold"

You may have heard it said that it is better to get pneumonia than a cold, because pneumonia can be treated with an antibiotic but the common cold is viral and therefore unresponsive to antibiotics. As a result we must grin and bear it.

Let's not stop there. Let's take a closer look at the common cold. We all know people who tend to get colds and people who seem to never catch one. You may know someone who is eighteen years of age and has five or six colds a year although he or she seems otherwise to be in perfect health. But a parent living in the same house, and who is twice the young person's age, may be able to count all the colds he or she has ever had on the fingers of one hand.

In my family medical practice I saw patients who had respiratory infections ranging from the sniffles, sore throat, and cough to full-blown cases of pneumonia. The organisms producing the infection ranged from bacteria, such as the streptococcus, to viruses, such as the flu. In almost every case the person believed that he or she had caught the infection from someone else, perhaps someone in the family or someone at work. But one of the major modes of spreading these infections is through the coughing and sneezing of the organisms into the air; it therefore follows that *I* should have had an upper respiratory infection just about all the time. Seldom did a day go by in which I was not coughed or sneezed upon, and certainly the enclosed space of my office contained large numbers of these little invaders riding on particles expelled into the air by my patients. But neither I nor the average doctor walks around constantly with a cold.

Other explanations are usually given by people who suddenly get a bug, such as, "My resistance is low" or "I've been run down lately." By run down, the person usually means tired or exhausted. Nevertheless, it's generally not the person who goes out and works eight or ten hours a day chopping wood, digging a ditch, or working on a construction job who feels run down. It is the business executive or office worker, who works a nine–to–five job, expending little physical energy, who feels run down. So lack of physical exertion does not result in an increased capacity to battle invading organisms. Let's examine this even more closely. Take the story of Sam, as an example. Sam has come to my office complaining of a sore throat. I can see little patches of white, indicating places where the streptococcus bacteria are growing. The throat is red and inflamed, and the lymph nodes in his neck are sore.

As we breathe in and out every day, we take in huge quantities of air laden with bacteria and viruses. One of the main functions of the cells of the pharynx is to conduct air, moisten it, clean it, and prevent infections from developing in itself. Because the throat is moist and warm and an ideal place for infection to begin, it's clear that these defense mechanisms are generally effective.

The idea that germs cause disease follows from experiments in which a few hundred bacteria are removed from an infected person and grown on agar in an incubator. Soon each germ cell has produced millions more in colonies. If we now scoop up a few hundred thousand and inoculate a well person (for example, paint the germs on the internal surface of the throat), that person tends to develop the disease the first person had.

Before we conclude that this is the whole story, we must remember that the first person was probably not inoculated with as many bacteria when contracting the infection. The first person probably came in contact with only a few organisms. Thus the situations that appeared identical at first have certain differences, and to assume that the presence of the bacteria is the whole story may be incorrect. In fact, it has been shown in the laboratory that a certain number of each specific type of organism must be used in inoculation to produce infection in 50 percent of the people. This may range from one organism (for example, tuberculosis may develop following the presence of a single bacillus) to several hundred thousand organisms.

Sam's infection, then, means either that a powerful germ has come along or that the defense mechanism has, in some way, broken down. If we were to culture the throats of the people in Sam's office and home, though they might feel completely well, we might find exactly the same streptococcus germ living there. Indeed, studies have shown that people can carry streptococcus around in their throats for months with no sign of infection. They may suddenly develop all the signs and symptoms of a strep throat, including the massive overgrowth of the organism, or they may never develop an infection and the bacteria may disappear.

To find a more likely reason for the development of this infection, we must go back to a few days before the sore throat developed. Sam stops at a bar on the way home from work for a couple of drinks. When he leaves the bar, he neglects to take with him his briefcase full of important papers that he is to complete at home. He comes back later that night but apparently someone has picked up his belongings, and Sam realizes that he is in big trouble at work.

Sam has real problems. This isn't his first mistake, and he's been warned several times about his unreliability. This latest fiasco might mean that Sam has to find a new job, not a happy possibility with his work history. Sam is afraid.

The next day, while driving to work, Sam concocts a plan. A young woman has recently been hired and is one of Sam's subordinates. "She has no dependents," thinks Sam. "She has much less to lose than I do."

On arriving at the office, Sam walks over to the young woman's desk and asks her in a loud voice, "Where are the papers for the briefing today?"

To the young woman's startled and confused reply that she has not seen them, Sam answers angrily, "I put them on your desk yesterday and told you to check them last night. Where are they?"

Sam reports this to his boss, who, of course, gets angry and tells the young woman that one more mistake like this could cost her her new job. Sam sighs in relief and feels that he has narrowly squeaked by.

Almost. Our understanding of coherency will give us a different picture. As Sam scolds the young woman, and as he tells the lie to his boss, he must use his vocal cords and throat to produce the words. Because Sam is lying, incoherent neural discharges are being sent to the throat and the vocal cords. By an act of will Sam is able to sound convincing, but the functioning of the pharyngeal cells has been altered.

For the next few days every time Sam speaks, especially at work, the incoherent mental image causes the proper functioning of those cells to be interrupted. The normal defense mechanisms are broken down as surely as if there were a partial denervation of the throat. Coherent neural patterns are necessary to permit the cells to perform their normal function of combating bacteria and viruses.

Perhaps there have been streptococci in Sam's throat for a long time, or perhaps he inhales a few during these days. The bacteria find, in the disordered cells of his throat, a comfortable place to grow. Having gained a foothold in the body, they may discharge their toxins into the bloodstream and cause further complications, such as pain in the joints or fever.

The secondary defense system, the white cells, are not as effective as the first line of defense in the throat would have been, and Sam comes to my office for an antibiotic to help weaken the organisms so the body can wipe them out.

Tensions other than lying can cause incoherent discharges to the pharynx. Often people will develop a cold several days before or after speaking or singing before a group of people. The stage fright focuses its incoherent patterns on the voice-producing area of the throat, and the defense mechanisms may break down, leaving the area susceptible to germs.

Even the fear of becoming sick can cause an upper respiratory infection. A person who has frequent colds might become worried several days before a vacation that a cold will come along to spoil the fun. The fear of being sick creates anxiety in the mind that is obviously related to the upper respiratory tract. Ironically, the resulting incoherent discharges can render this area susceptible to attack by a germ.

Whenever I see a patient with a respiratory infection, be it sniffles, sinusitis, sore throat, bronchitis, or pneumonia, I ask the following question: "For a few days prior to the development of your symptoms, did you have any psychological tension about a speech, did you have to verbalize a decision you weren't too sure about, or did you have any other fear associated with speaking, breathing, or singing?

Most people are surprised at the question, but a large percentage answer in the affirmative. When I explain my reason for asking, an aha! expression often lights up the patient's face. I then explain that he or she can help to eliminate the disease by rethinking the decision or by allowing himself or herself to feel more calm about the stressful event. Sometimes the patient leaves the office with such enthusiasm for the idea that he or she declines medication.

I have seen numerous people for Selective Awareness Therapy who, in addition to other problems, have had three or four attacks of colds, flu, or strep throat each year. Following the exploration and deconditioning of negative patterns related to speaking, such as memories of having been spanked for speaking out of turn as a child, being laughed at for making a mistake in school, or being threatened with physical harm if he or she uttered a word about something he or she had seen, the pattern is eliminated and the number of upper respiratory infections drops significantly.

Sometimes people come to my office specifically to trace the cause of their frequent upper respiratory infections. The instructions that I give to the unconscious following the initial induction are simple: "Go back to one minute before the feeling occurred that was responsible for the development of a cold in the past."

This information may not be available to the person consciously but the unconscious, of course, knows exactly when the feeling occurred. It is often able to take us through many repetitions of this same emotion, and we are able to trace it back to its origin in childhood.

The results of the deconditioning usually include greater self-confidence in speaking, elimination of certain maladaptive responses such as stage fright or inability to speak one's mind at certain times, and a marked decrease in frequency of infection.

I would not attempt to put every human malady in the category of psychophysiological illness. As the disorders that follow are examined carefully, however, we will see that a large percentage, in fact, can fit into this category. Much work has been done describing the other processes by which infections may develop; all I mean to present here is illustrative examples to show how the coherency theory may be utilized *when applicable.* The examples provide you with a framework for understanding the relationship between your mental and bodily processes and for understanding how healing processes can be accelerated. Each of the explanations and examples are based upon what I have learned from explorations performed in my office wherein symptoms responded to deep relaxation and imagery techniques.

Hay Fever, Allergies, and the Sniffles

Allergies are widespread in our present culture, and literature indicates that humanity has suffered from them for centuries. Traditional approaches to allergic reactions are the removal of the substance that causes the trouble or the administration of medication that prevents the body from responding to the substance. Allergies also represent a group of diseases that we, as human beings, seem to have much more frequently than do other animals. Let's take a look at allergies as understood through the coherency theory.

There are probably millions of different specific molecules to which a person could become allergic. We may become allergic to cat dander but remain nonallergic to dog fur; we may become allergic to walnuts but not to peanuts. A person who has been found to be allergic to grasses can often tell you exactly the species of grasses to which he or she is allergic. This can be determined by skin testing. The question arises, "Why does the body choose only a certain set of molecules to react against, ignoring other molecules to which it could have become sensitized?"

Those who work in the field of allergies know their relationship to emotional disturbances. Outbreaks of hay fever, asthma, and topical rashes often accompany emotional upsets. If you have an allergic condition, you might be able to associate it, by thinking back, with periods of great emotional stress in your life. Following is a theory as to how allergies begin.

The human being is perhaps the only animal who will remain immobile in an unpleasant situation. At work, on the freeway, in arguments, we stand still and experience levels of tension that would send any self-respecting dog running to the nearest door. We don't leave these difficult situations because doing so might bring about a worse situation or cause us to lose face. The decision to remain in a situation of fear and high tension is a conscious decision on our part; we believe we understand why we are staying. The unconscious and the body, however, are confused by this behavior.

Imagine a child standing in front of a parent or teacher who is yelling angrily, scolding him. He may be extremely frightened, but he does not run because leaving the situation would result in an even more unpleasant punishment. The unconscious and the body respond to the high level of tension as though it were a physical threat. They seem to decide that because the child is not running away, the tension that is being produced is from inside the body rather than outside. They then begin to search around for some possible cause of the tension. Let us further imagine that the scolding is taking place in a field of clover. In its search for an offending agent, the body may discover the protein molecules of the clover in the bloodstream, and because there seems to be no other cause for the tension, it may decide that this molecule is the source of the problem. This seems reasonable because a half hour ago, when the bloodstream was free of this protein, there was no tension. It draws the erroneous conclusion that the protein molecule is causing the disturbance. The body's way of responding to offending molecules, such as those of drugs, viruses, or bacterial products, is to form antibodies against them.

When we are infected with a virus or bacteria, the antibodies that are produced serve to inactivate the foreign protein molecules and also to act as a tag that attracts white blood cells. The white blood cells then gobble up the antibody-antigen complex, as the combination is called, and remove it from the bloodstream, like tow trucks taking away illegally parked cars. In the case we are describing, however, the protein molecule of the clover pollen is not actually a threat to the body, and nature has not provided a mechanism for completely inactivating the molecule. Instead the body can form only incomplete antibodies if it attempts to defend against the molecule.

The incomplete antibody only partially reacts with the molecule, and, as a result, a new molecule is formed, consisting of the combination of the protein molecule and the incomplete antibody. Ironically, the original protein molecule is thus converted to a substance that *does* cause an irritative reaction in the body. This reaction is characterized by the release of a substance called histamine. Histamine causes tissues of the body to become hot and swollen. It causes irritation of nerve endings, and the result is itching and malfunction of the organ to which it has been released.

Let us return once again to our naughty child. As he is being scolded he is crying, but trying to hold back the tears. The muscles of his forehead and those around his eyes are tightly constricted, and you might notice redness in this area. If we now take a look at his internal mental image, we find that, along with the emotional tension, there is an incoherency and spasm associated with this area of his body. The unconscious may then decide that the cause of his problems is located in this area. It immediately begins to search the upper respiratory tract for possible dangers. As it does so, it finds the clover protein on the surface of his mucous membranes. It then alerts the lymphatic system, which attempts to produce antibodies. This is an incoherent response.

Only incomplete antibodies can be formed. Of course the scolding lasts only a few minutes, but the allergic response is remembered by the body. When, a few weeks later, the child walks out into a field of clover, the body recognizes that the protein is present once again. It remembers the amount of tension associated with the presence of this molecule in the past, and the allergic response is activated. Although the child is walking peacefully through the field, the body begins to respond by sending the incomplete anti-bodies to the nasal mucosa. Within minutes the child's nose is running and he is sneezing.

Each time he is exposed to this antigen, the response grows stronger as the body tries harder to attack the invader, and the response is soon noticed by his parents. When this is brought to the attention of his doctor, he is diagnosed as having hay fever based on the results of skin testing. (Skin testing is performed by injecting small amounts of various proteins underneath a person's skin and then seeing to which ones the body reacts. Those injection sites that show redness, swelling, or itching indicate the protein to which the person is allergic.

The child is then treated with an antihistamine, which serves to block the effects of the histamine, and cortisone, which prevents the allergic response on the part of the body involved, in this case, the nose. A symptomatic cure is effected. The boy now remains allergic to the substance, and his only means of preventing problems is by taking these drugs. Is it any wonder that as a teenager the boy does not associate his hay fever with emotional problems?

Perhaps an actual example will help make this even more clear. Bob came to my office because his hay fever allergy of many years' duration had become so strong that he was unable to drive past a field of hay without severe symptoms. An exploration was performed in which I asked his unconscious to go back to one minute before the allergic reaction began on several occasions in the past. It turned out that in each memory, he was passing a field of hay. His reactions included stuffiness of the nose, redness of the eyes, and the production of tears.

Finally, his unconscious was requested to take us back to one minute before the very first time that this reaction had taken place. He described the following story.

"I'm about three years old and my father is asking me if I would like to go for a ride to visit my grandfather in the country. I am sitting next to him in the car, and we are riding past many fields and farmhouses."

"We are pulling into the driveway of my grandfather's house."

At this point Bob began to show signs of fear: his forehead wrinkled and his eyelids fluttered furiously.

"What do you see right there?"

"I see many bales of hay piled up in the yard. In front of them is a red tractor. Standing next to the tractor is something that looks like a man but is very frightening. It is dressed from head to toe in a gray suit, and instead of a head there is a huge cylindrical metal mask with a glass plate where the eyes should be. In its hand it's holding the end of a long wire coming from a machine making lots of noise. From the end of this instrument there is a blinding light."

At this point Bob began to cry and to show signs of great fear.

"What are you doing?" I asked.

"I think it's a monster with a death ray, and I'm hiding on the floor of the car. My father, grandfather, and the other men around are laughing at me. I feel very embarrassed, alone, and frightened."

Bob's signs of fear became even stronger.

"What's happening now?"

"My father and grandfather are opening the door of the car and they are dragging me out and calling me a coward and laughing at me. They are forcing me to look at the monster next to the bales of hay."

At this point the tears were running freely from Bob's eyes, and his nose had begun to discharge large quantities of mucus. His face over the area of his sinuses was red.

After erasing the image it was possible for Bob to become completely relaxed and to realize, with his adult mind, that what he was seeing was simply a man welding two parts of a tractor together. As a child his unconscious had picked up the tension and incoherency in the eye and nasal areas and attacked the protein molecules of the surrounding hay; thus his hay fever had begun.

Following a few days of deconditioning himself to various memories of reactions to hay, as well as various memories of feeling embarrassed and forsaken by people who loved him, his hay fever almost completely disappeared. His mind had been allowed to review a period of irrational fear and to reconstruct the memory along rational lines so that there was little need for the production of antibodies against hay protein.

Similar explorations and results have been obtained with allergies to food as well as to physical contact with various substances. Explorations focusing on attacks of sinusitis have produced similar findings and results. In each case a situation of high emotional tension was associated originally with the contact of a certain portion of the body with a foreign substance. Of course not everyone who has a high degree of tension in a hay field will develop an allergy to hay. Whether this happens depends also upon the person's genetic makeup, emotional history, past contacts with this molecule, prior tension-producing events, and so on.

Disorders of the Endocrine System

Since the turn of the century, we have heard a great deal about a newly discovered system in the body—the endocrine system. This consists of many glands, including the thyroid gland, pituitary gland, gonads, pancreas, and adrenal glands. The diseases associated with the endocrine system range from the common problems of diabetes mellitus and irregular menstrual periods to Addison's disease—a problem with the adrenal glands that gained much attention when President John F. Kennedy was said to suffer from it. And most of us have at least one friend with an underactive thyroid gland.

The endocrine system consists of glands that empty their chemical products, called hormones, directly into the bloodstream. These hormones control nearly every aspect of our body's functioning, including metabolism (thyroid glands), sugar usage (pancreas), and sexual functioning (gonads). The release of epinephrine, which we would feel, for example, a few moments after an almost fatal accident, is the result of a release of a minute quantity of the chemical from the adrenal glands.

When a nerve cell is stimulated, it conducts the discharge all the way from one end to the other. As it reaches the end of the nerve, this information must cross a small space, called a synapse, to another nerve, muscle, or other kind of cell. It does this by releasing an extremely small quantity of a certain chemical, such as acetylcholine or a form of adrenalin (depending upon the kind of nerve cell). It is this tiny amount of chemical that causes the next cell to realize that a message has come down the nerve fiber. In a way, each nerve is like a tiny gland!

The endocrine glands are richly supplied with nerves and are rigorously controlled by the nervous system; I often view them as huge nerve endings. Instead of releasing minute amounts of chemical, as the tiny nerve endings do, the endocrine glands may release much larger quantities. They are, therefore, able to adjust the person's overall activity in many ways.

Just as you are able to increase the activity of your hand by moving it back and forth and up and down, it is possible for the thyroid gland to increase the overall activity and metabolism of your entire body. If you have an overactive thyroid gland or if someone gives you thyroid hormone pills, you may find your arms and legs moving much more often, feel nervous and jittery, and always feel too warm even though other people feel comfortable. On the other hand, too little thyroid hormone can cause feelings of being slowed down or drowsy and make a person tend to gain weight. In a similar fashion, the other endocrine glands may be seen as superenlarged nerve endings that regulate a person's overall activity in one way or another.

Because of their close association with the nervous system, there is much opportunity for the function of these glands to become involved in conditioned reflexes. In other words, a person's glands may secrete too much or too little hormone, depending upon what kind of stimuli are in the person's environment and what kind of thought patterns the person has. I have worked with several people who had improper secretion levels of the endocrine glands. In the course of exploration we saw a pattern of conditioning that was similar to that discussed up until now except that a change in the secretion of the gland became one of the responses. Following exploration and deconditioning there was an improvement in glandular function.

We spoke before about such problems as muscle tension and spasm being due to a continuous tension maintained by the central nervous system. In other words, instead of there being just occasional impulses going to the part of the body that is in tension, the impulses tend to run continuously. Thus a condition of the body can be maintained by the nervous system alone. This, however, is the job of the endocrine glands. They function to provide steady, continuous conditions of the organism. They produce overall changes in general activity in the same way that the nerves produce intermittent types of activity. A disease of muscle tension that occurs in the presence of certain stimuli is there because there was a tension present at the time of some sensitizing event or at the time of a series of conditioning events. The tension is produced because the nerves to the muscle are functioning abnormally. Through the rules of negative conditioning, then, this may become more and more pronounced with each new trial. In the same fashion an interruption of the normal secretory patterns of an endocrine gland by negatively programmed events may also sow the seed for future dysfunction. Let's see how this might happen in a particular case.

Let us imagine that Betty has parents who, for some reason, are sensitive to any noise or activity above a certain level. Each time Betty begins to play and becomes very active or loud, her mother and father come in, yell at her, and tell her to go to bed. Thus several stimuli are becoming linked with a reflex in which enthusiastic activity causes an increase in tension, such as that which is experienced when the child is punished. Later on, then, being very active is associated with increased fear, and thus, through avoidance programming, the child becomes trained to be less and less active.

The gland controlling overall bodily activity is the thyroid gland. As this conditioning grows stronger and stronger through the years, the overall program, which the mind is carrying out, becomes less active. The way the body generally carries out the commands to become less active is to decrease the output of thyroid hormone. By the time Betty has reached twenty or thirty years of age, the program may be strong enough that its effects are noticed, and she may go to a doctor to learn that she has an underactive thyroid gland.

Other situations might cause an individual to develop an overactive gland. Graves' disease (thyrotoxicosis) is a malfunction of the endocrine system in which huge amounts of thyroid hormone are released into the bloodstream by the thyroid. This release is believed by many to be because of overactivity of the pituitary gland, which controls the thyroid. The pituitary, in turn, is controlled by way of the hypothalamus, a higher center in the brain. In many studies patients with hyperthyroidism relate the onset to *major emotional or traumatic crises* in their lives (that is, stressful situations that tell the unconscious that it should do something). Some of the symptoms seem like a prolonged negative (escape) response: elevated metabolic rate, increased sweating, diarrhea, rapid heartbeat, tremor, and apprehensiveness. Perhaps the unconscious believes that the crisis is here to stay and so it develops a lasting glandular alteration.

Or let us say that Betty, at the age of three years, discovers that she feels a pleasurable sensation when she plays with her clitoris. As she is experiencing this joyous new discovery, she is discovered by her prudish mother, who becomes horrified and spanks her, telling her she is a bad girl and forcing her to wash her hands and go to bed. Thus there is an association of the functioning of the sexual glands and the sexual parts of the body with the feeling of tension. As Betty grows older and finds herself becoming interested in boys, her mother's attitude makes itself felt in her life. All her endeavors to meet and go out with boys are greeted with maternal disapproval, leading to tension on Betty's part. In other words, whenever the sexual glands are functioning normally, which includes stimulating the body, there is an associated tension. As both a child and as a teenager, then, the activity of Betty's sexual glands and the sexual parts of Betty's body are being disturbed.

Because breast development is dependent upon the normal functioning of these glands, it would not be unusual to find that Betty's breasts were delayed in their development. Indeed, they might never develop fully until this conditioning is altered. She might well have difficulties in her marriage because of pain on intercourse or sexual nonresponsiveness, irregular and troublesome periods, and difficulty, both physical and mental, in bearing and giving birth to children. I find early sexual repression to be a common pattern when the presenting complaints are of this type.

The coherency theory gives us a way to visualize how a gland can be involved in a reflex pattern. At the time when certain stimuli are present and when the tension is felt, incoherent information is being sent to the gland that is being used at the moment, just as it is sent down the nerve to the spastic stomach muscle in the person with an ulcer. This means that repetitions of the same stimuli and emotion on future occasions will cause this reaction to grow stronger and stronger and, as the years pass, the gland will actually begin to become measurably abnormal in its secretions. It is even easier to visualize how when this stress occurs during childhood, while the gland is growing, its development can be influenced.

Like most physicians I have observed the close connection between a person's moods and feelings and the functioning of the endocrine system. Probably most people have known a woman who, fearing pregnancy, has missed her period by one, two, or three weeks, although her period may have been regular until that time. Often she will go to see a physician, fearing pregnancy. When informed that she is not pregnant, it is common for her to begin her period that very day. I feel that many glandular disorders may begin and end in response to stress or relaxation, but because the other glands don't announce their state of activity by such a dramatic and immediate change as menstrual bleeding, the connection is not as readily detected.

Chronic and Degenerative Diseases

Such health problems as high blood pressure, heart disease, and tremors appear more frequently as we grow older and are called the degenerative diseases. They are rarely attributed to any specific cause, and seldom is anything done to find the source of these problems. The treatment of them tends to be symptomatic and, in general, they tend to be progressive. Some may be fatal.

After watching the beginning and progress of these diseases and getting to know the people who have them, many investigators have become convinced that quite a few of them can be prevented, ameliorated, or even cured, provided the right approach is taken. We will now explore several common chronic diseases from the perspective of the Coherency Theory.

High Blood Pressure and Heart Disease

The major cause of death in this country is from diseases of the cardiovascular system, and the most common disease is high blood pressure, which causes inadequate circulation to the heart and overwork of the heart muscle. Some types of high blood pressure are due to glandular disorders, and these have specific treatments.

But the most common kind is called essential hypertension. Its cause is unknown. Although the name given to the disease makes it sound as though it is somehow essential to the person and incurable, I do not feel this is necessarily the case.

High blood pressure, or hypertension, is a condition in which the diameter of the blood vessels all over the body is made smaller by contraction of the muscles in the walls of these vessels.

But the elevated pressure does not come on all at once, nor does it simply become elevated and stay permanently high. On different visits to the doctor's office, the patient's blood pressure is sometimes elevated and sometimes not. The elevation of blood pressure occurs with situations of tension in the person's life. It is common for a person's blood pressure to go up when he or she is excited or nervous, and nervousness often occurs upon physical examination.

Many doctors have the patients take their own blood pressure at home, so reliably does it go up under the stress of being in the doctor's office. In fact, one of the first treatments the physician gives for high blood pressure is merely tranquilizer medication. By keeping the person calm, the blood pressure elevations do not occur as frequently, and the high blood pressure has been treated symptomatically.

The patterns that are causing the tension, however, are not eliminated by the tranquilizer. As a result, the contraction of the walls of the blood vessel may begin to recur as learned response patterns cause the tension level to break through the bonds artificially imposed by the tranquilizer. The blood pressure begins peaking more and more often, and the patient is begun on a diuretic, or water pill. One main function of this medication is to remove a certain amount of water from the body. It thus lowers the total volume present in the bloodstream, and through this, along with several other mechanisms, the symptoms of high blood pressure are again erased—for a while.

The blood pressure soon begins to rise once again, and more vigorous methods of controlling it are employed. Drugs may be used that function through their effect on the kidneys or the nervous, vascular, or endocrine system, but the blood pressure often continues to rise.

In some cases the rise in blood pressure continues to the point that severe headaches, brain problems, or kidney problems result. We can imagine the blood having to flow through all of the spastic vessels to reach the various organs of the body. It must then flow back through the veins to the heart to be pumped out again. As the muscles in the walls of the vessels begin to contract, it becomes more and more difficult for the blood to flow through them. Just as when the garden hose is kinked, the output of water decreases, so too is the volume of blood reaching various organs of the body diminished. In order to compensate for this decreased blood flow, the heart must pump harder. If you had to blow up a balloon through a small straw, you would have to blow much harder than someone blowing it through a larger straw in order to keep up with him or her.

This increased work, of course, falls on the heart muscle. The heart muscle is supplied with blood from arteries in its walls. Like all the other vessels in the body, these vessels may also be narrowed and in spasm. When this spasm has been present for a long time, it may become impossible for the vessel to ever again reach its original diameter.

The heart has to pump harder and harder with a smaller and smaller supply of blood to its own muscle. This is the situation seen commonly in people with angina pectoris. The chest pain is caused by a heart that goes into spasm, partly because it is not able to keep up with the work it is being called on to do. The problem may actually become so bad that a portion of the heart muscle dies, leading to a myocardial infarction, or heart attack.

It probably comes as no news to most people that heart attacks and high blood pressure are closely associated with each other and also very much associated with the amount of tension in one's life. Those people who live in a tense home situation or have tense and demanding jobs tend to have much more cardiac and high blood pressure disease than people in more relaxed daily surroundings.

Remember the negative conditioning of the dog back in Chapter 8? If we conduct this experiment with a special instrument on the dog to measure its blood pressure, we find that each time it gets a shock, its blood pressure goes up. Actually, the pressure can increase in all of us in any time of tension or fear, because it is part of the normal response pattern. If it occurs regularly, along with a programming stimulus, it becomes negatively conditioned. Soon each time the stimulus comes along, the blood pressure goes up. Perhaps in human beings we do not see continuous elevated blood pressure very often in younger people because it takes some time for this overall mechanism to become firmly established. In addition, the greater flexibility of the walls of the blood vessels of younger people give them much more ability to absorb periodic tensions. As one grows older, however, blood pressure elevations occur repeatedly, until the conditions of high blood pressure and its unhappy results may be produced.

You're probably asking yourself, "What about all the talk of diet, exercise, and heredity as related to blood pressure and heart disease?" These are definitely important factors, and should not be ignored by anyone seeking to maintain the health of the circulatory system. But in addition to the management of diet and exercise, management of emotions is important. The more unrelieved tension and incoherent response patterns in one's life, the more rapidly the blood pressure is likely to rise through the years. A person who has a genetic predisposition to develop these problems, or who has had early warning symptoms, has an important choice to make. That person cannot change his or her heredity, but he or she can decide whether to continue to be high-strung, hurry from one appointment to another, worry, and lose his or her temper. That person can begin, one by one, to eliminate these dangerous responses. My advice is that he or she learn to become a person who can choose to remain relaxed and calm even during stressful situations in spite of how uptight he or she may have been in the past. The person who follows this advice stands a much better chance of retarding any gradual increase in blood pressure and, perhaps more important, avoiding the emotional crises that may be the cause of the acute elevation in blood pressure responsible for heart attacks, strokes, cerebral hemorrhage, and kidney disease. Whereas it might be permissible for another person to worry, get upset, or feel tense, for an individual with hypertension, it may be more dangerous than walking on a broken leg.

This is not to say that the person should avoid all his or her usual pursuits, only that the person should become aware of any stress that creeps into his or her life and alter his or her responses through deconditioning (for instance, not getting upset if he or she is late) and positive programming (becoming as "patient as Job" and as "relaxed as a sleeping babe").

Martin came to see me because of a dual problem. He had known for years that he had hypertension, and he had attacks of sweating and pounding heart whenever he had to wait for anything. On his first visit he had one of these attacks as a result of sitting for one-half hour in my waiting room. His blood pressure was significantly elevated.

He told me that this response had been present for years, but that no one had ever told him it might be related to his high blood pressure. His emotions during these waiting periods were annoyance and impatience. The location didn't matter. Whether he was in line at the Department of Motor Vehicles, the post office, or the bus stop, he would get sweaty palms and armpits, his heart would pound, and he might even develop a headache.

Following a complete physical exam, including laboratory tests to rule out the curable causes of hypertension, I started him on mild medication and explained the possible mechanism of his disease. I sent him home with instructions on how to decondition this pattern and tapes for spasm relaxation and positive programming. Within a month he had all but eliminated the troublesome reaction. His blood pressure was well within the normal range, and I slowly weaned him from his medication. Repeated examinations have failed to detect any further elevation, even after long periods in my waiting room. Thus we have an excellent example of how the course of this problem may possibly have been altered; it would be premature to assume it has been cured forever. There may still be a continual climb over the years, but if there is, I believe it will be much more gradual than if he had not learned to relax.

Cardiac Disease

Through the mechanisms we have been reviewing, similar results can be obtained with heart disease patients. One researcher working at a cardiac care unit taught relaxation and positive imagery to patients who were admitted to recover from heart attacks. His findings included a dramatic reduction in complications, such as arrhythmias and successive heart attacks, that often follow an acute episode. If you imagine yourself suddenly lying in a hospital bed with chest pain, separated from home, work, and loved ones, and connected to all sorts of vital function measuring devices (the usual lot of the cardiac care unit patient), you can imagine the fear and tension that might develop.

To prevent negative changes in heart function and blood pressure, a group of these patients were taught relaxation induction and told to imagine a calm, relaxed, restful vacation stay in the unit—rather than the nightmare it could have been. The resulting coherent process of dealing with the situation took care of the remainder of the healing process, and avoided shocks to the system that might have caused sudden death.

As previously mentioned, it has long been known that people with certain personality traits involving tension tend to be at a much higher risk of developing heart disease. If more people are alerted to this relationship, perhaps they can change dangerous patterns or prevent them from developing. I feel this awareness will prove as rewarding in terms of health as diet and exercise prescriptions, and certainly more rewarding than the prescription of a tranquilizer.

Shaking, Muscle Tremors, and Parkinson's Disease

I have worked with several patients with Parkinson's disease, a disease that is generally thought to be of unknown origin but that causes a person to have severe shaking of the hands and severe difficulty in walking, especially in taking the first step. When Parkinson's disease patients wish to walk, they must begin to lean forward until they are off balance, so that a foot moves out to catch them. In other words, they are incapable of consciously initiating a first step. They can only push themselves off balance and let reflex mechanisms catch them so that they can continue walking. Once the walking is under way, it can continue quite well. Doesn't the inability to take a first step, the inability to initiate movement, seem the same as being trapped, not being able to move in any direction?

With one patient, explorations revealed that important memories were those in which he felt unable to make decisions involving physical movement. He had multiple memories fitting the pattern of an experience that occurred at the age of twenty, when his hand was caught in the gears of a machine. On reexperiencing and deprogramming this sensitizing event, the relaxation greatly diminished the tremor.

The senile tremor, or old age shake, is something we see often in persons aged seventy and older; we would be surprised if someone aged twenty-five had this same continual tremor. Once again, the name for the disease almost implies that one should expect it, that its cause and cure are somehow beyond us. Let's take a closer look.

How many people have you seen aged twenty, thirty, or forty who already have some shaking of the hands? Of course this is usually present only intermittently. You might notice it only during an argument. Or maybe it's only when a person is depressed that you notice a trembling of the hands or knees. Perhaps it is only after a long day of work that lasted well into the night that your hand trembles in the morning as you drink your cup of coffee. As the person grows older and older, and the conditioning grows stronger and stronger, the tremor may come more often. Noticing that one's hand is shaking is seldom taken as a sign that some permanent neurological condition is coming on, so people tend to ignore this shaking in the early stages. Nevertheless, look about and see how many people are beginning to shake. Also notice that it seems to be markedly increased at times of stress and that it can disappear when the person is relaxed. Does it seem that these tremors fit the pattern of negative conditioning? Doesn't it seem reasonable that these tremors are incoherent neural discharges being sent to various parts of the body, and that these discharges are just portions of negatively conditioned habit patterns? Time and again in exploration emotional tension is found at the base of such problems.

Many other diseases that we attribute to aging can be conceptualized in a similar manner, including that problem of old age called senility. When Charlotte is twenty-five years old, she is not a pleasant person to be around because she tends to be grouchy. By the time she is forty-five, she spends most of her time complaining about things. When she is sixty, she is very unpleasant to be around, even for her family and the people who love her, because

of her constant complaints and attacks on other people for not satisfying her needs. By the time she is seventy-five she is senile and
she sits in her chair in a nursing home, moaning and groaning and
complaining in a demented way, over and over, day after day. I think
that this is a particular habit pattern, with its tension getting worse
and worse, moving to its logical conclusion, in which the person
just sits and complains all day long. You can probably begin to work
out mechanisms for other diseases generally accepted to be con-
comitants of old age. As you do so, note that tension and negative
conditioning always seem to be at the root. Perhaps within the next
century or two, longitudinal studies will be done to test these
hypotheses.

The prevention of these diseases may be enhanced by beginning now to eliminate the deep-seated emotional problems you
uncover in yourself, before the development of physical symptoms
confuses the matter. If they have developed, however, the self-
healing methods we will discuss may be added to this program.

Skin Problems

Skin rashes and other problems and disorders of the skin constitute a large portion of diseases seen in general practice. The
problems range from simple hives to impetigo to more complicated
ones such as psoriasis. Many people with skin problems have noted
their tendency to vary in intensity, according to their mental states.
They also notice that their emotions react strongly to the presence
of the disease, especially when it makes them feel unattractive. On
the other hand, he or she may not be aware of such emotional connections. Careful investigation, however, often shows fluctuation
of a physical symptom along with an emotional state; perhaps incoherent information is being sent to the skin.

Actually, there is a large body of evidence in the literature of
medical hypnosis documenting resolution, following hypnotherapy,
of a large number of commonly occurring, noninfectious skin diseases. This is not surprising, because the majority of these problems
are actually just reactions of the body. A skin lesion, whether it be
a boil, an acne pimple, or a patch of psoriasis is composed primarily

of the cells of the body reacting to an agent, either an external agent or process (as in an allergy) or an internal, emotional one (as in neurodermatitis). Because these lesions are not performing any desirable function for us, we would rather be without them; that is, they represent incoherent responses (behaviors).

The drug most commonly employed to treat skin reactions is hydrocortisone. Its primary function is to paralyze the skin's ability to react. When the skin can no longer react, the dermatitis disappears.

A remarkable number of skin problems seem to prefer the face to other locations. Curiously, a large percentage of people with facial skin problems are the type who are self-conscious and easily embarassed by anything that is not "just so" on their bodies. It seems bad luck indeed that they tend to have their blemishes on the one part of the body that everyone can see! The following story, however, indicates that something more than bad luck may be involved.

Marjorie came to my office in tears, requesting cortisone for an unsightly skin condition that had appeared on her face. She had suffered intermittently with this problem since her teens. Her embarrassment was so evident that I pointed out it might be a good idea to investigate the emotions connected with her rash.

As a child she had been taught to be very conscious of her looks, and weeks before her first high school dance she began to fear something would go wrong with her appearance. Then one day on one of her frequent trips to the mirror, she noticed a small red patch of bumps and went crying to her mother. Whatever corrective responses her skin might have made were blocked by the incoherent process under way; the red bumps multiplied into many red marks and she was unable to go to the dance.

Marjorie felt miserable, but her unconscious saw things differently. It knew that if no rash had formed, it would have experienced worry and fear all the way up to the night of the dance. The unconscious, then, recognized this rash as an escape route. Thereafter whenever Marjorie had an important meeting or was to go to a party, the rash would tend to appear; not on every occasion, but enough to cause frequent unhappiness and self-consciousness. Gradually, she began to avoid these encounters.

Following her exploration, Marjorie could see this relationship, and how her feelings of inadequacy and embarrassment were so strong that the unconscious had come to her "aid" by producing a disease that would spare her the ordeal of facing anyone. It couldn't know that staying home with red blemishes on her face was not more pleasant for her. She began to realize that her emotions were the triggers for, rather than the result of her skin condition.

She rewrote her script by reliving all the times she could recall embarrassment, this time feeling secure and relaxed. She projected ahead to feeling at ease with people. She learned to smile at her face each time she passed the mirror, and to simply accept the rash in a relaxed manner, using it as an indicator that she needed to learn how to feel even more self-confident. As her internal self-image improved, the blemishes slowly faded.

Not too long ago I received a research paper in which a surgeon, who had become frustrated with the usual antibiotic treatment for acne had tried a new tack. He enthusiastically reported excellent success in shrinking acne lesions by teaching his patients to look in the mirror several times a day repeating, "That's just where it's supposed to be," each time they saw a new pimple. As a result of carrying out this ritual, the emotional tension lifts and the response is broken. His explanation was that the teenagers' embarassment was itself part of the vicious circle which gave rise to the disease, and by programming in a sense of acceptance this circle was broken.

Vision

Visual disorders also may be linked to negative conditioning. Some people who wear glasses are consciously aware of fluctuations in their vision according to emotional state or time of day. Let's take a case of nearsightedness. A two-year-old is taken to the zoo by his mother and father, and falls asleep on his mother's shoulder. As she speaks with her husband, she happens to turn so that the sleeping baby is facing the lion's cage. Before anyone realizes what has happened, the lion has come to the part of the cage nearest the baby and let out a deafening roar. The baby is startled into waking and finds himself faced with the lion's gaping jaws. He feels confused and extremely frightened. He now turns his head and sees his mother. As he does, his level of tension begins to decrease; he feels safer. In order to see his mother, however, his eyes must focus down from the distance at which he has seen the lion to the near focus of his mother. As we have all seen babies do, he turns back from the safety of Mother's arms to look at the frightening thing again and then rapidly back toward his mother for reassurance.

Each time that he looks at the lion, his eyes go to far vision and he feels tension. Each time that he looks at his mother, his eyes go to near vision and he feels a release of tension. Thus we have the beginning of a conditioning that can grow stronger and stronger throughout his life. The association of fear with the focusing of his eyes on a distant point may be reinforced by similar events, and by the time he is six or eight years old, he may notice that when he is very frightened or angry that his vision seems blurry. One would expect, from his conditioning, that situations requiring him to deal with difficult things that are at a distance would tend to elicit the program of fear and the focusing of the eyes to a near point as an escape behavior. This prevents the mind from seeing the object. When he reaches puberty and dating time comes around, he is faced with quite a challenge outside his home. This is one of the major times for youngsters to become so nearsighted that they need glasses—the time when they begin to become involved with things away from home. Or if the boy should be placed in a class that is too advanced, the pressure could produce a deterioration of vision; the blackboard could slip into blurriness. I have found that following the inductions at my seminars, some people have become so relaxed that they have been able to see perfectly without their glasses. In addition, others have experienced, through explorations, an improvement in their vision.

You can see the way in which various diseases can be produced through these mechanisms. It merely requires that a situation of unpleasant emotion be associated with incoherent patterns related to a particular organ. As this emotional state is repeated, the incoherent information is programmed more and more strongly, until finally an actual disease may occur in this part of the body. Of course, before performing an Exploration, we can never be sure whether the visual problem *will* be resolved, for many visual problems are not caused or maintained by negative programming. But we must consider the possibility that there is negative conditioning involved any time a disease becomes repetitive or chronic, as in the case of inadequate focusing of the eyes. In general, people who are aware of their vision changing occasionally especially in relation to their emotional state, stand the best chance of improving their vision through exploration and deconditioning.

Surgical Diseases and Surgery

In medicine there is a curious phenomenon called the gridiron abdomen syndrome, that is, the evidence of multiple abdominal operations. *Gridiron* describes the characteristic marks of the surgical scars crisscrossing each other. These patients may have had exploratory surgery on several occasions, along with removal of the gallbladder or appendix, or of other organs in the abdomen. Sometimes a diseased organ may have been found, sometimes only spasm and redness.

These people tend to have a similar personality pattern. They have a strong program linking daily tensions to the nerves supplying the abdomen. The result is disordered neural patterns that disrupt muscular, glandular, circulatory, and healing processes, which must function smoothly for health to be preserved.

The gridiron abdomen syndrome is, of course, an extreme example, but it serves to illustrate how negative programs can lead to the need for surgery. We have already discussed the development of ulcers, gallbladder disease, and hemorrhoids in Chapter 5. Any of these problems, if they persist, may require surgery.

Examination of the appendix under a microscope reveals that it too has muscular walls, and I suspect that spasm, decreased blood flow, and subsequent infection in this little pouch may underlie many cases of appendicitis. When I see patients with what appears to be a developing appendicitis, my first response is to teach them to relax this area and restore coherent patterns if these have been interrupted. Most doctors simply inform the patient that he or she may need to undergo a painful, expensive, time-consuming surgical procedure and recovery: this tends to create or intensify spasm and incoherent patterns through the emotional tension generated, possibly worsening the condition.

In general I suggest to my patients that, should they begin to develop a disease process that might require surgery or if they are admitted for a surgical procedure, they use repeated inductions, with visualization of the disease clearing rapidly or of the surgery being successful and followed by minimal postoperative discomfort and no complications. Fear about the hospitalization must be removed for maximum healing to take place. I have mentioned earlier the experience of surgeons who find complications, such as postoperative pain, infection, or poor function, much less common when the patient is prepared in this manner.

A person who has had two or more operations should consider exploring his or her health history through selective awareness (Chapter 10). This may reveal that programming is the understructure to the surgical diseases. In this fashion, he or she might avoid future surgery. The following case demonstrates how an individual may develop conditioning that leads to surgical operations at a later date.

In first grade Sally stopped on the way home from school and ate some green apples. By the time she got home, she had quite a stomachache. She went into her parents' bedroom to find them having a great argument. They told her that she deserved the pain for eating the apples and sent her out of the room, closing the door. Sally lay on the couch feeling lonely, rejected, and guilty, as her stomach reacted in a noncoherent fashion to physical and emotional irritants.

This provided an excellent opportunity for conditioning a powerful negative pattern linking these emotions, this kind of situation, and disorderly abdominal function. As she grew older, the usual childhood stomachaches tended to stimulate fear, which further incrased spasm and delayed healing. On the other hand, emotions of rejection, loneliness, or guilt tended to cause her stomach to knot up, as the program linked incoherent abdominal discharges to them. In fact, whenever her parents argued (and later, when she would engage in an argument), this same reflex would stimulate those same emotions and abdominal pain. The initial programming, which mismatched emotions and events, now caused her to feel guilty following all such arguments.

Other memories reviewed during her exploration revealed that days or weeks before her appendectomy and hysterectomy and the appearance of her ulcer and gallbladder disease, she had had an experience in which she felt these same feelings in a relationship with a loved one. The stimuli and tension resulted in incoherent information being sent to the abdominal area. Through the years the psychophysiological connections had become so strong that this was severe enough to actually initiate a surgical problem.

Following insight, emotional releasing and deconditioning, she has felt free of these feelings and has had no further internal problems and no surgery.

This case also demonstrates the reversibility of negative programs. If you remember, the essence of this conditioning is that when one or more of the physiological *or* emotional conditions that were present during the programming arise, the remaining ones tend to be elicited. Thus in this case feelings of guilt or loneliness could lead to physical dysfunction. Similarly, an unrelated, physically induced episode of abdominal pain, such as from a viral infection, would tend to induce the appearance of these emotions and create problems in a personal relationship. Further, if Sally should witness an argument between friends, or even in a movie, it would tend to stimulate both the emotions and the abdominal pain. The development of her surgical problems was thus a rather natural outcome of the strengthening of this negative pattern with time.

These concepts can be used to develop an approach to any upcoming surgical procedure. The fundamental principles that you can apply yourself if you require surgery for any reason are:

1. Removal by deconditioning of any maladaptive fear response, even if you have just been informed that surgery is required.

2. Visualization of the mechanism of the problem through what you have learned about spasm and incoherency, followed by positive imagery and a self-healing induction (see Chapter 13).

3. Positive programming of the surgery and postoperative course; your surgeon can help you with the details of what to expect

during and after surgery, so you can program a trouble-free experience. After the induction, imagine yourself calm as you are being wheeled to the operating room and comfortably drifting into a deep, relaxed sleep, with a minimum of anesthesia. Project yourself into the recovery room waking up feeling relaxed, comfortable, and hungry (to prevent postoperative nausea). Imagine yourself urinating immediately, hearing the trickle of your urine into the toilet or bedpan (to prevent postoperative urinary retention). See yourself so free of discomfort that you are telling the nurse you need no pain shots, and see the surprised look on the doctor's face as you are up and walking in record time. Visualize your doctor saying that he or she has never seen anyone recover so rapidly, easily, and completely. Finally, picture yourself happily bounding out of the hospital, as if you had simply been on vacation, knowing there can be no recurrence of this type of problem. (See cassette #203, "Successful Surgery and Recovery," Appendix p. 288.)

4. Exploration; this may be required if you have had multiple surgeries that could be related to negative programs and emotions.

Remember, these suggestions are preventive in nature, and you must supply your own motivation based upon the principles you have learned, the experiences of other patients and of doctors who use these methods, and your desire to avoid future problems. If you follow them, your only reward may be rapid recovery, normal functioning, and good health. Your mind may not tell you during your postoperative recovery period that had you not followed them you would have had a wound infection. Nor may it inform you, during some difficult personal situation later in your life, that you have succeeded in avoiding another operation. Your success must be judged simply on the basis of how well you were able to accomplish the relaxation, visualization, and positive programming in the time of stress, and perhaps an inner intuitive sense of "rightness."

Sometimes the success of surgery is limited by a negative program, as in the following case:

Todd is a young man who was injured in battle by a piece of schrapnel, which struck his leg. His immediate thought was, "I'll never walk again." He mentally flashed through many of his experiences of playing football, jogging on the beach, and dancing. Picturing himself a wheelchair-ridden cripple, he experienced an overwhelming feeling of loss and sadness.

He lost consciousness and awoke following surgery in a field hospital. The leg had been saved, but the circulation had been compromised by the wound. The surgeon expected a return of near-normal functioning, but this did not occur. (We might speculate on the role of negative conditioning in this disorder of the healing response.) Eventually, gangrene began to set in and, after months of futile attempts to save the extremity, it had to be amputated, just below the knee.

The return of adequate function with the use of an artificial limb is usually assured in a person of his age, but Todd had more problems. The end of his stump remained painful, and when he tried to use a prosthesis (artificial leg), the skin over the area would break down, requiring him to return to the wheelchair.

Eventually, he was referred to me by a surgeon who had guessed the connection between the months of delayed healing, Todd's depression, and his growing dependence on pain medication. In the exploration we reviewed many of his recent memories, which were filled with hopelessness, helplessness, and despair. Unknowingly, Todd had been continually programming himself to remain a cripple. He reviewed the day of the explosion and relived it, this time knowing that he was young and strong and expecting to recover, rather than the opposite. Finally, we reviewed a childhood memory of great pain, sorrow, and empathy, which found Todd witnessing the other boys making fun of, and pushing around, another child, who was crippled with polio. It was the hopelessness of this memory that had stimulated the powerful negative pattern at the time of his injury, and the pain at the time was sufficient to reinforce it, thereby interrupting the coherent flow to the leg. His unconscious was picturing Todd in the place of this child, who was helpless.

Within weeks following deconditioning and positive, instead of negative, visualization, Todd was completely off pain medication and walking comfortably with his prosthesis.

This case makes a strong point for the necessity of viewing any surgical or medical procedure coherently. The failure to do this is believed by many to be one of the most common causes of operative and postoperative problems.

Pregnancy and Delivery

As in surgery, pain often plays a large part in complications of pregnancy and delivery. In our culture deliveries and surgical procedures are carried out in similar settings. Thus the fear associated with doctors, caps and gowns, scalpels, surgical orders, injections, intravenous fluids, and anesthesia attend both. This fear and our social programming tend to intensify the experience of pain. The process of giving birth need not be an excruciating ordeal. It can be taken matter of factly, as part of the experience of life, or it can actually be an ecstatic, joyful event. Indeed, if one observes animals giving birth, or women of certain tribes, who stop on the way to work, deliver, rinse off their babies and wrap them in a shawl, and continue to the marketplace, barely stopping to rest until the end of the day, one realizes just how natural, normal, and positive the birth experience can be. These people and the animals do not experience the fear of childbirth that we find in our society.

The fact that this fear is so endemic in our culture might, however come as less of a surprise if we examine some of the programming of the modern woman. She is constantly presented with photographs and stories of malformed babies and women who have died during pregnancy. Even the uterine contractions that occur during the birth process are called labor pains, leaving nothing to the imagination as to what one's experience ought to be. And in our vernacular, anyone who is distraught and complaining might be described as having a baby.

Few have not heard a gory tale of a baby's head getting stuck or of a woman's vaginal tissues tearing during delivery, requiring painful surgical repair, though it is rare for serious complications to occur with our present level of obstetrical skill. What is not passed on with this information is that in many cases the woman's fear causes such tension in the vaginal area that proper passage of the baby is not possible. A woman who is very frightened at the time of emergence of the infant's head is much more likely to give a panic-stricken push rather than heed her physician's instruction to allow it to come slowly and smoothly. The resulting tear is then the focus of the story you hear from her, and the blame is placed on herself, the doctor, the baby, or the process of birth itself. But often tension, expectation, and mental imagery is at fault.

A few years ago it would have been almost medical heresy to discuss what is today commonly accepted as natural childbirth. Numerous different methods are available, including the well-known Lamaze and Leboyer techniques. All of them focus on the elimination of fear and the substitution of positive conditioning, a positive environment, and positive expectations. My approach to a delivery has been based on similar principles. First, I teach methods of deep relaxation.

After the relaxation, positive image visualization is used to help the unconscious to realize that pregnancy and delivery are normal functions of the body, and that uterine contraction involve no more discomfort than the contractions of the biceps or any other muscles of the body. The delivery is visualized as proceeding slowly and calmly. An understanding is developed that panicky feelings can actually hinder its progress and cause the very problems that the woman wishes to avoid. Suggestions similar to those given for use prior to surgery are used, along with visualizations of a comfortable birth and relaxed rest period following that. I also make clear the fact that *the less fear present in the mother at birth, the more unlikely the child is to be in any distress when born,* and the fewer complications for both.

As with the imagery and relaxation used prior to surgery, the images used during pregnancy tend to act as posthypnotic suggestions, and the delivery itself is much more comfortable, even with no further conscious effort on the part of the mother. Generally things can be made even more comfortable and pleasing if, during the "labor" (actually this need not be "work" at all) contractions, the Selective Awareness methods of relaxation are used, using the breathing and the contractions themselves as signals to increase the relaxation.

One of the major causes for fear and tension and their complications is that the mother-to-be often feels apprehensive, as though she should be doing more, and because there is nothing to do, tension results. A more rewarding approach is to recognize that she is free to concentrate on her own relaxation. The proper contractions will occur as automatically as her heartbeat. She can thus save her energy for the time when she will be asked to push, which does not occur until near the end of the birth.

When the physician or midwife is aware of the principles of relaxation, the birth can be a pleasant, smooth event. The practice prior to delivering concentrates on relaxation and the awareness that the birth will feel different from her everyday experiences, but that it will not necessarily be uncomfortable, because it is a natural process. She is then encouraged to visualize the proper muscles contracting at the proper times. As each stage of labor and delivery are reached, the physical changes reinforce the imagery and the ability to flow with the experience increases.

I suggest the induction of a deeply relaxed state just before going to the delivery room or at the onset of labor. I also request that the lights in the delivery room be kept as low as practically possible, that the voices of others in the room be kept low, and that the nurses refrain from using such words as *pain, hurt, labor, shot,* or other expressions that imply that there will be discomfort or disability as a result of what is going on. The reason for the dimming of the lights stems from a finding common to many individual Explorations that have led back to the birth experience. Many of my patients have said that at birth they were very aware of the frightening aspect of the white or green delivery room and the surrounding masked faces.

Also stemming from these experiences is my current practice of giving the infant to the mother as soon as possible following birth, because numerous times I have found among my patients lifelong feelings of rejection and loneliness dating back to being carried off by an indifferent nurse after delivery.

Following a delivery, suggestions are given to ensure adequate stoppage of bleeding and rapid healing. As with all surgical wounds, small vaginal lacerations or episiotomy repairs heal much more rapidly when they are not associated with fear. Often, even when stitches are present, the woman is able to stand up following delivery and walk comfortably to her bed.

The main principles, then, in pregnancy and delivery are:

1. Elimination of fears regarding pregnancy and delivery through Exploration and deconditioning.

2. Positive programming and elimination of negative expectation (such as sickness, pain, or a damaged child).

3. Extensive practice in deep relaxation, focusing on breathing, with suggestions to produce anesthesia, beginning months before delivery when possible.

4. Visualization of rapid healing and return of strength following birth.

The baby's father can be included in all visualizations, including those of delivery, the postdelivery period, and the baby at three or four months. (See the cassette "Great Expectations," Appendix p. 287.)

The Autoimmune Diseases

Autoimmune diseases are among the most mysterious in the field of medicine. They include several familiar and many unfamiliar diseases, such as rheumatic fever, rheumatoid arthritis, glomerulonephritis, lupus erythematosis, polyarteritis nodosa, scleroderma, and myasthenia gravis.

They are generally characterized by a curious condition of the immune system in which certain of its cellular or chemical elements begin to react against and attack the body's own tissues. In some processes, such as in lupus erythematosis, *we can even see certain of the white cells of the body devouring other white cells.*

It seems that for some unknown reason, in this kind of disease, the body becomes sensitized to its own cells and attempts the destruction of those tissues to which it has become sensitized. The course of these diseases is generally downhill and sometimes ends in the death of the patient.

The mainstay of their treatment is hydrocortisone, a chemical similar to that produced in the body by the adrenal glands. As mentioned before, by diminishing the capacity of the immune, inflammatory, and repair systems it prevents the body from harming itself.

If you have ever had poison oak or poison ivy, then you may have been given hydrocortisone by a physician. With these rashes the body is attempting to react against the oil from the plant. The inflammatory chemicals released in the process of reacting themselves turn out to be irritants to tissue, giving rise to the characteristic itching lesions. It is really not necessary for the body to defend against this substance, as there are many people who are not affected by prolonged or even frequent exposure to poison oak or poison ivy. It has been demonstrated that in many cases deep relaxation and imagery can often help terminate or diminish allergic manifestations, such as skin reactions, asthma, and allergic rhinitis.

When hydrocortisone is used in the treatment of autoimmune disease the results are often different from those obtained with self-limited diseases, such as poison oak or poison ivy. The autoimmune process tends to become continually worse, and higher doses of hydrocortisone are needed until the side effects of the hydrocortisone itself, such as the weakening of bones, psychological disturbances, abnormal deposition of fat, and loss of muscular strength, become major problems.

I have worked with several people with these kinds of diseases. A common factor brought out in the explorations has been an intense anger toward themselves, often traced back to some insignificant act during childhood. As they have grown up, they may have had a continued tendency to be down on themselves, to internally upbraid themselves for even the smallest error. Although my experience has not included a large enough sample to draw a general conclusion, those with whom I have explored the psychophysiology of their autoimmune processes have tended to be easily embarrassed around people, thinking that they have committed some faux pas by, for example, simply being present at a party or having a small stain on the hem of a dress. As a rule they have tended to feel trapped in social situations and have frequently (especially in the case of arthritis) felt as though there was no direction in which they could move—frozen in their tracks. Most are quite skillful at hiding these conflicts from their associates.

When a person is angry, he or she has the urge to lash out at something or someone. When the anger is at oneself, the body may respond by attempting, through its antibody-producing system, to form antibodies against bodily proteins. This is comparable to the example discussed earlier of the antibodies that were directed against the protein in a foreign particle, the clover pollen. As a result of the combination of the antibody with the body's protein, the affected organ becomes inflamed and the autoimmune disease pattern follows. The goal of the Exploration, then, in these disorders, is to investigate the emotion that the mind associates with each attack or exacerbation of symptoms. This emotion is often anger. Deconditioning consists of imagining, during deep relaxation, past events and future ones without such anger. A case that demonstrates this is that of Maria.

Maria was born out of wedlock and was cared for entirely by her alcoholic mother. Her mother lived on credit, and there were frequent and sudden moves from town to town and county to county whenever the creditors got too close. Maria was quite dependent on her mother, who was the only constant figure in her life. She never went to school, partly because of the incessant moving, and partly because her mother did not want there to be any records by which she, the mother, might be traced.

When Maria reached the age of eleven, she was becoming a very attractive young woman, and her mother began offering her as a prostitute in bars. Although Maria intensely disliked this, she had never been permitted to say no to her mother, and she felt she had no choice. Her dependency was kept complete—she was not allowed to make phone calls, handle money, or even take the bus alone.

The symbiosis grew tighter and tighter as the years passed. Maria felt intensely ashamed of herself, and ashamed of what she was doing with her body. Her anger and rage at her mother was present, but could never be expressed. As a result it all turned inward, and Maria felt helpless, hopeless, depressed, and inadequate. Her body and her mind, however, found a way out of this impasse.

At the age of twenty-five, two things began to happen. Maria began to gain weight and became less and less attractive. She also began to develop strange muscle pains throughout her body. The combination of her increased weight and the inflammation of her muscles totally immobilized her, and she was capable only of lying in bed. Physicians verified the fact that she had a serious collagen disease and was creating antibodies to her own bodily tissues.

On previous occasions when Maria had attempted to put some distance between her and her mother, by going out on a date or by attempting to develop a friendship with someone, her mother would "have an accident." This would consist of lacerating her arm with a carving knife, falling off a ladder, or tripping and tumbling down a flight of stairs. She would then tell Maria that it was her fault. This would give rise to guilt, and Maria would abandon any plans that she had made on her own behalf and stay home to care for her mother. Now, however, her unconscious mind and her body had found a solution. She could not go to the bars with her mother, her mother could not have an accident, she did not have to face the cruel world alone (remember, she had had no schooling whatsoever), and the symbiosis could be maintained.

When I first saw Maria, she was thirty-eight years old and was still living with her mother. They were both working as domestics on a large estate. Maria was still suffering from flare-ups of the autoimmune disease, and was still afraid of separating from her mother. During our work together Maria learned to put herself into a state of relaxation and enjoy positive imagery. The tape recordings that we made she kept secret from her mother, and by using them was able to diminish the frequency and severity of her attacks, and to shorten those that did occur.

She began to understand the meaning of individual responsibility, and in the course of time Maria found her first boyfriend, and after careful consideration of the consequences moved away from her mother. Her mother promptly dropped a large trunk on her foot, shattering several of the bones. Following this, Maria suffered a brief flare-up of the autoimmune disease, but this was something she had already worked through in imagery. She did not move back in with her mother, but visited her from time to time.

Maria's story is typical of my patients with an autoimmune disease in her feelings of intense self-anger and helplessness. This state of affairs is usually present for many years before the signs of the disease begin to develop. The more years that the negative pattern has been present, the more emotional investment there is in the disease process, and the more areas of the individual's life have become connected to it. Thus although we may understand the mechanism by which the physical problem developed, many months or years might be necessary to decondition and write a new script. Thus far, although the results of using deconditioning, deep relaxation, and imagery have been promising, my experience with these problems has been of a short-term nature. Although improvement has occurred, perhaps a total resolution would require a more intensive course of therapy and a total change in way of life. Whereas in many diseases only a few specific types of events can trigger their onset, the more chronic a disease the larger the number and type of stresses that can trigger it, and the more therapy the individual needs.

Tumors and Cancer

Some of the most tragic stories one will ever hear in medical practice are those of cancer patients and their families. Unfortunately, the tragedy is often the result of the impact on people's lives not only of the disease but also of the treatment, as well as the failure of the current medical model to deal with preventive factors and emotional issues.

Although even the most conservative groups acknowledge that at least 80 percent of our cancers are premature and could be prevented by eliminating smoking, adopting a healthier diet, and avoiding certain exposures to radiation and cancer-producing hydrocarbons. In fact, in 1987, the New England Journal of Medicine published results of two studies indicating that women who consumed three to six alcoholic drinks per week experienced a 30 percent to 60 percent increase in likelihood of breast cancer.

Still, the notion of teaching people to care for themselves and to prevent these cancers seldom receives more than lip service from the orthodox medical practitioner. Instead, the overwhelming bulk of money and attention expended in the field of cancer is directed toward treatment. And as many cancer patients will tell you, the treatments are often as bad as the disease—extensive surgery to remove the cancer and all lymph nodes to which it has spread, radiation and x–ray treatment, which can burn and destroy normal tissue, and metabolic poisons, which poison not only the cancer cells but also many of the body's healthy cells. And because, with the exception of surgery, none of these treatments is expected to actually produce a cure, no matter how grisly was the last treatment, the cancer patient generally feels he or she has only two options for the future: an even more unpleasant course of treatment or death.

It has been said that when the only tool you have is a hammer, you tend to treat everything like a nail. Similarly, when the kind of medicine you have developed is designed to attack invaders (such as bacteria and bullets) the same logic is carried over to the treatment of cancer.

Although there is some theoretical support for the belief that at least some cancers may be triggered by viruses, what we do know is that in all cases of cancers the cells that cause the problem are cells from the patient himself or herself. Whatever the etiology may be, the final common pathway for the disease is that the normal rate of growth is changed and the healthy destruction of abnormal cells is inhibited in some way. As a result, large masses of cells are formed and appear as benign or malignant tumors.

Ordinarily, in nearly every organ of the body, cells are constantly dividing, producing new cells. Simultaneously, other cells are being destroyed as they grow older. This balance is also maintained by other, poorly understood factors, such as contact phenomena, in which the presence of a certain number of cells seems to inhibit the formation of new cells.

When we examine the cells of a tumor beneath the microscope, we find that they appear quite different from normal body cells. These changes are even more marked if we are dealing with a malignant tumor. The drawings on page 242 will give you an idea of some of these differences. These abnormal cells seem to ignore the usual rules, the normal cellular structure is lost and there appear to be no restrictions on their growth.

The appearance of abnormal cells is not, however, a rarity in anyone's life. Each day, of the hundreds of thousands of new cells that appear in our bodies, a certain percentage are abnormal and are destroyed by the body, either through its immune mechanisms or through the action of phagocytic cells. Thus, as many investigators believe, we may be producing many potential cancerous cells each day.

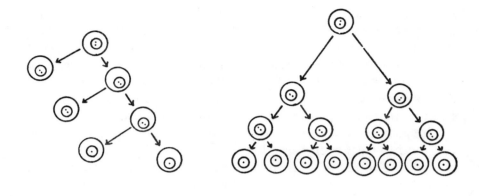

NORMAL   **MALIGNANT**

Only one cell re-divides   *All cells re-divide*

What leads to the breakdown in the controls that usually limit the rate of reproduction of cells? What paralyzes the body's ability to recognize these abnormal cells? Why is it that the body, which is capable of recognizing and identifying the difference between such infinitesimally small particles as molecules of clover and rose pollen, fails to recognize the rather obvious differences between tumorous and nontumorous cells, even though this difference is often obvious, even to the inexperienced eye, when viewed through the light microscope?

As we mentioned before, the development of the body proceeds gradually from fertilization, and the development of each organ and each cell of the body is closely associated with nerves and nervous discharges. We might, then, suppose that the coherent information traveling down the nerves maintains a coherently growing and functioning set of organs. We might also imagine that certain kinds of incoherent patterns, when they become closely associated with a particular organ, might produce a breakdown in these normal control mechanisms. This would allow the abnormal cells to multiply seemingly undetected by the body, in much the same way that any other unwanted symptom, habit, or emotion might become firmly ingrained in a person's mind without the person's being able to do anything about it.

I have had an opportunity to work with many people who had tumors of various types. Because of the long natural course and the possibility of sudden appearance and disappearance of this kind of problem, it is difficult to draw any firm conclusions at this point, though the response to Selective Awareness Exploration seems to be beneficial indeed.

The most significant traits that seem to be common to these people are:

1. Very high degree of intellgence and/or imagination.

2. A strong, often uncontrollable, fear of death, or fear of loss of love.

3. A strong mind–body connection (although it may be totally unconscious).

4. Frequent experiences characterized by inwardly directed anger (guilt, depression).

5. Often multiple frightening dreams and nightmares during the year or so prior to the discovery of the tumor. (Other researchers note, similarly, that a large number seemed to have a devastating emotional trauma the year or so prior to the development of the cancer.)

6. Frequently, a history of fear associated with an altered state of consciousness such as anesthesia, drug usage, dreams, or emotional trauma to the nervous system.

My feeling about these diseases is that their appearance may often follow a breakdown in the usual defense mechanisms, much as I believe a breakdown in defenses may be the predisposing function in a viral or bacterial infection. Indeed, many investigators feel that many cancers are themselves viral in nature.

This breakdown in defenses seems to occur due to tremendous fear, which is present while the attention is focused on a particular organ of the body. It seems as though the mind-body complex may actually attempt to ignore the existence of one of its organs. As a result, the organ may be free to grow unhindered by the control processes that would be present if the body were "aware" of its presence.

The cancerous process then, may be viewed as dependent upon several factors including:

1. Genetic factors (some tumors seem to run in families).

2. The presence of irritants (such as tobacco smoke).

3. The presence of certain viruses.

4. The reaction or nonreaction of the body to abnormal cells produced through the above factors.

5. The effectiveness of the removal of abnormal cells through medical treatment such as surgery, radiation, or chemicals.

Support for the theory that the person's mental state may be partially responsible comes from recent research such as that of Dr. Carl Simonton in Texas, and the Cancer Education and Support Center in California, which report excellent results by combining deep relaxation techniques, imagery, emotional releasing, and group support with traditional therapy. Other experimenters have found that tumors often become smaller and may disappear when simple hypnotic suggestions are used. Another study was performed in which a group of women with abnormal Pap smears of the cervix were divided into two sections. One group was told that their Pap smears were improving, the other group that their Pap smears were showing an increased abnormality. When Pap smears were taken a few weeks later, it was found that the women who were told they were doing worse actually showed more malignant cells under the microscope, whereas the women who were told they were improving showed improvement or no change. (The experiment was immediately discontinued, of course.)

Dr. Howard Miller, working in New Jersey, has published a report showing marked improvement of patients with cancers of the cervix and uterus following simple hypnotic suggestion. (All these women had previously refused surgery.) Cervical cancer is present more frequently in women who have early and frequent sexual relationships, perhaps related to the emotional aspects of this socially tabooed activity. Uterine cancer is more prevalent in women who have borne no children, almost as though the body felt it necessary to have something present in the uterus in the absence of the normal fertilized egg.

The chance of finding cancer cells in the bowel of a person with ulcerative colitis increases on the average, at the rate of 3 percent for each year in which the disease is active and severe, and ulcerative colitis is widely accepted as directly dependent upon psychological factors. This risk of tumor formation disappears if the disease is halted. The tension associated with bowel function, toilet training, and cleanliness in our culture might help to explain the generally high incidence of rectal tumors and cancer.

Two of the most important locations of primary cancer lesions are the prostate gland in the male and the mammary gland in the female, both of which are organs closely related to the sexual system, the source of many anxieties in our culture. One might even speculate that those heavy smokers who get lung cancer may be the ones who inhale at the time of high emotional tension and fear.

Further evidence to suggest mind–body relationships are found in a recent study showing that children who develop leukemia seem to show a higher-than-average incidence of the loss of a beloved family member during the first two years of life (during the time that the thymus gland, a respository for white cell development, is present). Coherency Theory gives an excellent way of explaining these various phenomena. The limitation of cell growth and the destruction of abnormal cells is a function of the organism as a whole and is probably also at least partially under the control of the central nervous system. We might view the essence of this control as related to the genetic picture of the organ and its cell but, as in the other disorders discussed, dependent upon many other factors, including learned patterns. Even as a breakdown in coherency can render an organ susceptible to viral disease (such as mononucleosis, which is related to psychological factors as well as to the virus believed to cause Burkitt's lymphoma), it may also perhaps, predispose to the development of groups of abnormal cells.

In the same way, as a person may have obvious psychological "blind spots," as in the case of a person with severe temper problems or the alcoholic who seems unable to recognize that he or she has a problem, the obviously abnormal cells may develop a physical blind spot. Perhaps research in the next few years will prove that persons with these tumors can learn to strengthen their resistance and perhaps even eliminate the process all together through the methods of meditation, hypnosis, deep relaxation, and Selective Awareness.

I am the first to admit that this aspect of the Coherency Theory is by far the most speculative, yet the correlations and mounting evidence certainly indicate a certain consistency. I would, however urge caution to those who, trained in conventional medical views, would scoff at these ideas without careful research. The history of modern medicine is already scarred by too-hasty rejections of innovative ideas by the conventional medical establishment. Medical science's initial rejection of Pasteur's germ theory and Lister's sterile techniques are but two examples!

Further, my suspicion that there is a significant blind spot regarding cancer is well supported by my experience as the medical director of the Cancer Support and Education Center in California. In spite of the clear evidence of the improved quality of life of these patients and their improved ability to withstand treatment, only a minority of the physicians in our area refer patients regularly. Indeed, physicians who don't make the time to investigate approaches that offer relief to their patients simply because the approaches are slightly unfamiliar may well lack the caring to explore other perspectives that hold promise of improved healing. Many techniques that make use of healing factors available within patients themselves have indeed shown great promise both clinically and in the laboratory. (Dr. Stephen Locke of Harvard University has published a review of 3,000 scientific articles that address these issues— *Psychological and Behavioral Treatments for Disorders Associated with the Immune System*, published by the Institute for the Advancement of Health, 1986.)

The approaches suggested here provide a valuable alternative to the present hopelessness and inadequacy of the merely palliative medical techniques that have not been measurably altered in decades. Here, again, the cornerstone is the elimination of useless fear.

Dentistry and Oral Diseases

The applications of relaxation techniques and deprogramming of previous frightening dental experiences by patients has been well explored. The expectation of pain and discomfort will only decrease the ability to comfortably handle an experience with a dentist and will tend to leave the person open to complications and delayed healing. Using Exploration, deconditioning, and positive visualization techniques should be simple for you in view of what you have learned thus far.

In addition, suggestions of anesthesia of the appropriate sections of the mouth will greatly reduce the need for pain medication. Consulting the section entitled "Surgical Diseases and Surgery" earlier in this chapter should provide help for you if you are expecting to have dental work done. Many dentists are schooled in hypnotic techniques and will be happy to assist you by giving you appropriate suggestions, perhaps in combination with analgesics and nitrous oxide.

After inducing the relaxed state, you may wish to visualize your teeth as blocks of wood and your gums as being frozen numb; any other images you associate with numbness may be used instead.

Disorders of One's Way of Life

Psychological factors are often obvious in diseases that develop as a result of an individual's haunts and habits. As modern technological medicine makes us safer and safer from the complications of trauma and communicable diseases, people are living long enough to suffer the consequences of an unhealthy and immature way of life. Thus, instead of polio, our wards fill with the complications of obesity—hypertension, cardiovascular disease, hyperlipedimia, heart failure, and orthopedic problems. Instead of being centers for the treatment of tuberculosis, medical wards are filled with people suffering from the results of tobacco smoking: lung cancer, emphysema, chronic bronchitis, cancer of the larynx, and peripheral vascular disease. People who have chronically used alcohol to solve their emotional problems contribute cases of liver disease to the medical wards and cases of nerve and spinal cord disease to the neurology wards.

These are obvious complications of an improper way of life. Yet we can add to this list other disease processes a little less obviously connected to maintenance of a healthy way of life. Among these are cardiovascular problems, including heart attacks and the complications thereof, which are more prevalent among those who do not do aerobic exercise. We can also say that many gastrointestinal disorders are the result of years of ignoring the body's need for regular deep relaxation—living continually under great stress with no relief sets up the conditions for hypersecretion of gastric acid, muscle spasm, and the other precursors of gastrointestinal disease. Even the majority of people sick, injured, and hospitalized as the victims of "accidents" are generally there because someone lost control of a car or their temper. The pressures of the world, stress, and the resulting distraction and irrational reactions are at the base of most accidents.

We could extend the list on and on—failure to develop a mature way of life based on the principles of self-care is as foolish as not maintaining an airplane. Indeed, it would make a great deal of sense to develop a personal checklist to be used like the pilot uses a checklist before taking off. The list might be divided into four major categories, with numerous subdivisions under each (according to the way of life you wish to develop).

1. *Deep relaxation/Meditation/Imagery*—Experiences of these should occur at least once daily. They are important for unstressing, charting one's life course, clearing the mind of unnecessary thoughts, enhancing creative potential, facilitating healing, self-exploration of attitudes, developing opinions, formulating plans, and so on.

2. *Movement/Exercise*—Moving the body is essential for maintaining mind, body communication, and physical good health. It should include several different varieties designed to accomplish specific functions: slow stretching (for example, yoga, joggers' stretching for flexibility), aerobics (based upon heart rate and designed to maintain cardiovascular reserve, for example, swimming, jogging, dancing), movement that emphasizes being in

the flow of life (for example, t'ai chi, aikido, improvisational dance, which develop a gracefulness that carries over into other aspects of one's life), and rhythmical movement (for example, t'ai chi, slow dance, Feldenkrais). The body is like a self-sharpening razor—it will maintain itself if it is operated in the proper fashion on a regular basis.

3. *Nutrition*—One should eat enough, but not too much of, the proper foods. This subject is too vast to be covered here, but here are a few guidelines. Special care must be used in the consumption of refined starches and sugars, foods that give empty calories and may cause emotional instability in some people.

   Animal fat and saturated fat have been shown to be harmful to cardiovascular health, and should form only a small portion of one's intake. Charred meat and other foods cooked at high temperature seem to set the stage for cancer. Fiber, cruciferous vegetables (cauliflower, broccoli, Brussels sprouts, cabbage), fish oils, and legumes (beans, peas) seem to promote good health, and should make up a sizable proportion of one's diet.

   Foods are best digested and processed by the body when meals are eaten according to a schedule. Fasting may be useful for some people.

4. *Ecology/Environment/Relationships*—Because our thoughts, emotions, behavior, and health are dependent upon our internal images, and because these images result from our interaction with the people, objects, and events in our environment, this category is a most important one. Wellness is promoted by an environment that is supportive both physically and personally. A rewarding community life and a trusted circle of friends with whom one can feel free and cared for and supported is as important as the ability to frequently experience the beauties of nature. Close relationships that are open, honest, sharing, and loving do a great deal to promote a sense of inner calm and belonging that stimulates positive feelings and a love of life.

Deep relaxation and imagery can be used to implement the preceding habits—it's like rewriting your own script. It's best to work on one category at a time. Develop positive exercise patterns by deeply relaxing and enjoying in imagery regular exercise, and then wait until this new habit is established before shifting to imagery designed to change eating habits. Remember, we are dealing with patterns that have existed for many years; change therefore will be gradual.

CHAPTER 13

Wellness, Self-Care, and Optimal Performance

I n our culture we tend to think of health in a negative way. We define it as the absence of any signs of disease. When symptoms arise we tend to seek treatment for them, and when they disappear we feel there is no further need for the care of our health.

Popular interest in self-care, fitness, and wellness is a new phenomenon in our culture. This new focus bespeaks a growing awareness that there are things that we can do, mentally, physically, emotionally, and spiritually, that will help us produce a higher resistance against problems in these areas and provide us with a reserve of energy that will help us perform at our peak. As we have already observed, how we image ourselves can inhibit or enhance the healing of a disease process. Once signs of disease have disappeared, however, the same principles of relaxation and imagery can be used to facilitate personal growth, self-actualization, and development of a way of life that enhances our wellness and our happiness.

Our goal, then, should not be to keep ourselves from becoming sicker than average, but of being more well than average. Rather than trying to avoid delayed healing of a wound, we should aim at healing faster than average. Rather than trying to avoid complications of a bad cold, we can aim our imagery toward healing the infection faster than others around or to resist catching the cold.

Heal faster than normal? Isn't normal about the best we can hope to achieve?

In answer to this question, I offer a metaphor. For many years it was widely accepted that humans could not run a mile in fewer than four minutes. Then one day, to everyone's surprise, one man did what was beyond normal. Roger Bannister broke the four-minute mile and collapsed from the strain as he crossed the finish line.

This was a first, but only a first. Normal had been redefined, and through the expansion of their awareness of what was possible more than 15 men ran the mile in less than four minutes during the following year!

Nowadays it is not unusual to see a person shave several seconds off the four-minute mark and then jog a lap around the track to cool down slowly.

Can a change in our awareness really speed up the healing process beyond normal? If so, how can such a phenomenon be explained?

How can a broken limb, which ordinarily takes six weeks to heal, be mended in four weeks or less? How can a person recover more than twice as rapidly from an operation and still develop a scar that is much smaller than someone who does not know these methods?

We earlier discussed the fact that we have a clear image of our bodies and other facts about ourselves in our minds. We discussed the fact that our bodies and other properties about ourselves can be altered merely by altering the image in our minds. We have also experienced that spot in the middle of our heads at which we feel most free from any outside concerns. We have imagined ourselves as projecting outward from that point through our image out to our bodies, which then imitate whatever is programmed into the image, in the same way as the image on a screen is formed by a projection from a slide.

In Selective Awareness we have an excellent tool for focusing our awareness. Our awareness can be focused on that image in our minds. Instead of being aware of our entire body, we can become aware of just one part of our body, as though we were illuminating only that part—as though we were projecting only that part of our body on a screen. We can imagine that if we have a disease in that part of our body, or if it has been injured or operated upon, that it needs an extra supply of coherent images, or information. We can imagine that we flood the area with coherent discharges, open all the gates to coherent information. We may imagine that the incoherent information which may have been present in the organ or in the nervous pathways leading to it, is pushed out of the way and replaced by health-giving coherent information.

The sources of harmful, incoherent patterns are numerous. Have you ever seen a person accidentally injure himself or herself, for example, striking a thumb with a hammer, and then swear at the injured part or at the hammer? Perhaps an impatient oath or criticism ("Oh, what an idiot I am!") is uttered almost automatically. This, together with the pain of the accident and the brain's awareness of the injury, serves to create (or sustain) a negative program involving this part of the body. Thus, until the injury is completely healed, there will be an incoherency in the very discharges needed to resolve the injury. As you might expect, such injuries heal more slowly. This kind of attitude toward a temporarily disabled organ tends to produce the same type of pattern as was true of the war veteran, previously discussed, whose leg failed to heal well after amputation.

Less detrimental to healing, but still important, are the usual tension and fear responses to an injury. A person who receives a shock while fixing a lamp usually jerks the hand away with a force and speed far out of proportion to the intensity of the jolt itself. The person who inadvertently steps on a tack demonstrates a similar tendency to overreact. This unconscious withdrawal response is actually adaptive, for an instant. If we add an image of negative expectation to this, however, we may produce a maladaptive physical response.

An example of this is the pianist who injures a thumb and immediately thinks, "Oh, no! If this is still sore on Saturday, I will probably give a poor performance and lose my scholarship!" In such cases, the fear may well slow the healing through the incoherency it promotes. Even if the imagined consequences are not realistic, this thinking is maladaptive because it can slow healing.

No matter how small the degree of tension, healing is better served by immediately inducing relaxation and coherency. The brick-layer who is hopping about on one foot, groaning in pain, is responding maladaptively. He should immediately sit or lie down and induce a state of relaxation, especially in the injured part. He should experience the pain impulses simply as a signal that there has been an injury, and try not to tense up against them. He should picture that part healing rapidly. All fear should be eliminated, by showing the unconscious that it is OK for the entire body to be relaxed. The awareness that proper treatment will be given, that the danger has passed, that the time has come for healing, rather than tension and withdrawal, will allow him to relax the body.

Of course if immediate first aid is necessary, such as for the controlling of bleeding, this should be accomplished followed by a relaxation induction. A few minutes later further examination and treatment can be carried out. In other words, *restore relaxation and coherency as soon as practical.*

You might wonder, "How, in the presence of acute pain, can anyone relax? Isn't that hard?" By *hard,* you mean that there's a natural tendency toward tension that follows an injury, and that to relax in the face of it requires work. But this kind of work is the very *essence* of deconditioning and positive programming. It's like fighting your way upstream, but you will be successful if you are powered by your rational reasoning, recognizing that the current you are fighting is just the flood of incoherent patterns that might otherwise slow your recovery. The conscious work you do in relaxing, not tensing yourself in response to the injury, serves to speed up the unconscious healing processes in the same way that pedaling a bicycle uphill enables you to later coast rapidly downhill. In other words, the work will pay off—try it!

Some people carry their maladaptive reactions to extremes, and may spend the entire next week crying the blues, telling everyone they meet of their misfortune. This is an escape mechanism the unconscious uses to enlist the sympathy, friendship, and attention of others for secondary gain, *but it intensifies incoherency.* How much more rational it is, in light of this fact, to be aware that other options exist, and say, concerning your injury, "Oh, yes, I bruised my toe yesterday, but it's nothing significant. In fact, it seems to be getting better already." How much more sensible this is than saying, "I really smashed my foot yesterday!" In fact, if you tell many people about it, then you are actually benefiting from the disease—it gives you something to talk about. You wouldn't tell other people if the telling didn't give you some kind of pleasure. If you do, your unconscious may figure that the injury is valuable (because it gives you some pleasure) and actually *retard* the healing or see to it that other injuries occur!

Probably the most effective thing to do during the days following an injury is to experience deep relaxation and healing imagery several times a day. This will serve to mobilize the body's proper responses. (See cassette #16, "Healing Journey," Appendix p. 288.)

The results of this approach are well demonstrated by the woman who, following delivery, walks comfortably back to her room in spite of the fresh sutures in the vaginal area; the man who recovers from complicated surgery without needing pain medication; and the emergency room patient who, with minimal anesthesia used, experiences rapid healing, with no infection, after having a laceration sutured.

The method is simple. First allow your mind to become totally quiet, and then begin to bring in the pertinent part of your body on the screen in your mind. As it comes in more and more clearly, you'll notice that you can feel the disease and experience it, in fact, you'll see that the disease is dimming the image. As you let the image grow in intensity, begin to illuminate this part of your body with health and let the unhealthy shadow fade away. As you do this, you will tend to restore a coherent neural flow to this part of the body, allowing it to respond at maximum speed and capacity.

I have had the opportunity to personally use this approach on a number of occasions. Once I contracted a severe case of laryngitis. I was scheduled to speak on a radio show that night, and so I listened to a tape of a self-healing process a few hours before going to the radio station, envisioning myself speaking to the audience with my normal voice. I found, as the radio show began, my laryngitis cleared up completely, and stayed clear for the remainder of the show. Then, as soon as the show concluded, my hoarseness returned. This tendency for the body to interpret images in a literal fashion is an important one to remember (in my image I had pictured myself speaking normally *on the radio*).

On another occasion I was injured playing basketball and was hardly able to walk. I knew that I had a hematoma (internal bleeding into the tissue) in one of my muscles, and had learned from previous experiences that it generally takes several weeks before this problem disappears. I used the "Coherency" healing imagery twice over the next twelve hours to limit any damage and to begin the restoration of normal neural impulse flow. I found that the following day my leg felt the way it usually feels after a week, and within several days it was completely better. Many others have had similar results with this method.

To visualize how positive imagery affects the physical response, imagine a guitar, piano, or other instrument upon which a chord can be played. Imagine that some of the strings are out of tune. Even if our hands are in the right position, even if we are truly expert at playing the instrument, the fact that the strings are out of tune will cause the resulting sound to be far less harmonious (indeed, even painful to our ears) than it would be if the instrument were properly tuned. On the other hand, when the instrument is in tune and a chord is played, there is a particular harmonious quality to it.

Incoherent neural impulses may be thought of as a sort of disharmonious chord, whereas the normal neural impulses to an organ are in special harmony, the harmony required for perfect functioning of that particular organ. As you imagine sending coherent information to the organ you wish to heal, think of the neural impulses going there as gradually beginning to form a chord. Pretend that your mind is tuning the nerves going to that organ, just as one might tune a guitar. By using this image, you enable the unconscious to make the correct adjustments and changes to bring about the necessary alterations.

Of course there's nothing sacred about the metaphorical images that I suggest. You might instead imagine coherent neural impulses as being clear white light. Or it may be more effective for you to imagine a clear stream of water, or a warm wave of energy. In general, whichever images come easiest to you and you are most easily able to experience are the best ones to use. Remember, it is unlikely that we will ever be able to fully understand the means by which the human body accomplishes its remarkable feats; our attempt here is just to develop some imagery that can help conceptualize the healing process and let go of the disease process, thus facilitating positive change.

You might find that an amazingly rapid healing occurs, one in which only a matter of hours elapses between your awareness of a disease in, or injury to, an organ, and its resolution. For most problems, however, particularly chronic diseases and problems that involve the breaking of the skin, as in cutting oneself, days or weeks may be needed to bring about a complete healing. During this time it is preferable to repeat the healing imagery process a number of times using the images of the coherency theory. Imagine that each time this is done, the healing will be accelerated even further. In situations involving broken bones, it's a good idea to repeat this imagery at least three times a day. The fracturing of the bone usually means a certain period of immobility at the outset, which provides an excellent opportunity to focus healing attention on the injured part.

Coherency Healing Imagery

Of course the ideal time to experience healing imagery is when a part of the body needs to be healed. But if you have no need at present to perform a self-healing, just imagine an injury, perhaps one you've had in the past. You can practice with this fantasy ailment now, and use the principles later, if necessary, on a real one. This is simply a form of image rehearsal, do not fear creating a disease, this will not happen if you are using the deeply relaxed state. Having learned the basic principles, they will be available to you whenever needed.

The fundamental purpose is to relax, to experience the body as a cohesive whole (rather than letting fear alienate you from an organ), and then to focus the awareness on that part of yourself most in need of coherency. Accept the present state of that organ and "see" the transformation to health. Finally, imagine the healing has already happened.

EXPERIENCE TWENTY-EIGHT
SOFTWARE FIVE: SELF-HEALING

*Experience the healing imagery that follows, or that on tape 10 or
tape 16 (see the list of tapes on pages 285 and 288). Repeat this
Experience several times in a week so that its principles are understood. The images used are based upon the concept that the coherent
energy that formed your body can be focused by creating your internal
image of the organ becoming healed, then letting the body (which,
after all, has had vast healing experience) allow this to come about
through positive programming. Reinforcement stems from your internal desire to get well fast, and your joy that your body is healing
rapidly.*

*This Experience is based on the kind of healing imagery that has
been used by many cultures around the world for many centuries.*

A. Physical Relaxation

*Begin by being aware of the area or process within your body in
which you wish to facilitate healing. Allow your body to sit or lie
comfortably and let your eyelids close. Allow your eyes to roll upward
behind your closed eyelids, and imagine you can see the word* Relax
*on the inside of your forehead. When you feel your eyelids have
become so relaxed they don't want to open at all, gently test them,
and as you do, let a wave of relaxation flow throughout all the rest of
your body. Feel it flow into the forehead, scalp, muscles of the face,
lips, and jaw muscles. Feel your jaw gently dropping open.*

*Let the relaxation flow down into your neck and your shoulders,
and let it cascade over your back like a cape. Allow relaxation to flow
down your arms to your wrists, your hands, and your fingertips.*

*Take a deep breath in, draw the relaxation up from the tips of your
fingers into the center of your chest, and as you let this breath out,
let it be a feeling of letting go, like a balloon letting out all the air,
becoming completely flat and relaxed. Let the air breathe for you. Feel
the rising and falling of your abdomen with each breath, and let this
rising and falling relax your internal organs.*

With each breath let the air breathe for you. Let the air breathe relaxation to the pelvis, thighs, knees, legs, ankles, and feet, all the way down to the tips of the toes.

You may double this relaxation, if you wish, by opening and closing the eyelids and again sending relaxation from the eyelids throughout the rest of the body. (Three to five minutes)

B. Mental Relaxation

Imagine you are standing at the top of a circular staircase at the edge of a beach. Count from ten down to zero. As you count, imagine you are descending the staircase, walking slowly down and around. Feel yourself going deeper, and any time unnecessary thoughts enter your mind, imagine an ocean wave washes through, erasing the thought like words being erased from the sand. You should feel extremely calm when you reach the count of zero; if not, you may take ten slow steps along the beach, sensing the soft sand and the warm water and letting them relax you. (One minute)

C. Imagery: Healing

Imagine that you can travel down inside your body. You might imagine that your consciousness enters a little submarine about the size of an aspirin. Imagine swallowing the submarine and it shrinking to become so small it can enter your bloodstream. Imagine traveling through your bloodstream to the area of your body in which you wish to facilitate the healing.

You may find other imagery that appeals to you for getting a look at this part of your body. You might imagine that you are riding on a small balloon the size of a molecule of oxygen, and that by taking a deep breath in, you breathe yourself into your body, and travel through the wall of your lung to the part of your body that needs to be healed. Or you may imagine you have inside your body a little television camera that can show you the image of the part of your body you wish to heal. You may use these or any other images to help you form an image of this area of your body.

See the area of your body that needs to be healed, and form an image in your mind of what it will look like when healed. It may be a realistic image—you may form an image of blood vessels, muscles, bones, and so on. Many people, however, choose more symbolic images. A cut may be visualized as a tear in a piece of cloth or a split in the Earth after an earthquake. A cancer may be visualized as an army of invading soldiers dressed in black or as a piece of discolored hamburger meat. A broken bone might be visualized as a cracked piece of pottery. Once again, the image that will be most effective for you, generally speaking, is the one that comes to you most easily while you are relaxed.

Now that you have an image of the disease process in its present state, imagine how the body will look when totally healed (pottery glued together so tightly that it will not break at that point again, all the invading enemy soldiers dead, and so on).

And now imagine a process by which this transformation to health can be visualized to occur. You might imagine an army of soldiers dressed in white shooting and killing the invading army. You might imagine the pottery being glued together with a super glue. If your imagery is realistic rather than symbolic, you might imagine increased blood flow carrying white blood cells and antibodies to an area that needs to be healed. Let your imagination and creativity work for you. This is essential to mobilizing the full healing capacity of the mind. After two or three minutes of visualizing the transformation to a higher level of wellness, again visualize this part of your body as healed. Form an image of yourself in a place you'd like to be, doing something you'd like to be doing, using this part of your body in some way. Choose an image in which you can see clearly that you are totally restored to health. Allow yourself to imagine very strongly that the healing has already taken place, allow yourself to feel a sense of accomplishment. The more strongly you can let yourself feel that the healing is real, the clearer the model presented to the unconscious. (Five minutes)

D. Returning to Your Usual State of Consciousness

Now form an image of yourself several months or years in the future. Imagine yourself looking the way you'd like to look, feeling the way you'd like to feel, and dressed the way you'd like to be dressed. Imagine yourself doing whatever it feels most pleasurable to be doing. Let yourself into this image, allowing yourself to have the mind, the body, the emotions, and the spiritual awareness that you would really like to achieve.

This is the person you really are down deep inside, and each time you allow yourself to see this person, you will become more and more the person you want to be. When you feel relaxed and at home in this image, then you may gradually allow it to disappear and allow your awareness to return to your physical surroundings. Tell yourself that as your eyelids open you will feel completely wide awake, refreshed, alert, and more and more like your true self. Affirm to yourself that it feels good to know that you have taken one more step on the road to maximizing your level of wellness.

It is helpful to repeat this experience (or use tape 16) two or three times a day during the healing process, especially in case of a serious threat to your health. (Two minutes)

CHAPTER 14

Now Open Your Eyes

This book might not have been written had our methods of raising children been evolved in harmony with the way our minds and bodies are constructed and interrelated. We might not need a special state of mind to return to ourselves the capacity for rational thinking; we might not have to eliminate maladaptive responses.

The existence of such patterns within ourselves, and their resistance to our conscious attempts to eliminate them, point up the need for the altered state of consciousness that is reached through Selective Awareness. In fact, because of programming not to relax, many of us may find it difficult at first to produce that comfortable state of relaxation that is our birthright.

As mentioned earlier, the state of mind we have been exploring is a physiological one, one available to every individual. Just as you wouldn't expect to be able to operate a typewriter or computer in a day or two, you should have patience in learning to think and visualize in this fashion. Progress in the world results from rational thinking, and if rational thinking proceeds best during a relaxed state of mind, it then seems only logical that each person should learn how to achieve this state.

Changes that you make in yourself through the use of the approaches we have discussed may be viewed as new options for behavior. You are not forced to continue the new behavior, you can always revert to the old way. You will still be able to choose to lose your temper and punch a hole in the wall. You will still have the option of being afraid in front of a group of people. You will still have the potential to develop an ulcer or heart attack. But now you will have the ability to choose, consciously.

Most people will find it simple to relax under most circumstances after completing the reading and experiences up to this point. Practicing relaxation and imagery several times a day for a few months will make this natural state of mind even more available to you, permanently. Every moment spent in learning these techniques will be repaid a thousandfold. What's more, you'll probably find you need less sleep, and the greater alertness following a period of deep relaxation will allow you to function more efficiently and with more enjoyment.

The final goal of Selective Awareness and induced states of relaxation is not, however, to spend a portion of each day with your eyes closed. Although this is useful for learning to let go of daily stress and tension, you will gradually become familiar with the state of mind and method of thinking. Just as your typewriting speed increases with practice, your speed at reaching the state of relaxation will increase, until you are able to accomplish it in a moment. You will then be able to use it when necessary, and will know the proper time, just as a carpenter knows when to use a hammer.

Ongoing Deprogramming

Maladaptive responses are most efficiently extinguished if we focus on them as they arise. Remember that the unpleasant feeling, the tension, is the energy that keeps these patterns going. Our goal, then, is to release this energy whenever we find it arising. Take the following example:

Bob has been happily shopping for Christmas presents on Main Street. He returns to his car to find that he has been given a ticket for inadvertently parking a foot closer than is legally allowable to a fire hydrant. He begins to feel rage, frustration, and a sense of loss (of $15 to the traffic court).

As these feelings begin to develop, Bob stops and realizes they are unpleasant, unwanted, and not at all helpful. He sits in his car and, before driving off, leans back and closes his eyes. He relaxes his body and clears his mind of all thoughts. He does this because he knows that this emotion, if allowed to persist, could cause him to make other mistakes. Perhaps tomorrow he will forget to lock his office or neglect to make an important phone call. He realizes that the only way to avoid this progression of symptoms is to be rational.

In the relaxed state he allows his unconscious to calmly adjust to the fact that there is no way to avoid paying for the ticket, unless he takes the day off from work to go to court, which is even more costly in terms of time and money, and not likely to succeed. He realizes that to continue feeling frustration about this little piece of paper under his windshield wiper could cause him to have an upset stomach, fail to enjoy his dinner, be unable to relate with his children, and be peevish with his wife.

Instead of frustration, Bob begins to feel triumphant over this little piece of paper that could have sent someone else into an unpleasant state of mind and a useless behavior pattern (even if this just involved retelling the story to seven different friends). He opens his eyes and calmly drives off—whistling.

In other words, as soon as you find an emotion, habit, or symptom that is not helpful to you, your first response should be to relax yourself. Perhaps it will not be as effective as was Bob's relaxation; you might even still feel some of the emotion after opening your eyes. Nevertheless, it will be less than it would have been otherwise, and you will be slowly chipping away at the strength of this general response pattern.

Achieving Rapid Relaxation

The following image may help make it clear how a rapid change of state is possible. Picture a worried father-to-be who is pacing up and down in the waiting room, sweating, trembling, and feeling fear. This is because of chemicals being produced in his body. One of the major chemicals responsible is epinephrine (adrenalin).

If we now picture a man waiting at the finish line of a race at the time his horse wins, we see another reaction, one of total explosive joy. This emotion, too, is dependent upon the release of epinephrine.

Let us imagine that our bodies have within them two kinds of receptors. Let's call one kind negative receptors and the other positive receptors.

We can imagine that the man in the waiting room has his negative receptors open and his positive receptors closed, because this corresponds to the image within his mind. It is an image of fear and possible danger. The epinephrine within his body is triggering these negative receptors, causing the body to produce increasingly negative emotions. Although he is not under any physical threat, though these emotions cannot possibly help him, they may, in fact, be preparing him for even worse repetitions in the future if they persist.

The man at the finish line has his positive receptors open and his negative receptors closed. The same chemical causes him to feel exhilarated and comfortable. These receptors are in these states because of his mental image of the world at this moment.

Though not absolutely physiologically correct, this analogy suggests imagery that may give us a way of changing our feelings when we are experiencing maladaptive emotions. If the mind has the ability to open or close the positive or negative receptors, depending on the image, we can develop a voluntary response pattern to help us when any unwanted emotions arise.

We simply imagine, if we are in an unpleasant frame of mind and experiencing tension, that our negative receptors are open and receiving the epinephrine within our bodies. We become aware that there is an opposite state of mind possible for us if we close these receptors and open our positive ones. Practice the following procedure a few times, then use it as the need arises. As you practice it, take about a minute. When you actually use it to deal with a stressful situation, the entire procedure might take only five or ten seconds.

EXPERIENCE TWENTY-NINE
SOFTWARE SIX: INSTANT RELAXATION

Wherever you are, allow your eyes to find a point opposite you. It might be a flower, the edge of a person's eyeglasses (if you are facing someone), or a point on the horizon. As soon as you find that point, allow everything else within your visual field to grow blurry except that point. Imagine that there is a parallel universe available to you, one almost exactly like the one you're in. Exactly the same people are around you, the weather is the same, you are in the same location. The only difference is that instead of the unpleasant emotion, you have a positive, exhilarated emotion. Although the environment, with its pressures, is the same, you are feeling calm and confident, and you are thinking clearly.

The point you have chosen is a pinhole leading through to that other universe. When you are ready to go to that other universe, allow your eyelids to close and imagine yourself being drawn rapidly forward toward that point.

Imagine that you are shrinking down as you approach it, and imagine that you are going through a funnel. As your eyelids close, feel this happen rapidly and imagine you are becoming too small to hold the unpleasant thoughts that were in your mind. Let them escape and remain in the old universe as you burst through the pinhole.

As you imagine yourself going through the tiny hole, take a deep breath and imagine yourself exploding through on the other side. Imagine yourself having the feeling you get when you hear some tremendously good news—such as receiving a substantial raise in pay. Let that feeling replace all feelings that were present a few moments ago. Let it flow throughout your body. Then open your eyes.

Anyone watching you will be aware only of the fact that you closed your eyes for three or four seconds. He or she would probably be unaware that your eyes happened to focus in one place for ten or twelve seconds. On the other hand, you will find a remarkable thing tends to happen. Suddenly, a solution to the problem may develop, a solution previously hidden by the negative emotion. At the very least, you will have experienced some improvement in your relaxation, an improvement in your ability to handle things in an adult, rational fashion, and you will be moving ever closer to being free of the negative programming that could remove you from the control of your responses. Eventually, you will not have to use this technique; you will have a general control over almost all situations.

As mentioned earlier, the normal state of consciousness of the average person is one in which the conscious mind is filled with a continuous clutter of events past, present, and future. They arrive in the mind in a seemingly random fashion and the mind tries to deal with them as they come up.

While I am washing the dishes, several kinds of thoughts are entering my mind. I am thinking of the next dish to be washed, the temperature of the water, the cleanliness of the dish, and so on. At the same time thoughts of my speech tomorrow night enter my mind. My talk, however, has been well prepared and I have even spent some time visualizing the desired outcome. The thoughts at this time are merely anxious ones, and are useless to me. I decide to use the waking induction. Each time a thought about my speech comes along, *I become aware that I am thinking the thought.* This little maneuver takes my attention off my thought and focuses it on my awareness. I then redirect this awareness to what I am doing. I am giving a dish its final rinsing.

I focus all my attention on the exact details of what I am doing. I feel the warm water running across the surface of the dish, feel its touch on each of the fingers of my hand, and feel how far the dampness extends up my wrists. I rub my fingers over the surface of the plate and try to detect the smallest irregularities, which indicate the presence of residue. I become aware of the exact shape of the dish, of the light coming in the window, and of the light's reflection in the surfaces of each soap bubble in the sink of water. I smell the soap in the steam of the water.

This awareness floods my mind with stimuli from the activity I am performing and completely replaces, momentarily, the unwanted thought. Of course it may return in another form, the worry of whether Ms. Smith will like my presentation. I immediately become aware of this thought and redirect that awareness, this time to the feeling of the dish towel as it glides across the surface of the dish, the colors of the dish towel, the texture of the towel, the temperature of the dish, and the sounds of a car going by outside, allowing each thought to relax me.

Doing this several more times results in that thought leaving, just as surely as if I had erased it by using the counting-down-from-one-hundred method. My mind allows me to erase that thought because it knows I will spend time thinking about it when I am not doing dishes if and when it is appropriate. My unconscious realizes that I do not intend to ignore what it considers to be so important, but that I wish to approach it in a relaxed fashion. Redirecting my attention several times teaches my unconscious that this is what I want it to continue to do, and these thoughts do not arise again. I become aware of all my perceptions of my environment: the feeling of my shoes on my feet, the feeling of my interacting with the dishes, and so on. My actions feel significant, and they keep me in the here and now.

Any repetitive activity that is likely to become boring gives you an opportunity for great growth. If you perform an activity and allow yourself the negative feeling of boredom, you will find that the activity becomes more boring as time goes on. As much as you feel it is necessary to continue to perform this activity (washing dishes, driving, addressing envelopes, watching children, cooking, and so on), these negative emotions will cause it to become more and more painful. But if you use the instant relaxation process, you may erase the thought of other activities your mind was comparing with what you are doing. As you do this, it cannot possibly compare unfavorably and therefore cannot be boring, because *an activity must be boring with respect to some other possible activity.* Nearly any activity, viewed from the proper perspective, can be interesting and relaxing.

In addition, you'll find that during this time of freedom from intellectual thought, during this time of freedom from having to figure anything out (a kind of time that people in our culture experience rarely), the unconscious will be able to work on possible solutions to the problem you have set aside. Later, when you return to it, you may find solutions waiting, just as a temporarily forgotten name returns to you if you relax and think about something else for a while.

Problem Solving, Test Taking, and Learning

This gives us an immediate clue as to how to approach situations in which the memory and calculation abilities of our unconscious are most important. As in other situations, feelings of tension and anxiety will decrease the ability of the mind to perform rationally. (Actually, some motivational pressure is necessary to get the mind to think; the kind we wish to eliminate is the *negative* tension.) During a test this may mean the inability to recall the answer to a question. During learning this may produce doubt; the mind may assume you doubt its ability to learn, and thus may learn ineffectively, so as to live up to your image of it.

If you feel great stress or tension about a problem, your mind, instead of feeling free to enter the problem, explore it, and solve it, may tend to see the problem as an area of fear (it realizes that you feel fear as you bring the problem up, and so may conclude that the solution will be painful). It thus may retreat from the proper solution, perhaps giving rise to further problems to compound the matter.

Whenever I have a significant problem upon which I am unable to focus, one in which the solution is not at all clear, I allow myself to relax and clear my mind of all thoughts. Following this, I merely focus upon the problem as though it were written on the page of a book. I do not allow myself to develop an unpleasant, useless emotion about the problem; I depend upon my internal motivation to provide the energy necessary to solve it. After focusing on the title of the problem and the things I know about it for one minute, I erase the problem from my mind without trying to solve it. As the problem is being erased, I suggest to my mind that it work on some solutions to present to me later. I then visualize myself going through the next five minutes or hour without having to think about the problem (obviously, the time allotted depends upon the situation).

Think of how, when you've forgotten someone's name, you say. "It will come to me," and you focus on something else. Well, exactly the same thing happens here. A little while after the induction, after I have not been thinking about the problem for some time, suddenly the answer pops into my mind—an alternate way of looking at the problem, a piece of needed information for solving the problem, or the realization that more research is needed. In this case the unconscious is treated like a computer; both do their best work when we allow them to operate automatically (like a musician playing an instrument without concern).

Similarly, when I have to learn something or take a test, I make sure I stay completely calm during that period of time. Sometimes I do an induction just before learning, then continue through my learning, focusing my attention, in a relaxed fashion, on what I am doing—in much the way previously described in doing the dishes. The result must be experienced to be appreciated. Try it!

Selective Awareness Compared with Traditional Medicine

I am often asked how I feel about the kind of medicine I learned in medical school. How can I think of using traditional methods of diagnosis and treatment, having discovered the importance of the Coherency Theory and the psychological processes of my patients?

Although the majority of diseases in our culture are produced or aggravated by negative programs, this is not true of all diseases. We may never find a psychological cause or cure for liver flukes or the plague bacillus. We *need* antibiotics.

A fractured arm will still need a cast for proper healing. And even some of those problems that seem to stem directly from psychological causes may still need medical attention. The ulcer may be eliminated in its early stages, but once it has made a hole in the wall of the intestine and the hydrochloric acid is pouring into the abdominal cavity, surgery is necessary.

Many people use the supposed shortcomings of the medical and surgical fields as an excuse to avoid seeing their physicians, although they have symptoms they do not understand. This, of course, can lead to a worsening of the underlying process. A disease that is curable in its early stages may develop to the point where it is no longer so, or complications of the process may ensue. The woman with unexplained soreness in her legs may be able to get along for months with untreated inflammation of the veins, but it would be well for her to have this soreness evaluated by her physician before the possible complication of an embolus (blood clot) to the lung supervenes and changes a temporary problem into a more permanent one.

The fact that most headaches are merely symptoms of negative programs and their resultant tension does not negate the necessity of having a doctor, trained in diagnosing, determine that the headaches are not due to dangerously high blood pressure. Untreated, the elevated blood pressure could give rise to a heart attack or stroke.

Thus medical diagnostic techniques are most useful to assure us that the problem we are working on is indeed approachable through relaxing, unstressing, and internal healing experiences. In fact, generally speaking, you will be unable to adequately relieve symptoms within your body unless the unconscious is convinced that there is no dangerous underlying process being masked or left untreated. It is thus important to find a physician who you trust, both for his medical and diagnostic skills, and for his ability to relate with you as a person. He should be willing to recognize *your* responsibility for your health and be willing to serve as a trusted advisor and consultant.

Treatment with Medication

When the prescribing of medicines is the most appropriate solution to a health problem, I do not hesitate to do so, but I maintain a certain philosophy in regard to them. I view medications merely as aids to the natural healing function of the body. One type of medication, the antibiotic, provides an excellent illustration of this principle.

Your body is in constant battle with microorganisms (bacteria, fungi, and viruses). It attempts to maintain a balance with them. Generally, this means keeping the interior of your body sterile, free of foreign substances. Thus any organisms that manage to get past the barrier of the skin must be quickly gobbled up by the appropriate white blood cells.

The presence of an infection is an indication that this balance has become upset, and the body has begun, in some way, to lose the battle (though not necessarily the war). Thus vaginitis, the common cold, sinusitis, and a boil merely represent the result of:

1. A breakdown in normal defenses because of physical factors, such as injury or a decrease in blood flow, or mental–emotional factors.

   or

2. The body's contact with an organism too powerful for its natural defenses.

Now a steady state no longer exists. The body's secondary defenses are called out as it attempts to isolate the area of infection. If you are to survive, the balance must be shifted in favor of your body. If this is done soon, no permanent disability will result. If this is done too late, then a permanent handicap may be sustained.

The return of the balance and the ultimate victory by your body may take place without any treatment. Perhaps only the normal responses of the body will be necessary, as is true of the usual case of the mumps or measles. Only rest and time may be needed.

Perhaps the restoration of mental and emotional balance will aid in allowing the return of the normal defenses and the elimination of the disease process.

In certain cases medication may be needed to help restore this balance. The treatment of meningitis is one such process. Prior to the discovery of antibiotics, certain forms of meningitis were almost uniformly fatal; they are rarely so these days when antibiotics are properly administered.

The antibiotics, however, don't provide the cure. Only your body can do this. The antibiotics are merely substances that slow the growth of the organism within the body so that the body's own defenses may gain the upper hand. Once this has been done, the antibiotic becomes unnecessary and may be discontinued.

In prescribing medicines, then, we must be careful and judicious. We must be careful that we are not, in doing so, hiding the symptom of some more fundamental process. Attempting to eliminate the headache of high blood pressure by covering up symptoms can produce serious or even fatal consequences, just as the hiding of symptoms by a tranquilizer can cause a worsening of a deeper emotional problem. The person who has chronic acne may be done a disservice if he or she is placed on antibiotics for the infection but never allowed to see that it is a basic feeling of embarrassment and insecurity that caused and maintains the process. Continuous suppression of a vaginal infection by medicines can delay the impetus for a woman to examine an unsatisfactory relationship.

Medications should aid your body, not hide the symptoms of disease. Feel free to express this philosophy to your doctor. Most of the time your doctor will be happy to find someone who feels as he or she does. The majority of his or her patients have been taught that they don't have any part to play in the healing process. They merely want "a shot of penicillin." Sometimes they want it so badly that they threaten to go to another doctor if the first will not give it to them. Let your doctor know that you are interested in playing a part in the healing of your own body. He or she will give you even more hints on how to do this.

A Final Step

As you learn more and more through the use of Selective Awareness, you will find more and more situations in which you can relax, where previously you would have been tense. Because the brain learns better when you are relaxed, your learning speed will begin to increase. And the similarities between yourself and other people will become more and more obvious.

You will begin to see that the problems you experienced are experienced by many other people in only slightly altered forms. You will begin to realize that you live where you live, eat what you eat, and do what you do because of the work of untold numbers of people who have gone before you and left something behind.

You will begin to feel the fundamental rightness of things, and the ideas in this book will take on a deeper, more personal meaning for you. You will be able to express these ideas in your own words and may find yourself doing this more and more often to help others.

Once, while walking down the street, I passed a man who was repairing the engine of his car. He was trying to thread a nut onto a bolt located in a tight corner. Each time he slipped and dropped the nut, he would display frustration and anger. I stopped and watched. When he got to the task of filing down a corner of the engine he found his elbow bumping into the hood, and this gave rise to further frustration and oaths.

I went over to him as he seemed ready to throw his hammer at the windshield, explained that I could not help overhearing him, and suggested he make a single change—that he try smiling each time he made a "mistake." I explained that his mind would thus feel motivated to learn more instead of becoming afraid to try doing the job correctly. I passed that way the next day to find him whistling happily. When he saw me he ran over and heartily pumped my hand up and down, exclaiming that my advice to him had been the best he'd had in years. This had been the first time he'd ever really *enjoyed* working on a car.

As I walked away I looked down at my hand. The palm and fingers were greasy and black from the hand of the mechanic, and I had touched and stained my trousers. Nonetheless, I felt a warm and pleasant feeling inside. I knew that sooner or later I would find some way to remove the grime. In the meanwhile, I figured, each time I saw the dirt on my hand it would remind me that I had helped another human being feel a little bit better.

BIBLIOGRAPHY

Chapter 1 - The Psychophysiological Approach

Kroger, William. *Clinical and Experimental Hypnosis*. New York: J. P. Lippincott Company, 1977.

Describes the use of medical hypnosis, an excellent demonstration of how imagery and deep relaxation can be used in a clinical setting. Filled with specific research references.

Kroger, William. *Hypnosis and Behavior Modification*. New York: J. P. Lippincott Company, 1976.

Locke, Stephen. *Psychological and Behavioral Treatments for Disorders Associated with the Immune System*. Institute for the Advancement of Health, 1986.

Chapter 5 - Tension, Anxiety, and Physical Symptoms

Cannon, W. *The Wisdom of the Body*. New York: Norton, 1967.

Dr. Cannon first described the "fight or flight response" in this book.

Morris, Desmond. *Naked Ape.* **New York: Dell, 1969.**

By looking at the functioning of the various systems of the human body, comparing those to how these systems function in lower animals, we can learn much about how we need to change our responses to today's high-speed environment.

Selye, Hans. *The Stress of Life.* **New York: McGraw-Hill Book Company, 1956.**

The book on stress by the man who invented the word.

Simeons, Albert T. *Man's Presumptuous Brain: An Evolutionary Interpretation of Psychosomatic Disease.* **New York: Dutton, 1961.**

An excellent book showing how the brain, if we do not discipline it to serve us, will make decisions which are not the best.

Chapter 6 - Transforming Tension and Spasm into Relaxation

Benson, Herbert. *The Relaxation Response.* **New York: William Morrow and Company, Inc., 1975.**

This book by a Harvard professor describes the role of relaxation in protecting against and resolving cardiovascular diseases.

Chapter 7 - Positive Imagery: Visualization and Projection

Maltz, Maxwell. *Psychocybernetics.* **North Hollywood, CA: Wilshire Book Company, 1960.**

One of the first books to really approach in a scientific way the manner in which one's thoughts can have an effect on the human biocomputer.

Samuels, M., and Samuels, N. *Seeing with the Mind's Eye.* **New York: Random House, Inc., 1981.**

An excellent book on the use of imagery and visualization.

Sheikh, Anees A. *Imagery: Current Theory, Research and Application.* **New York: Wiley & Sons, 1982.**

Shorr, Joseph. *Psychotherapy Through Imagery.* New York: Thieme-Stratton, **1983.**

Chapter 8 - Maladaptive Patterns (Negative Programs)

Miller, Emmett E., with Lueth, Deborah. *Self-Imagery, Creating Your Own Good Health.* Berkeley, CA: Celestial Arts, 1986.

Satir, Virginia. *People Making.* Palo Alto, CA: Science and Behavior Books, Inc., 1972.

An excellent book to learn better communications using the systems model and family therapy.

Wolpe, J. *Psychotherapy by Reciprocal Inhibition.* Stanford, CA: Stanford University Pess, 1958.

This book was very important in the development of basic Selective Awareness techniques. Describes the functioning of the nervous system and how imagery and relaxation can be used to alter one's responses to the world.

Chapter 10 - A Look at Yourself: The Exploration

Kurtz, Ron, and Prestera, Hector. *The Body Reveals.* New York: Harper and Row 1976.

Using deep tissue massage (Rolfing), Dr. Prestera describes how painful experiences are remembered in the body's musculature, and can be released through massage and imagery.

Chapter 11 - The Coherency Theory

Jaffe, Dennis T. *Healing from Within.* New York: Alfred A. Knopf (Distributed by Random House), 1979.

An excellent book describing the mechanisms and approaches associated with self-healing.

Pribram, K. *Languages of the Brain.* Englewood Cliffs, NJ: Prentice-Hall 1971.

An excellent introduction to the holographic nature of the way the brain works.

Chapter 12 - Emotions and the Diseases They Cause and Cure

Cousins, Norman. *Anatomy of an Illness (As Perceived by the Patient).* New England Journal of Medicine, 1979.

Describes how Dr. Cousins helped to facilitate his own healing through taking charge of his own treatment and using humor.

Cousins, Norman. *Anatomy of an Illness.* New York: Norton, 1979.

Friedman, Meyer, and Rosenman, Ray H. *Type A Behavior and Your Heart.* New York: Knopf, 1974.

This is the book in which Type A behavior and its effect on the cardiovascular system was first described by these two cardiologists.

Locke, Stephen. *Psychological and Behavioral Treatments for Disorders Associated with the Immune System.* Institute for the Advancement of Health, 1986.

Locke, Stephen, and Douglas Colligan. *The Healer Within.* New York: Dutton 1986.

A professor at Harvard Medical School, Dr. Locke has written both of these books about the new field of psychoneuroimmunology. He presents literally thousands of abstracts from the research elucidating the effect of the mind on the immune system.

Pelletier, Kenneth R. *Mind as Healer, Mind as Slayer.* New York: Delacorte Press-Seymour Lawrence, 1979.

Remen, Naomi. *The Human Patient.* Garden City, NY: Anchor/Doubleday, 1980.

Simonton, O. C., Matthews-Simonton, S., and Creighton J. *Getting Well Again.* Los Angeles, CA: J. P. Tarcher, 1978.

An excellent book for patients with cancer, showing how they can, by taking charge of their lives as well as their treatment, help to participate in their return to health.

Chapter 13 - Wellness, Self-Care, and Optimal Performance

Ardel, Don. *High Level Wellness.* Emmaus, PA: Rodale Press, Inc., 1977.

One of the first and best books that describe what high level wellness is and how wellness centers operate.

Dossey, Larry. *Beyond Illness.* Boston, MA: Shambhala, 1984.

Ryan, Regina Sara, and Travis, John W. *Wellness Workbook.* Berkeley, CA: Ten Speed Press, 1981.

Still the best workbook available for learning what wellness is, evaluating your current level of wellness, and initiating change to create a wellness lifestyle.

Smolowe, John S., and Deliman, Tracy. *Holistic Medicine, Harmony of BodyMindSpirit.* Reston, VA: Reston Publishing Company, Inc., 1982.

Chapter 14 - Now Open Your Eyes

James, Muriel. *Born to Win.* Reading, MA: Addison-Wesley Publishing Company, 1971.

Can help you to develop a healthy attitude.

Pelletier, Kenneth R. *Holistic Medicine, from Stress to Optimum Health.* New York: Delacorte Press, 1979.

Software for the Mind Cassettes by Dr. Miller

Let Dr. Miller's voice guide you in developing your own personal programs for bringing your best to life. Since 1972, Dr. Miller has developed and produced the finest and the most highly acclaimed audio and video cassettes for personal development, wellness, and self-care. Discover why these cassettes have remained the first choice of health professionals the world over.

Each of us, whether we are awake or asleep, is continuously recording "mental videotapes" and storing them with a selectivity and speed of retrieval that staggers the imagination. These stored images are the models upon which all our actions and reactions are based.

The essence of Dr. Miller's work is the study of the nature of these "mental videotapes," or images, to determine which are most regularly associated with good health, high-level wellness, and optimal performance.

The tapes listed below present these images, or "programs," through the medium of audio and video cassettes. The Selective Awareness state of deep relaxation is often used to increase the depth of penetration of these models and to provide ongoing stress reduction. Further, it provides a calm space in which to access one's deeper values and personal mission. The resulting self-healing, inspiration, enthusiasm, and sense of wholeness are then integrated into one's mental, emotional, and physical life through effective, yet simple, visioning techniques.

The lapping waves of the Caribbean Sea, birds from mountain meadows, and other nature sounds, along with sensorily rich music and visual images, are used to maximize enjoyment of use. We are certain you will find these programs highly enjoyable, easy to use, and very effective.

To learn and apply the material presented in this book on a deeper, experiential level, Dr. Miller suggests you begin with one or more of the following programs: Power Vision (#650), Healing Journey (#16), Letting Go of Stress (#23), Writing Your Own Script (#202), Health and Wellness (#18), The Ten-Minute Stress Manager (#53), or select one of the programs that focuses on a specific problem you may have. Complete instructions for use of all tapes are included with each program.

To order, or for more information about Dr. Miller's work, write or call:
Source Cassettes
P.O. Box W, Dept. 602
Stanford, California, 94309
1-415-328-7171 - For Information and California Orders
1-800-52-TAPES - For Orders Only (outside California)

A sampler cassette of Dr. Miller's programs is available for $2.00 then redeemable with next order.

EXPERIENTIAL AUDIO CASSETTE LISTING

Stress Management

Letting Go of Stress. This program teaches a logical progression from simple to sophisticated techniques for stress management. It includes methods to help relieve anxiety, tension, and the physical symptoms of stress. #23.
$10.95

The Ten-Minute Stress Manager. Each ten-minute experience is a quick battery charge for executives, students, managers, and homemakers. #53.
$10.95

The Source Meditation. "Opening Gates to Universal Energy - Life, Breath, Creativity, Wisdom." Provides meditations based on Yogic, Zen Buddhist, and other approaches. #42. $10.95

Easing into Sleep. Those who have used it call this tape "the closest thing to a cure for insomnia." Experience a process that melts away restlessness and leads to deep sleep. #20. $10.95

Rainbow Butterfly. To enhance and deepen meditative skill, to help improve a bad day or lighten a mood. Journey through the color spectrum, and the metamorphosis of a butterfly. Help color your future bright and beautiful. #11. $10.95

Behavior Change

Tools for Taking Charge. An introduction to techniques of managing stress energy through deep relaxation, meditation, autogenic training, guided imagery, and Selective Awareness (no music). #10 $10.95

Writing Your Own Script. Eliminate unwanted attitudes, emotions, and habits by replacing negative self-images with exciting new self-concepts for the future. #202. Two Cassettes. $15.95

Smoke No More. Quit or cut down using the simple process that replaces the false relaxation of smoking with techniques for utilizing natural stress energy to create the self-image of a healthy nonsmoker. #221. Two Cassettes. $15.95

Imagine Yourself Slim. This program treats overweight as a symptom, not a cause, and promotes change of self-image and eating habits. Learn to eat only what you need, independent of emotional triggers. #19.
$10.95

Sexual Intimacy: Relaxation and Imagery to Enrich the Experience of Making Love. The experience of making love can be more than merely physical. It can be a richly rewarding emotional, mental, and even spiritual experience. The experience of this kind of sexual intimacy can only be described as magic. Listen—experience it yourself and with a loved one. #52. $10.95

Accepting Change, Moving On. Changes in life, in a relationship—separation, or even death—can be met with acceptance and experienced as positive challenges. You are guided through the process of putting the past to rest and awakening to a brighter future. #48. $10.95

Freeing Yourself from Fear. Fear is the greatest obstacle to personal progress. Some people fear rejection or failure. Some have phobias about people or situations. This program is an antidote for fear, utilizing a powerful step-by-step approach to ensure victory over potentially threatening situations. #338. Three Cassettes. $27.50

Blossoming, Growing Beyond the Limits of Your Family. Designed to help adult children of alcoholics lead more satisfying and productive lives. Developed in conjunction with family therapist David Shearer, this series of eight experiences, selected from Dr. Miller's self-imagery programs, helps to correct the negative impact of growing up in an alcoholic home. Best used in conjunction with individual or group therapy or counseling, this program helps reshape negative thoughts, attitudes, reactions, feelings, and self-image. #400. Four Cassettes. $37.50

Peak Performance

Power Vision. This program provides an excellent introduction to effective techniques of self-relaxation, a step-by-step development of your ability to create mental images and techniques for accessing your power from the past and projecting it forward into the future. Features nearly four hours of fascinating, entertaining, and highly informative lectures by Dr. Miller, as well as six different imagery experiences and a special cassette of music and affirmations for use as you prepare for work (the "Drivetime™" cassette). #650. Six Cassettes and workbook. $49.95

Optimal Performance, Reach for Your Goal. "Go for the Gold!" Whatever your job, profession, hobby, sport, or activity—this cassette can help you become a winner. Learn how champions reach their goals—and how you can do the same. An exciting motivational experience for those who strive for excellence. #54. $10.95

You Deserve to Be Rich. "The Inner Path to Wealth." Become attuned to your deeper values and discover your personal mission. Commit to honest sharing and true wealth will flow to you. Deprogram negative attitudes about money and create a prosperous self-image. #50. $10.95

Healing the Planet. The time is right to share a global vision. Words and music combine for a beautiful inspiring look at our potential as a global human family. On Side Two, a meditation on love as the source of peace. #101. $10.95

Winning at Learning. Accelerated learning, peak performance, test-taking skills, and stress reduction. This program offers powerful aids for those endeavors where retention and retrieval of information is vital—school, business, sports, acting, public speaking. #207. Two Cassettes. $15.95

High Performance Sports. Techniques for using stress energy to achieve your optimal performance. Learn focused concentration and guided imagery skills. Used by competitive and recreational athletes. #228. Two Cassettes. $15.95

Health & Self-Care

Down with High Blood Pressure. Powerful drug-free techniques for controlling high blood pressure. Clinically proven. Change your reaction to life's stressors. #03. $10.95

Healing Your Back. Four Parts—Music and imagery to relax away pain and tension; tracing your symptoms to their source; special morning and evening experiences to keep you well. #05. $10.95

Great Expectations. "The Joy of Pregnancy and Birthing with Techniques for an Easy Delivery." A loving guide through pregnancy. Consistent with Lamaze and other childbirth methods. #30. $10.95

Headache Relief. Powerful techniques for headache relief through tension reduction methods with morning and evening exercises. #12. $10.95

An Answer to Cancer. Based on his work with patients as medical director of the Cancer Support and Education Center, Dr. Miller has created a special version of his widely acclaimed *Healing Journey* cassette. Side One features the popular "Healing Image." Side Two features "Targeting

Your Treatment," which presents special imagery for cancer patients as an adjunct to medical treatment. #29. $10.95

Healing Journey. Learn techniques for active participation in your body's healing process, especially valuable for acute or chronic conditions. #16.
                                                                     $10.95

Successful Surgery and Recovery. Condition the mind and body to achieve maximum benefit and speedy recovery from surgery. Techniques to minimize anesthesia, postoperative swelling, pain, bleeding, and infection. #203. Two Cassettes. $15.95

Health and Wellness. Techniques for reaching high levels of wellness including personal approaches to diet, exercise, motivation, and stress management. Restore balance to your life. #18. $10.95

Change the Channel on Pain. "Managing Pain Successfully." Your mind receives pain messages much like a TV receives a broadcast signal. Using this tape, those with occasional or chronic pain can learn to "change the channel," tune out pain and tune in relief. #46. $10.95

Special Lecture Programs

Self-Hypnosis and Personal Development. Recorded live at the University of California, Berkeley, this has been acclaimed the finest course on the use of self-hypnosis for personal growth offered anywhere. A lively, enjoyable program in which the humor, student participation, and fun have been carefully preserved. Techniques for stress reduction; imagery; using disease as a teacher; neutralizing fear, phobias, and other negative feelings; overcoming obstacles to personal development; cultivating a positive self-image; and writing your own script. #803. Eight Cassettes in a custom case. $59.95

Right Imagery - Wisdom of the East as a Basis for Healing Imagery. Dr. Miller's keynote address to an audience of physicians and other health professionals at the Second International Conference on Eastern and Western Approaches to Healing. He compares his experiences of Eastern disciplines with their focus on "being" with the Western emphasis on "doing," which is a fundamental cause of stress. #CL-1. $10.95

Achieving Mastery. Health professional seminar, recorded live. Using the Selective Awareness approach, Dr. Miller teaches powerful techniques for application in your daily practice and in your life. Included are practical perspectives and skills for supporting true healing, the integration of mental, emotional, physical, spiritual, and social aspects at the highest level. #CL-2. Eleven Cassettes in a custom case. $75.00

Healing Imagery and Personal Transformation—*Deep Relaxation, Imagery, and Selective Awareness; Techniques for Health Professionals.* A training in the principles of human healing and wholeness. Focuses on the individual and families that present primarily with a physical symptom. #CL-3. Nine Cassettes in a custom case. $59.00

Letting Go of Dis-Ease. An interview with Dr. Miller by Michael Toms of the New Dimensions radio show on the meaning of healing and the body as a "symptom." #ND-1. $10.95

Awakening the Healing Within—*1986 Lectures at the Cancer Support & Education Center.* Dr. Miller shares his twenty years of clinical experience supported by the latest research in psychoneuroimmunology. Topics include the power of awareness and attitude, healing imagery, self-expression and the immune system, and the role of faith. #229. $15.95

EXPERIENTIAL VIDEOS

A beautiful sequence of visual images has been developed with the award-winning cinematographer Glen Carroll.

Dr. Miller's soothing voice and a stereophonic high fidelity soundtrack welcome the viewer to a gently flowing montage of nature images . . . rippling streams, crashing surf, golden hills, and peaceful sunsets. This sequence, "Watervisions," provides the visual portion of the following video cassettes. Each contains skillfully chosen narration to create the inner experience suggested by each title. Available in VHS and Beta (additional charge for ¾" format).

Relation and Inspiration. Discover how quickly you can let go of stress. Dr. Miller guides you to a deeper inner awareness of peace, inspiration, power, and healing. Excellent for a 15-minute midday mini vacation, or use the entire 25 minutes (the final 10 minutes feature gentle music and visuals only) to unwind at the end of a busy day. Soothing both as a participatory experience and as a background piece that turns your television into a work of art. #944 - 25 min. $24.95

INDEX

(A)

activities (programs), 29–31
adrenalin, 266
age regression, 24, 157–159
allergies, 208–213
American Medical Association, 19–20
American Society of Clinical Hypnosis, 20
analytical thinking, 43
animal magnetism, 8, 18
antibiotics, treatment with, 272–274
antihistamine, 211
anxiety, 57–74
    defined, 57–58
autoimmune diseases, 236–240
autonomic nervous system, 136, 186–187
    self-induced programs in, 187–188
avoidance response, 130
awareness, states of, 40–44

(B)

Bannister, Roger, 252
blood/blood vessels
    emotions and, 190–191
    spasm of, 68–69
    See also heart; high blood pressure

(C)

cancer, 240–246
cardiovascular system. *See* blood/blood vessels; heart; high blood pressure
chemical changes, conscious control of, 8–11
chest, spasm in, 64–66
Christian Science Church, 2
chronic diseases, 217
civilization, disease and, 72–73
coherency, 4
    healing imagery, 257–261
    See also incoherency
Coherency Theory, 185–202
concentration, passive, 43
conditioned stimulus, 94
conscious mind, exploring, 27–38
contractions. *See* muscles; pain; spasm; tension
cortisone, 211
critical thinking, 43
cybernetics, 92

(D)

data (information), 28–29
daughter cells, 193
deconditioning. *See* deprogramming
deep relaxation, 248

291

ABOUT EMMETT E. MILLER, M.D.

Emmett Miller is a physician, mathematician, musician, and poet who has won international acclaim as a pioneer in Humanistic Psychology and the emerging "New Medicine."

Dr. Miller's instruments are not scalpels and drugs, but words and experiences, images and memories — techniques which teach people to relax and inspire them to take charge of their lives and realize their full potential.

A feature unique to Dr. Miller's work is his use of audio cassette tapes to enable his patients to practice image rehearsal at home between visits. These tapes, which weave Dr. Miller's soothing and inspiring voice through a rich tapestry of music and nature sounds, are in widespread use by medical centers, wellness clinics, and individual health professionals, and are available at thousands of bookstores throughout the country.

For many years a practitioner of family medicine, Dr. Miller currently resides in the Stanford area of California where he practices his subspecialty of *psychophysiological medicine*, the use of self-care approaches to create balance and health among the mental, physical, emotional and spiritual aspects of human life. He is a member of the California Commission on Self-Esteem and personal and Social Responsibility, and teaches public and organizational seminars on Personal Excellence™.

ALSO BY EMMETT E. MILLER

SELF-IMAGERY: Creating Your Own Good Health

Here is an updated edition of the classic in the field, revised in 1986 for this edition. It advocates taking responsibility for your own health and turning it around to make yourself feel—and be—better.
$8.95, 272 pages, paperback

To order send check or money order to:
Celestial Arts
P.O. Box 7327
Berkeley, CA 94707

Postage and handling: **UPS** (street address only)—$2.25 for the first book, .50 for each additional book. **4th Class Book Rate**—$1.25 for the first book, .50 for each additional book.

California residents include your local sales tax.